Sustainable Management, Wertschöpfung und Effizienz

Reihe herausgegeben von
G. Weber, Breunigweiler, Deutschland
M. Bodemann, Breunigweiler, Deutschland
R. Schmidpeter, Ingolstadt, Deutschland

In dieser Schriftenreihe stehen insbesondere empirische und praxisnahe Studien zu nachhaltigem Wirtschaften und Effizienz im Mittelpunkt. Energie-, Umwelt-, Nachhaltigkeits-, CSR-, Innovations-, Risiko- und integrierte Managementsysteme sind nur einige Beispiele, die Sie hier wiederfinden. Ein besonderer Fokus liegt dabei auf dem Nutzen, den solche Systeme für die Anwendung in der Praxis bieten, um zu helfen die globalen Nachhaltigkeitsziele (SDGs) umzusetzen. Publiziert werden nationale und internationale wissenschaftliche Arbeiten. Die Reihe *Sustainable Management, Wertschöpfung und Effizienz* wird von Gregor Weber, Markus Bodemann und René Schmidpeter herausgegeben.

This series is focusing on empirical and practical research in the fields of sustainable management and efficiency. Management systems in the context of energy, environment, sustainability, CSR, innovation, risk as well as integrated management systems are just a few examples which can be found here. A special focus is on the value such systems can offer for the application in practice supporting the implementation of the global sustainable development goals, the SDGs. National and international scientific publications are published (English and German). The series *Sustainable Management, Value Added and Efficiency* is published by Gregor Weber, Markus Bodemann and René Schmidpeter.

Weitere Bände in der Reihe http://www.springer.com/series/15909

Markus Bodemann

Management in Public Administration

Developments and Challenges in Adaption of Management Practices Increasing Public Value

Springer Gabler

Markus Bodemann
Breunigweiler, Germany

Dissertation, Bucharest University of Economic Studies, Bucharest, Romania, 2016

ISSN 2523-8620 ISSN 2523-8639 (electronic)
Sustainable Management, Wertschöpfung und Effizienz
ISBN 978-3-658-22686-2 ISBN 978-3-658-22687-9 (eBook)
https://doi.org/10.1007/978-3-658-22687-9

Library of Congress Control Number: 2018947744

Springer Gabler

This Springer Gabler imprint is published by the registered company Springer Fachmedien Wiesbaden GmbH part of Springer Nature
The registered company address is: Abraham-Lincoln-Str. 46, 65189 Wiesbaden, Germany

Dedication

This work is dedicated with love and gratitude to
my wife Eva,
my parents Franz und Barbara Bodemann
and Prof. Dr. Marieta Olaru;

all for individual reasons they know well.

Table of Contents

List of Abbreviations

AIRMIC	The Association of Insurance and Risk Managers
ALARM	The Public Risk Manager Association
APA	American Planning Association
BIP	Bruttoinlandsprodukt
BSC	Balanced Score Card
CEO	Chief Executive Officer
CFO	Chief Financial Officer
CGC	Corporate Governance Codex
CIO	Chief Information Officer
COSO	Committee of Sponsoring Organizations of the Treadway Commission
CSR	Consumer Social responsibility
DRG	Diagnoses Related Groups
ERM	Enterprise Risk Management
ETA	Event Tree Analysis
EU	European Union
EVA	Economic Value Added
FAZ	Frankfurter Allgemeine Zeitung
FTA	Fault Tree Analysis
GDP	Gross Domestic Product
HAZOP	Hazard and Operability
HGB	Handelsgesetzbuch (German Commercial Code)
IRM	The Institute of Risk Management
IPSAS	International Public Sector Accounting Standards
ISO	International Standardization Organization
KGSt.	Kommunale Gemeinschaftsstelle für Verwaltungsmanagement
IRM	The Institute of Risk Management
KPI	Key Performance Indicator
NAO	National Audit Office
NPM	New Public Management
NSM	New Steering Model
NYSE	New York Stock Exchange
OECD	Organization for Economic Cooperation and Development
PI	Performance Indicator
PISA	Programme for International Student Assessment
PM	Prime Minister
PMPA	Public Management Policy Association
PPP	Public-Private-Partnership

PRIMO	Public Risk Management Organization
PRP	Performance-Related Pay
PSA	Political Studies Association
PSE	Public Sector Efficiency
PMPA	Public Management Policy Association
PMS	Public Sector Management
RAROC	Risk Adjusted Return Of Capital
RORAC	Return Of Risk Adjusted Capital
SOE	State-Owned Enterprises
SOX	Sarbanes – Oxley – Act
TVÖD	Tarifvertrag Öffentlicher Dienst (Germany)
UK	United Kingdom
USA	United States of America
VAR	Value- At- Risk
WTP	Willingness to pay

List of Figures

List of Tables

Introduction

Since fifty years the reform ambitions in public sector in general and in public local administration in particular are intensified, caused by fiscal, public and political pressure. Governance is regarded as in a steady transition; some indicators show a trend towards post-bureaucratic organization. The financial crisis in 2008, combined with the bankruptcy of one of the established bank Lehmann Brother, was one significant turning point which forced and offered a never known transparency and insight; for finances and financial behaviour of the financial sector, of the private sector, and even of the public sector. In the aftermath, shares by public organizations were calculated and the outcome for each citizen presented. Some argued that this event was a turning point to be more aware of the third sector, others draw conclusions for the investment in real estate and the behaviour of credit institutes. The call for new and efficient tools for prevention got louder and louder, especially because the direct links of bankruptcies of private organizations caused countermeasures in public sector. Urgent demands of valid models and methods to analyze previous developments and to forecast the full spectrum of future events are raised. The following impact of the budgetary crises in Western government led to acute and amplified public and political concerns about public financing and spending, although reforms were initiated few years ago. Expected objective was citizen-centred, result oriented and decentralized provision of public services and products while in-creasing public value.

The crisis revealed the vulnerability of both private and public sector to certain con-junctures. Neither global players nor national to local governments are spared from international crisis, the global network of businesses follows own rules.

Despite all changes in business management that have been going on since the 50ies of the last century, data collection and processing, global and local businesses still face uncertain environments and factors in the aftermath of decisions once made. Anticipation of developments leads themselves to a variety of fronts.

Parallel to the different and dynamic situation of private organizations, the public sec-tor is increasingly under pressure to cope with more complex duties and to proof competitiveness in comparison to organisations and performance measurement of the private sector. To seek for tools to increase efficiency and effectiveness in public sector is a steady task, dis-cussed on administrative and political level. One important step to create more transparency and comparability was the adoption of the double-entry-accounting, introduced in Switzerland already in the 70ies of the last century, introduced in Germany since the beginning of the 21st century, followed

M. Bodemann, *Management in Public Administration*,
Sustainable Management, Wertschöpfung und Effizienz,
https://doi.org/10.1007/978-3-658-22687-9_1

by Austria currently. Among the accounting techniques tools are converted to be applied in public sector increasing the ratio between output and input, to accelerate processes, to recognize public needs and interests with one final mandatory goal: By increase the productivity by anticipating future states and preventing surprising risk factors management of risk should contribute to increase public value or welfare. Especially the latter ones determine the peculiar situation of public administration. Under the label of New Public Management known and working management tools are transferred and introduced in the public organizations. For example delegation of responsibility, creating cost/ profit centres, outsourcing, and privatization. But it remains the question whether these tools would lead to the intended results and which specific features and objectives are intangible and traditional ones.

The following work gives perspectives to the following objectives: First the current tendencies in converting and adopting business practices in public administration are presented, followed by estimations whether or not business practices will work in a public administrative environment. A further limitation to risk management addresses general approaches to risk management in private sector and attempts to augment current public sector reforms by risk management tools. By a field research and an analysis of annual status reports public sector awareness and the bandwidth of risks are elaborated and evaluation and conclusions draw for necessary further developments.

As result these key scientific research areas are addressed in the thesis paper:

- Definition and meaning of efficiency and effectiveness in the context of local public administration
- Enclosing of purposes of private sector and public sector organizations and enterprises
- Adoption of management tools for public administration and the boundaries for application
- Interpretation of current studies regarding the introduction of New Public Management tools in general and the New Steering Model in Germany in particular
- Measurement of success for public administration, considering public and individual welfare
- Risk awareness in public administration, based on annual status reports
- Avoiding of and/or preparing undesired developments and their effects to public value as substitute to economic value in private sector

The author of this paper has worked as project manager for the introduction of the double-accounting-system in Germany as one segment of the New Steering Model (NSM), main emphasis on local public administrations in North Rhine-Westphalia. All local public administrations in this state were legally forced over a period of five years to convert their former cash-accounting system technically and systematically between 2005 – 2009 to start with a standardized balance sheet; one year later to integrate all subsidiaries to a consolidated balance sheet. Further he was elected to join a task force for risk management in public administrations by the Kommunale Gemeinschaftsstelle für Verwaltungsmanagement (KGSt.). The project for elaborating and presenting risk management overviews and tools is separated in three stages; the last stage, risk controlling, is planned for the second half of 2016. The KGSt. is a nation-wide non-for-profit organization which is largely funded by contributes from municipalities and counties. It focuses on providing advice and consultancy to the local governments particularly in organizational matters.

Despite the theoretical approach and background, the author was ten years member in a county parliament, including a membership of the commission for regional economic development. During this period he was allowed to act as interface between politics and society on county level, recognizing effects of parliamentarian decision to individuals and groups of individuals.

During different occasions, such as symposiums, public sector conferences and other networking opportunities, he was able to discuss the approach and results of the research with scholars and practitioners from the overlapping areas between business and public sector. In various presentations and following discussions the author met representatives of various public organizations, from local public administrations to state-owned energy providers.

Alongside the combination of business experience and practical work on local public level as elected politician in combination with working for and in public administrations al-lows the author to understand and to estimate the challenges and to identify the adjustment screws, but also traditional, legal, organizational, and financial boundaries to increase efficiency and effectiveness. During the study the author was responsible for introducing a new accounting system for the archdiocese Paderborn, a public corporation with an annual budget of more than a half billion Euros. Currently he works for a state-owned data-centre in North Rhine-Westphalia. This centre provides application and infrastructure for every state department in the state of North Rhine-Westphalia, Germany.

This work is dedicated to my wife Eva, my parents Barbara and Franz Bodemann, and, especially, to Prof. Dr. Marieta Olaru, who had in an outstanding way supervised and supported the progress of this work. Without her help the presented version would not exist. At least this work is dedicated to all responsible individuals and commissions who are involved in the process to increase social welfare. May they have some use of the results and ideas for the execution of their own tasks.

1. Current tendencies in business practices in public administration in a global economy

1.1. Characteristics of public administration an the influence of the environmental and juridical framework

1. 1. 1. Specific issues of public administration

Discussions of public sector organization and the distinction to private sector organizations need an agreed notion. Broadbent and Guthrie offers the following to define the area of the research: "The public sector is that part of a nation's economic activity which is traditionally owned and controlled by the government...The public sector is composed of those public organizations which provide utilities and services to the community and which have traditionally been seen as essential to the fabric of our society." Especially the terms government, utility, and society will dominate the task and the result of the research. The bandwidth and depth of public sector varies in the different counties, but the given aims above create a useful limitation.

Since it is one of the general fields of research interests, this paper focuses on the public sector and the ability to convert and apply management tools for more efficient use of resources, funded by the public. Different from private sector, public sector organizations are subject to a relatively homogenous definition. The OECD (The Organization for Economic Cooperation and Development) defined the following determining branches for the public sector in 2013:

- Health care
- Justice sector
- Education
- Tax administration

All of them give no answer to the question, what has to be the main effort of public sector. The National Audit Office in the United Kingdom points out that "...the main focus of private sector risk management is on maintaining and enhancing profitability – in contrast in departments the focus is on implementation of objectives and services to the citizenry."[1] This depiction considering the term risk could be used for the general description of tasks for the public administration in the same way. In this interpretation provision of the mandatory services has priority. But in general the ob-

[1] National Audit Office, *Supporting innovation: managing risk in government departments*, National Audit Office, London, 2000

M. Bodemann, *Management in Public Administration*,
Sustainable Management, Wertschöpfung und Effizienz,
https://doi.org/10.1007/978-3-658-22687-9_2

jective is very similar: While the public-oriented purpose can include provision of services and products and the benefits to particular classes of individuals or the whole society by subsidized prices, the private sector organization follows the fiduciary idea to maximize shareholder's wealth, after the legal theory of the firm.[2] Others, like Wilson (1889), introduce the radical distinction between policies and administration as unique selling point for public administration.[3] Stiglitz (2000) suggests to distinct the sectors by the concrete activities, different from the model to compare the strategy and motives. He summarizes the activities as follows:

- providing a legal system
- Production (own provision or by a third person as contractor) of goods and services
- affecting what the private sector produces, through subsidies, taxes, credits and regulation
- purchasing goods and services from the private sector, which are then supplied by the government to firms and households
- Regulation and subsidization of private production
- Redistribution of income; that includes payments, such as unemployment benefits to particular groups of individuals. redistributing income[4]

To summarize the given objectives and duties at local administration Burgi (2012) suggested the following content:[5]

- Self-administration/ provision of basic services
- Safety and regulatory services
- Police and fire departments
- Planning of municipal infrastructure
- Provision energy and water/ disposal of waste water
- Protection of historical landmarks and monuments
- Social security services
- Education and culture/ sports
- Support and stimulation of local business

---

2 Moore, M. & Khagram, S., *On creating public value*, Working Paper No. 3, March, p. 12, 2004

3 Ostrom, V. and Ostrom, E., *Public choice: a different approach to the study of public administration*, Public Administration Review, Vol. 31, No. 2, p. 203 -216, 1971

4 Stiglitz, J., *Economics of the public sector*, 3rd edition, Norton & Company, New York, p. 27, 1999

5 Burgi, M., *Kommunalrecht,* C.H. Beck, Munich, p. 19, 2012

This list shows the exchange and overlapping areas of execution between different level, consisting of mandatory and sovereign duties. As discussed above and based on the legal framework local public administration is not autonomous in the meaning of entrepreneurship. This point contributes to a model of absence of responsibility.

Denhardt and Denhardt (2009) compare both sectors by the monetary results: They point out that in most businesses the bottom line profit is the basic measure to evaluate what the organization is doing and with what kind of resources. For public or non-profit-organizations losing money for example is not the main criterion for assumed success or failure.[6] Further differences lay in the pluralistic decision making and the extensive visibility for decisions and evaluation of results.

For a direction, which is supported by a vivid result- and outcome-oriented management, we need a measuring tool. On the highest national abstract legal level, welfare to the people is main objective for political and governmental action. But welfare to the people is a vague expression and leaves the diffuse notion what increases and what decreases welfare or to assess the current status of welfare. The absorption and evaluation of social benefits remain an almost subjective estimation. The different geographical, social, marital, or financial situations of citizens are rarely to compare rather than to get a consensus of acceptance, support and approval of decision for projects or measures.

Mark Moore deployed his model of the strategic triangle; in these compound governmental agencies create public social value in 1995. He presented different examples how to create and, finally, to measure, or to compare a public value status and the deviation during a certain period of time.

---

[6] Denhardt, R. & Denhardt, J., *Public administration: An action orientation*, Thomson Wadworth, Belmont, p. 5, 2009

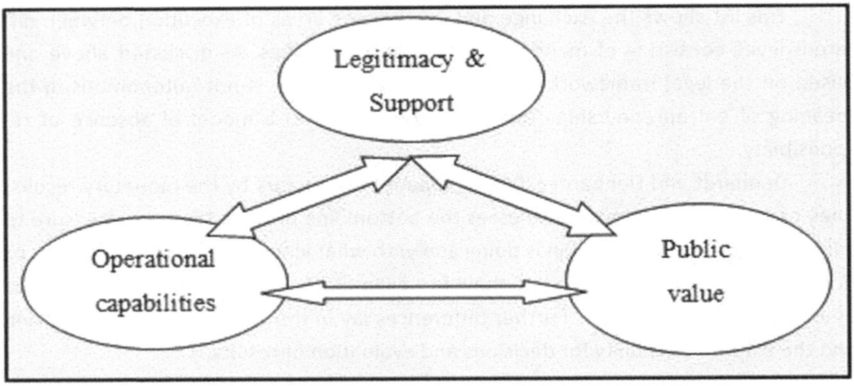

Figure 1: Strategic triangle
Source: Benington, J. & Moore, M. (eds.), *Public Value - Theory and practice,* Palgrave Macmillan, Basingstoke, 2011, p.5

Ten years later, Reichard (2004) describes the network, a public administration is working in and what can create events which could cause desired and undesired consequences, as follows:

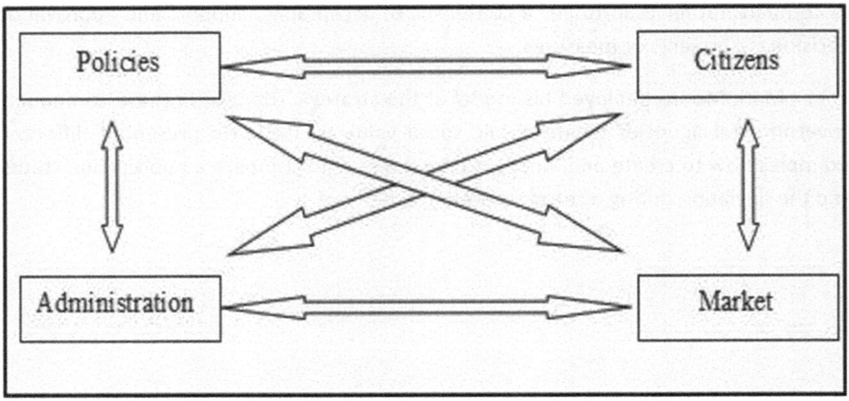

Figure 2: Framework for public administration
Source: Reichard, C., *The New Steering Model and the Citizen*, Deutsches Institut für Urbanistik, 2004

Further, Bozeman (2007) claims in his explanation, that the focus to public value and public interest should be a counterweight for the increase of economic individualism.[7] Introducing the model of the creators of bureaucracy, the ideas of Taylor

[7] Bozeman, B., *Public value and public interest*, Georgetown University Press, Washington, 2007

and Weber have to be considered: For Taylor, the division of responsibility between groups of managers and the group of executers on operational level is one important factor for efficient work; that factor is to replenish by detailed information of work processes, analyses, and guidelines for the most efficient way. Weber argues that bureaucracy is a social phenomenon, too. After a period of authority based of tradition, charisma, and qualified career officials, a structured hierarchy, rule-based duties, and procedures should form the organization and processes of public administration. He intended to increase precision, speed and clarity of execution, combined with a reduction of costs.[8] Critical for execution of public administration is the area of conflict, based on the function of responsiveness to public's wishes on the one hand and interests and responsiveness to the interest of the government and the execution of political programs on the other hand, often accompanied by different interests.

Schütz (2006) uses the following criteria each municipality faces in its own and unique environment:

- Geographical enclosed area
- Self interest
- Execution without hatred and passion
- Absence of profit motive
- Sovereign duties enshrined in the law
- Political Influence
- Multiple and conflicting interests of stakeholders
- Absence of competition/market conditions
- Efficiency in execution
- Bureaucratic environment[9]

Flynn (2007) argues that the boundaries between both private and public sector are neither defined nor permanent in place.[10] More important is the influence of the external environment, dominated by influential share- and stakeholders of the public administration. Local administration is exposed to a wide variety of interests and pressure groups. Following influence groups are named exemplary and could

[8] Rainey, H., *Understanding and managing public organization*, John Wiley & Sons, San Francisco, 2009
[9] Derived from: Schütz, Martin, *Risikomanagement im öffentlichen Sektor*, Schweizerische Gesellschaft für Verwaltungswissenschaften SGVW, Rufenacht, Switzerland, 2006 http://www.sgvw.ch/d/dossiers/Seiten/dossier_22_sgvw_jahrestagung_fachartikel.aspx?print=1,retrieved 03.01.2010; Fry, B. & Raadschelders, J., *Mastering Public Administration*, CQ Press, Washington, p. 36, 2008
[10] Flynn, N., Public Sector Management, Sage, London, p. 1, 2007

vary, depending on size, location, and managerial and financial conditions of a public administration:

Table 1 Interest groups and stakeholders in public administration
Source: by author

voters:	inducement for politicians: likelihood of re-election
taxpayers:	Public services to individuals and for general welfare
employees:	Interested in their own working conditions, salaries, and perks; compensation and benefits, non-financial benefits
customers:	Examining and evaluating specific goods and services for personal use and need
grant-givers:	Providing services to target or general population
bond-holders:	Interest payments, principal repayments
entrepreneurs:	individual interests in customized treatment and infrastructure as providers of products and services interest in long-lasting contracts and guaranteed payment
vendors:	payments or promises of payments
unions:	collective wage agreements for whole sector
boards:	power, prestige, service to constituency
politicians:	acting as strategic managers of the public administration in combination of the function as overseeing authority
government:	The body that provides the needed resources to execute political and legal programs
financial sector:	They evaluate the probability of loss to rank the individual municipalities and decide on conditions for loans extended to the municipalities (for example Basel II +III)

Following diagram should illustrate the trajectories of influence to the public administration. The level of pressure depends on the size. Larger cities have considerable more pressure groups; in addition, smaller pressure groups are easier to convince. Lobbyists and associations can be detected on all governmental level, while influential persons and arguments on federal level are quite more powerful than on local level as executive level. On the other side, participation on local level can be more directly and effectively than on governmental level.

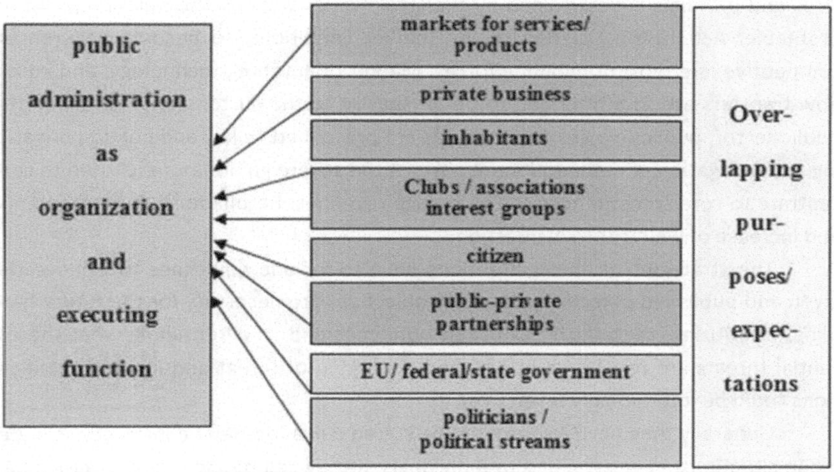

Figure 3: Influence and pressure groups for public administration
Source: by author

The internal environment is influenced by:

- general interest groups
- business interest groups
- unions
- citizen's needs and demands
- elections

Other influence factors are:

- constraints of laws and regulations
- rigid hierarchical structure
- promotions, determined essentially by department heads and the mayor, though in consonance with the regulations
- lack of assessment of individual outputs

Rules and regulations could stifle dynamic initiatives to improve services. Through notionally, as per laws, all citizens are to be treated equally, civil servants have their own pressures to cope with – consequently some sections of the society are served better than others. Irrespective of the degree to which such an equal treatment materializes in reality, the mandate, by itself, is a key distinction between the public administration and the private business, where the entrepreneur or owner could decide about a customer to take.

For private management the lists of pressure groups, operating conform to legal environment, is comparatively shorter; analogue, the influence to provide services and products is determined by the legal framework and the main target to be profitable. Action and reaction to the market conditions, to become and remain competitive, are most dominating forces. Market orientation, technology, and know-how transfers are to attract and to be persuasive to the customers, contrary to the public sector; public services and products are prescribed by law and politics; privatizing and delegation of more and more parts of the sovereign duties are chosen to concentrate to core competences and to reduce revenues. Results for public acceptance and increase of welfare are in question.

The strategies of all organizations have to include guidelines to achieve the given and published objectives. Strategic objectives are necessary for the future handling, prioritizing, ranking the expected outcomes and to determining what the essential threats are for the objectives and what kind of threat and inhered ramifications could be intentionally taken over.

Generally they have to describe the stated risk appetite and instructions in decision situations, in general and to individuals, if they can be identified. Decisive factor for public sector, driven by politics and managed by public administration, is the identification of what type and grade of deviation from current state are acceptable, considering law, resources public interests, and public value. They also have to calculate and present the promised personnel, physical, financial and information resources, recognizing the legal requirements and fitting in with the formal structure of the organization. Thus after closing of certain periods, a mapping of planned and reached goals is necessary for evaluation and further adjustments.

As Hill (2003) pointed out, risk management for the public service is the handling of all events, decisions and activities, which could affect these objectives and which could prevent the local body from providing the services expected of it to the citizens on a daily basis.[11] The sustainable cost-effective provision of those services is a cornerstone of strategic planning.

Whatever the compulsions: The board of directors or the mayor, the councillors and the CFO, and the political community of interests, have to develop a mid- and long-term strategy, which will contain all main and measurable objectives and values. According to the ISO 31000 they have to set organization's objectives against an uncertain environment.[12] In addition they have to estimate fiscal incomes for the realization. Numerical values can be created and enhanced by calculating the possible impact of a decision in question on financial status and potential earnings, the proba-

---

[11] Hill, H., *Finanz- und Haushaltsrisiken*, Proceedings of the symposium „Aufgabenkritik, Privatisierung und Neue Verwaltungssteuerung", German University of Administrative Sciences, Speyer, 02.-04.04.2003

[12] Purdy, Grant, *ISO 31000:2009 – Setting a new standard for risk management*, Risk Analysis Vol. 30, No. 6, p. 882, 2010

bilities of achieving the goals, and also the likelihood and significance levels of each known and predictable development.[13]

Knowing the potential effects for individuals or the society contributes to the appropriate assessment of outcomes and public acceptance in the case of deviation. But the outcomes are multidimensional, so effects are widespread and have different distinctness. A measurement of efficiency will be proportional difficult to private sector with a focused view to economic targets.

This will, in turn, demand at least creating a sophisticated overview of the current welfare status, including the valuation of uncertain factors and their potential effects to the results and outcomes to the public as target system. The internal and external environments have to be taken into consideration to identify the influenced fields and also for a clear and precise qualification and quantification of each particular result.

In general, the environment is structured as follows:

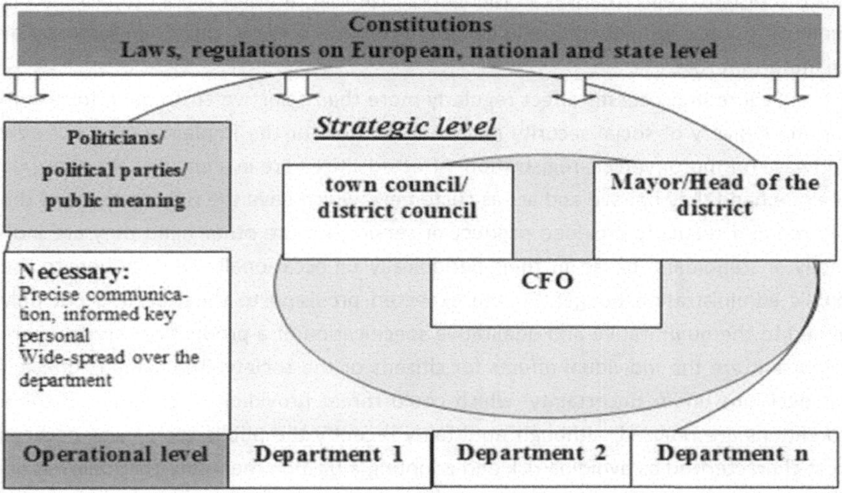

Figure 4: Systematic structure of influences from strategic to operational levels
Source: Simon, H., *Organizations and Markets*, Journal of Public Administration, Issue 5, No. 3, pp. 273-294, 1995

The role of the stakeholders is important when it comes to the external environment: Knowing as exactly as possible the internal and external environmental fac-

[13] Barton, T./ Shenkir, W./ Walker, P., *Making Enterprise Risk Management Pay Off*, Prentice Hall, Upper Saddle River, p. 12, 2002

tors will enable the managers to define the possible threats to objectives and goals the public administration wants to achieve.

Public organizations act in their given legal and physical environment and have a mandated purpose, given by law. These purposes vary, depending on location, size, duty, legal and political importance. They tend to act as Weber demands as exactly as possible as a machine within prescribed routines. The system was designed to deal with a wide variety of work in routine. Strict guidelines are set and impersonal rules limit the interpretation of operations and processes; in addition, processes should be freed of personal irrationalism or emotions. They are more perfect the higher the grade of depersonalized processes. It is expected by the public that the managerial processes are as close as possible to be fail-save and risk free. That means that the public administration should be excluded of searching for opportunities and chances to reduce certain essential expenses.

This is an initial contradiction what has to been solved politically and legally.[14] But the research and treatises of theorists prove that, also for the external environment of a public administration as for the internal processes, uncertain factors play an important role.

Failure in processes affect regularly more than selective customers, for example the delivery of social security payments on time or the implementation of new software for motor vehicle registration. Affected citizen are in a peculiar situation. On the one hand they behave and act as customers, which have the right to demand the offered and regularly provided product or service; on the other hand they are indirectly shareholders, based in their periodically or occasionally contribution to the public administration budget. So the expected provision to the citizen is not only aimed to the quantitative and qualitative specification of a product or service; more important are the individual effects for citizens or the society. The same is relevant for decisions under uncertainty, which could threat providing of products, if some conditions are realized, although until fairly recently the public sector was perhaps best characterized as avoiding risk and adopting a bastion mentality that delayed acceptance and adoption of new instruments and tolls to enhance the managerial quantity and quality.

In Switzerland, after three stages of reforms considering the accounting system on local, cantonal and federal level and the introduction of a system of cost-benefit-analysis, the Swiss Confederation followed the next necessary step: To evalu-

[14] The active seeking for chances and intentionally using uncertain decisions is generally prohibited, resulting from the trustee position. But being more effective and efficient and to be market oriented and acting entrepreneur-like need a switch in the legal and political commission of the public administration.

ate the service and products; not by their monetary value based on the costs for providing, but evaluate the results of providing goods, the outcome.

For that purpose Buschor (2004) uses following dependencies of processes and instruments:

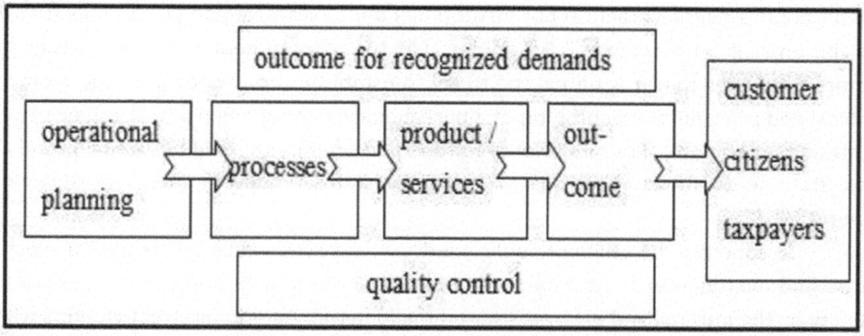

Figure 5: Administrative processes
Source: Buschor, Ernst: "Neues Haushalts- und Finanzmanagement in der Schweiz", Zürich, p. 15, 2004

The outcome of a product-consumption could be ensured by some criterions which are determined to be important for the potential users. The specification of a product or machine offers such criterions. For example the use of a modern processor structure in a PC, combined with other relevant and coordinated parts, could lead to a better performance and faster results; for example calculating the technical stability of a bridge or a building.

But how to measure progresses considering public services and products? And, how to identify influence to public welfare? What are indexes or signals to use for analyzing and evaluating the progress? In the case of risk management it has to be evaluated the not-realized products and services and the ramifications of the failure to do so. How to evaluate reasons for not realized projects or partial projects which caused other reduced utility for the citizens?

Already in 1970 Arrow and Lind proposed that the evaluation of utility by an individual will be more or less identical with its expected value. But the use of a service is very diffuse in a municipality: Streets are less useful if they head in an undeveloped area, the personal estimated value of a dame will more valued if the majority of citizens or important infrastructure are threatened by flooding, social aids are critical valued by people who are not depending on. Woodrow Wilson (1889) stated that the search of models and progress in administrative sciences was based in the facts that an institutional separation between policy function and administrative function exists.[15]

But the relevance of this classical assumption is fading in Western democracies. It is accepted that both functions are performed by both sectors, a stringent separation is neither practical nor institutional appropriate. Simon (1995) rejects the dichotomy of both sectors.[16] He argues that the environment has since changed; more he argues that it is unrealistic to try to establish a total control of the hierarchical and procedural organization of a bureaucracy without any political influence by this administration.[17] For him priority for decision premises should be factual premises, statements about observed or to observe status or developments in the real world.

To concrete the utility of public goods and services will be create a diffuse picture and even harder to measure with objective criterions because of the assumed utility by the internal and external user on the long run. Additional street workers will affect the social life in some focal points in a long term; the reduction of traffic in certain areas of town is often measurable very fast. But what is the utility as value weighing up the alternatives in a decision under uncertainty? And how to distribute public funds in the case of reduced tax income, for example stopping completely of projects in favor of specified projects which spends more assumed public utility than others? The individual valuation could influence the risk management, but the welfare as whole should be priority for public decisions.

Similar to Switzerland, Germany is in a transformation process to evaluate political and economically products and services according to their future outcome: From the former input orientation of administrative focus over the output-orientation to the outcome-awareness. Potential results and consequences of acting and omission for the society and infrastructure become more the focus of decisions and investments. Collected data will contribute to process all variables and expected outputs and outcomes. Currently different theorists work since the 90ies of the last century on modernizing and public sector, to reach a higher level of effectiveness and efficiency.

The general political environment remains most challenging: Public organizations and public managers are expected to remain open to new ideas and to respond

---

15 Wilson, W., *The study of administration*, Political Science Quarterly, June 2nd, 1889

16 Simon, H. A., *Organizations and Markets*, Journal of Public Administration, Issue 5, No. 3, p. 273- 294, 1995

17 Fry, B. &./ Raadschelders, J., *Mastering Public Administration*, CQ Press, Washington, p. 219, 2008

in various ways, contrary to the expectation to act in a prescribed way. Another area of conflict is public's wishes and the interest of the government.[18]

Analysing and suggesting ideas to improve organizational or procedural states have to include solutions for this tension.

1. 1. 2. Comparison of private and public sector objectives

As Peter Drucker (2008) pointed out, a firm or organization has to focus to only two aspects: The customer and a fitting product. Both contribute to remain in competition. He criticizes the focus only to the target to be profitable. This motivation is for Drucker irrelevant; contrary to the general theory of the firm, like Knight proposes.[19]

For the public administration profit is neither of prime importance nor a purpose. Among others reasons are the provided public funds and the origins. Financed services by the citizens should not aim to make any profit to the burdens of the citizens. At least the profit and benefit were taken from the citizen. Danielsson (1977) distinct both sectors by the way they finance the execution of their tasks: private sector is therefore market-oriented and driven, public sector is budget-driven, mainly without direct service in return.[20]

Political and societal outcomes are more important than profitability. Both represent a general improvement of increasing welfare in the meaning of utility to the citizenry. Alford and Hughes states that the consumption of a provided service or a product determines the term and the grade of affection considering public value (2008).

Already in 1970 Arrow and Lind mentioned that the intentional taking of opportunities, linked with potential disadvantages, must be established and maintained in accordance with other social target or strategies. Similar to Alford and Hughes Arrow and Lind proposed that benefits minus costs depend on the individual's share of the offer of public services. Hansson (2002) uses in the context of risk a definition concerning the direct exposure of an individual: "Nobody should be ex-posed to risk unless it is part of an equitable social system for risk taking that work for her advantage." In the later assessment of public value and the model to convert subjective estimations and expectations in an objective value the priority of common improve-

---

[18] Rainey, H., *Understanding and managing public organization*, John Wiley & Sons, San Francisco, 2009

[19] Drucker, P., Management, rev. edit., Collins, New York, 2008

[20] Monsen, N., *Public Management von Einnahmen und Ausgaben*, in Hilgers, D./ Schauer, R./ Thom, N., (eds.), Public Management im Paradigmenwechsel, Trauner Verlag, Linz, , p. 225, 2012

ment before individual choice will be discussed. The sum of all individual net outcomes will lead to an objective estimation of consequences of a decision. Weighing up these results creates more transparency and comparability, although the serious estimation of the citizens, collecting, and processing remains critical.

Beneath the examples given to determine differences between both private and public sector, traditional differences have to be considered: The core objective of public administration is to provide public goods which can be consumed without rivalry. As one effect responsibility to customers is not directed to a single or a group of citizens or users, but directed to a 1 x n relationship, each linked with an individual utility of that specific outcome of a product or service. As given by the constitution responsibility rather directed to concentrate to a market share or earnings, it is more linked to a sustainable and economic provision of these goods. A balanced budget including the guaranteed execution of mandatory tasks, as best practice a surplus to reduce the debt level, can be used as indicator for a peculiar customer-oriented responsibility; current numbers and indicators from all over Europe are sobering, so the orientation to the customers starts at intention to stay in budget.

Impacts or the outcome of a service are hard to define in the case of public services: Individual grade, duration and intensity differ; evasive action to another product is in most cases not possible. A highway could improve the situation of a logistic firm located in a city; its environmental burden will disturb the life quality citizen in the vicinity in many ways. In both cases the public administration has to balance the effects to cope with the expected consumer responsibility. Moreover in the case of not certain developments, concerning finances or environmental pollution, risk awareness will become an important feature in the relationship to citizens. Combined with a non-evasive opportunity and the monopoly for strategic planning, preparation, execution of such projects, especially infrastructure projects, a peculiar relationship exists. In the case of detected and published minor quality of products on the private market a quick loss of customers will be the inevitable consequence; but in public services and products the quality is hard to define, at least in the case of public goods which cannot be compared to a standard market good. Further the cost orientation leads to a reduction of public services: Concentration to the business-like "cash cows" and to a defection on activities that are not profit making is contrary to the idea of welfare state to every people and in every region.

To create a useful and effective system of public management targets and indicators to measure success or failure have to be defined clearly. Investigating measurement of public sector is based on the measurement system, the applied and agreed indicators. Using same measure for different purpose could lead to diffuse results.[21] As pointed out above, the targets of private and public sector are different, but to remember Stiglitz, public sector and private sector are linked together because both have intersections and influence each other; for example economic crises will affect private and public sector and their available resources, by tendency with a time gap. The different targets could be managed and indicated by the different products and services the individual sectors produce. Public sector provides mainly products and services which are public goods, defined by non-rivalry and no exclusion-principles. The production of these services of general interest is no allowed to be delegated to private sector and is a fundamental task for the public sector, for example energy or waste water disposal. But this distinction is currently blurring; for example education or health services are delegated, because of the capacities and the costs of providing these services to the people. On the other hand, public sector recognized that the production of electricity could be a productive part; they invest in windmills or watermills and offer the energy at a public market. The blurring in providing of products and services leads to the conclusion that the product portfolio could not be used to distinct both sectors; but it also closed the gap of comparability, applied same terms for both sectors for efficiency and performance. Many researches try to show the benefits of different public sector projects. But in most cases the results are sobering. For example in transportation projects, observed in the research mentioned above, nine out of ten projects passenger-related forecasts were overestimated.[22] Probabilities of inappropriate estimations in these public projects point to areas in need of improvement in the public sector, especially in the areas where the provisioning can be privatized and are therefore in a direct competition to private vendors.

Business targets could be interpreted also in a wider range. Some will argue that the main goal is to maximize the revenues and therefore the wealth of the investors or shareholders, after the legal theory of the firm, as Moore and Khagram (2004) point out.[23] Hall et al. (2007) define the goal as increasing the shareholder value. So for private sector various perspectives for organizations are in use to specify the goals; at least in business plans, the nature and the objectives are presented.

---

[21] Micheli, P. & Neely, A., *Performance management in the public sector in England: Searching for the golden thread,* Public Administration Review, July/ August, pp. 591 – 600, 2010

[22] Flyvbjerg, B./ Holm, M./ Buhl, S., *How (in)accurate Are Demand Forecasts in Public Works Projects, Journal of the American Planning Association,* Vol. 71, No. 2, Spring, p. 133, 2005: For example: The "Skytrain" in Bangkok provides much longer platforms than needed.

[23] Moore, M. & Khagram, S., *On creating public value,* Working Paper No. 3, March, 2004

It remains the constitutional goal for public sector organizations to contribute to increase public welfare, to an individual, to a group of individuals, but also to the society as a whole. This abstract objective and mandatory orientation for every governmental activity will be the cornerstone for a development and maintaining of vivid management for public sector organizations. For private sector organization, the success of production could be measured by generally accepted calculations. Indicators for success can be the market shares, increase or decrease of earnings, number of innovations and inventions and many more. For the sustainable operations in private sector the economic growth and overall profit are the most important numbers; for public administration it is different: Especially public goods are hard to measure by individual and personal utility rather than by economic values. The try to distinct or categorize the offered activities shows evidently that economic use of resources, to stay in budget or an orientation to a competitive market is not primary focus for the public sector. Main goal is to fulfill the obligatory tasks; secondary are costs, quality and outcomes of the activities. Diefenbach (2009) complains about that with the introduction of NPM additional systems and processes of auditing, control and regulation are implemented; for him it is a try to convert public administration to industry and quality standards and performance revisions. Application of all these instruments ignores the most of intangible assets and traditional values public administration is based on; including fairness, dignity, equality, and justice, quality of live, participation, trust and freedom. Beneath progress in processes disadvantages in losing the own culture have to be handled. Van Dooren et al. see the measurement of public sector as to evaluate an agent in a societal process.[24] Denhardt and Denhardt (2009) offer three reasons to distinguish both sectors:

- Ambiguity: Making or losing money is not main criterion to evaluate progress or success of a public or non-profit organization
- Pluralistic decision making: several groups and individuals have direct or indirect access in the process as basement of a democratic government.
- Visibility: discussion and decisions are executed with a greater visibility, often accompanied with a public discussion in the media.[25]

Operating with public funds target of public administration is the local welfare state; existence guarantees and the almost unlimited resources frame the execution. In contrast private sector organizations have to be profitable to compete and survive. Loss of resources increases a threat of existence.

---

[24] Van Dooren, W./ de Caluwe, C./ Lonti, Z., *How to measure public performance*, Public Performance & Management Review, Vol. 35, No. 3, pp. 489 – 508, 2012

[25] Denhardt, R. & Denhardt, J., *Public administration: An action orientation*, Thomson Wadworth, Belmont, p. 5, 2009

Moore draws two images of the execution of services by the public administration: The public servant acts a faithful manager of their political masters, the moral duty to lend substantive and administrative expertise as contribution to achievement of objectives; framework for execution are laws, elections, courts; for the execution every own interest has to be supressed to the favour of public interest

Public executives as independent moral actors are requested to express their own views of what is right and good.26 Both kinds enclose different advantages and disadvantages, i.e. whether a public manager could act separated from his own estimation and private interests; in best way he acts in the favour of public interests if arguing against some politically planned projects.

Similar to the explanation made for business goals, the affection of stake- and shareholders will be also various. But not only the passive stance of stake- and shareholder, the activities to influence the strategy and the operational goals by vocalists and influential stakeholders have to be considered during the development of an effective risk management system.

One important difference between citizenry and share- and stakeholders is the exit-option. If shareholders or investors disagree with strategy, with products or the way of the production, he can withdraw his investment and leave the firm. Similar to other stakeholders; they can try to influence the strategy and product direction of the firm, by individual or collective influence, during the operations and during the annual stockholder's meeting. Moore and Khagram (2004) complain about the missing of conceptions of strategy in the public sector.[27]

Strategy is bound to the ability to carry out some combined operations to fulfill targets and to establish a clear view of a company. In public sector the way of receiving tendencies for strategies and the often changes in the political leadership, combined with ideological frameworks, tend to show a diffuse and time-limited realization. The affects for the citizenry is therefore in tension between influence by individuals and by representatives and the task environment, build by the mandatory and voluntary political task. Both strings are dominated by the financial, personal and material resources a public administration is able and willing to spend. So prognosis and forecasts are made for a short period of time, based on the time-limited political will and scarce resources. The ramifications, in a passive and active way, will create the environment for management in general, but for a risk management in particular.

---

[26] Moore, M., *Creating public value: strategic management in government*, Harvard University Press, Cambridge, p. 294, 1995

[27] Moore, M. & Khagram, S., *On creating public value*, Working paper No. 3, March 2004, John F. Kennedy School of Government, Harvard University, p. 12, 2004

1. 1. 3. Considerations on performance indicatros used in public administration in relation to private sector

After centuries the public sector replaces step by step the input orientation to output orientation, based and measurable by the use of double-entry-accounting. On long-term development and accompanied with better use of information technology this change can lead to an outcome orientation. This will include a movement from a simple productive system to a more intelligent and dynamic system with feedbacks about the results and impacts of the inner and outer environment. The following figure shows the possible evolution from an administrative organization to an effect-oriented organization. Based on increasing more complex accounting systems, associated with more sophisticated tools for evaluation, sources and effects can be analysed and estimated with more reliable data. In Germany the CFOs of public administrations are convinced by the expected effects of accrual and double entry accounting as more transparent and appropriate for better control; but they are less convinced that key performance indicators, derived from the accounting systems, can be applied for inter-communal comparison and competition.[28]

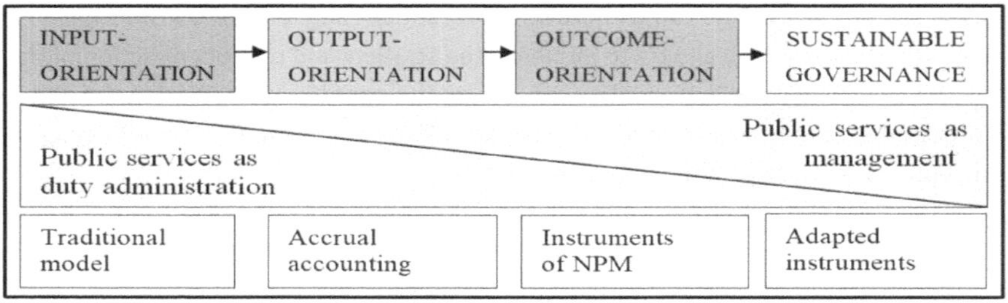

Figure 6: Transformation of applied managerial tools and aims in public administration
Source: Bodemann, M., *NKF-Klassenziel erreicht ?* , NKF-Zeitung – Journal für Doppik in Ländern und Kommunen",No. 2, Behördenspiegel, Bonn/ Berlin, p. 10, 2009

But currently the outcome is neither measured in an appropriate way nor regulated by activities nor by consequences or impacts to the society. This is another implicit distinction between public and private sector: To be aware of the consequences of products and services to the society. Private sector has in focus the function of a product, promised specifications and expected utilities; public sector has to bear the consequences of those products to the society or the individual. Although

[28] Burth, A. *Die Kommunalverschuldung wirksam begrenzen – Entwicklung des Modells einer doppischen Kommunalschuldenbremse* in: Hilgers, D./ Schauer, R./ Thom, N., (eds.), Public Management im Paradigmen wechsel, Trauner Verlag, Linz, , pp. 209 – 224, 2012

some borrowings from the private sector to establish and to present in the annual status only a few addressed the threats; in concrete for the provision of a product and for the outcomes expected by decisions as Bodemann, Olaru und Pirnea (2015) found out recently.[29]

In 1993 the US Congress had mandated the Government Performance and Results Act (GPRA) with the objective to make governmental agencies more accountable for results to their stakeholders, customers, the citizen and taxpayers.[30]

For that purpose a comparison was summarized to the similarities but also to accept differences, which make adoptions difficult:

Table 2 Comparing strategies in private and public-sector organizations by aims
Source: Arvenson, P., Translating performance metrics from the private to the public sector, www.balancedscorecard.org, retrieved 07.02.106

Strategic Feature	**Private sector**	**Public sector**
General strategic goals	Competitiveness	Mission effectiveness
General financial goals	Profit, growth, market share	Cost reduction, efficiency
Values	Innovation, creativity, good will, recognition	Accountability to public, integrity, fairness
Desired outcome	Customer satisfaction	Customer satisfaction
Stakeholders	Stockholders, owners, market	Taxpayers, inspectors, legislators
Budget priorities defined by	Customer demand	Leadership, legislators, planners
Justification for secrecy	Protection of intellectual capital, proprietary knowledge, growth rate, earnings, market share	National security, best management practices
Key success factors	Uniqueness, advanced technology	Best management practices, sameness, economies of scale, standardized technology

This framework can be applied with minor adoptions to public sector organizations in almost all developed countries. In question is whether it is possible to trans-

29 Bodemann, M./ Olaru, M/ Pirnea, C., *Risk awareness as competitive factor for public administration - a German case study*, in "Proceedings of the IE 2015 International Conference", p. 499, 2015

30 Arvenson, Paul, *Translating performance metrics from the private to the public sector*, www.balancescorecard.org, retrieved 07.02.2016

late or convert the language of private sector terms to reach an increase of the results; one step further to measure the results in terms of private sector.

Performance measurement in non-profit organizations will remain a steady challenge for organizational researches and new paradigms to reform. Van Dooren et al. describe performance indicators as increasingly used in public sector. Complex realities could be present in a tangible way and support to held actors accountable.[31] Efficiency and effectiveness in public administration are in doubt; but the Weber's separation of politics and administration, extended by the bureaucracy paradigm of Wilson and the standardisation of Taylor are globally accepted and applied in organizations, especially in developed countries. A dilemma occurs where performance measurement is on one hand neither legally and politically nor opportune or the results are illusive; on the other hand, services and products and their desired outcome are only vaguely described. How to estimate performance without concrete and relevant references to compare with the expected and desired results? This situation is amplified for instance in deviations from a decisional situation: If politicians or public managers are forced to decide under circumstances without references, what kind and what grades of chances or threats are to be expected and who will share the desired or undesired results? Critical to these developments Pollitt summarized the missing framework in 2012: For him the public sector reforms are based of three question marks: There is no need for it, specific targets are absent and there are no costs of reorganization.[32]

As Diefenbach (2009) points out, public sector has three orientations to be considered in every decision situation and in the evaluation of performance of public sector:

- Market orientation (commodification of services and products to the people, ratio of value for money)
- Stakeholder orientation (meeting and maintaining the objectives and policies of influential external stakeholders, like industry, lobbyists, and other persons and groups)
- Customer orientation (service delivery under the perspective of customers / citizens)[33]

---

[31] Van Dooren, W./ de Caluwe, C./ Lonti, Z., *How to measure public performance*, Public Performance & Management Review, Vol. 35, No. 3, p. 501, 2012

[32] Pollitt, C., *40 years of public management reform – what we have learned, what have we forgotten*, 40th Anniversary Conference "40 years of policy and politics" , 19.09.2012, University of Bristol, UK

[33] Diefenbach, T., *New public management in public sector organizations – the dark side of managerialistic 'enlightment'*, Public Administration, Vol. 87, No. 4, pp. 892- 909, 2009,

All of the three contribute to public welfare as overall target; the grade of customer orientation differs, because of the organization success oriented intention of the first two one. Thus to measure the effects to each individual is difficult and results will be processed and presented delayed.

There is a prevailing perception that non-profit organizations, especially governmental institutions and their output, have to be measured by peculiar indicators. The absence of competition, virtual unlimited resources, and the guarantee of existence, make public administration an untouchable, politically trusted, and secured organization. But Diefenbach (2009) focus to the traditional and fundamental objectives of public sector organizations. According to them, public services have to be provided regardless of the gravity of need, cost or ability to pay.[34] Current public projects (i.e. in Germany the exploding costs and multiple missed timelines at the Berlin municipal airport, or the absence of a marketing strategy for the Elb-Philharmony, a concert hall in Hamburg) show the magnitude of decisions and improper management. The expected and desired outcomes of such projects could have a very wide spectrum: Reputation, increase in the range of infrastructural or cultural services, attraction for jobseekers or companies and other collateral outcomes. Especially the increased global and regional competition force public administration to provide excellent conditions for investors and citizens. Tax legislation on governmental and fast internet on local level are only a few issues. The issue of wrong estimation of the volume and timetable could cause waste of additional resources and major distrust in public organizations and qualified personnel. In the consequence resources are retained, the ratio between output and input decreases, the potential grade of welfare is reduced.

Considerations about outcomes to interests and values will support the path for regaining responsiveness; this will further contribute to faster orientation and better guidance, with focus on society, on fulfilling fundamental objectives and increasing the welfare of the citizen. Because of the diffuse expectation and ability to absorb the effects of public services public organization have to do more to seek, prepare and to address the multidimensional expectations of their customers, the citizens and entrepreneurs.

Grüb suggest an adoption of a Balanced Score Card for development of performance indicators. Similar is already applied in health management in a Bavarian region in Germany. Following perspectives are considered and modelled:

---

[34] Ebd. p. 894

Figure 7: Perspectives of performance measurement
Source: Grüb, B., *Performance Measurement in Gesundheitsnetzwerken* in: Hilgers, D./ Schauer, R./ Thom, N., (eds.), Public Management im Paradigmenwechsel, Trauner Verlag, Linz, p. 403, 2012

Disparate to private sector the measurement of success of public administration is based on a wide variety of assessment by persons, which personal intentions and expectation are also very vague. The following graph by Christopher Pollitt & Geert Bouckaert (2011) shows the trails of values created by public administration and their potential monitoring points. The socio-economic situation, as substitute of welfare, could be measures by different indicators, including average income, school system, housing situation or violation of public order. The traditional process from input to outcome could be applied to every organisation, the sustainability and cost effectiveness is anchored in the legal environment. The analysis and prioritization of needs is delegated to politics, the expected effects to the society are on gap risk management in public administration, beneath others, can fill. They define efficiency as ratio between input and output, regardless of the outcomes to the addressed individuals.

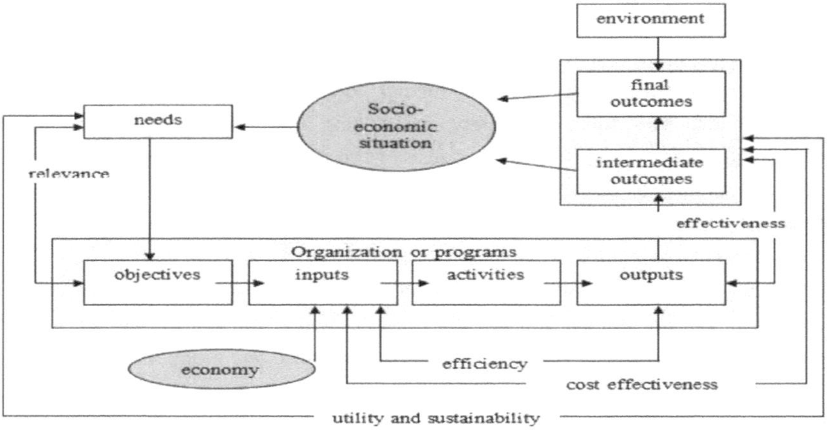

Figure 8: Conceptual framework for performance
Source: Pollitt, C. & Bouckaert, G.: Public Management Reform, 3rd Edition, Oxford University Press, New York, p. 133, 2011

As Moore (2013) points out, government faces a diverse and volatile political and social environment.[35] A changing environment has already direct influence to demand and supply of service and goods. It challenges in specific the public manager in a decision taking situation. The expected or processed deviation of public value could be used as guidance to better estimation of ramification of decision, collectively and individually, under conditions of a changing environment and demand. Changes in external environment have great implications to performance, output, and outcomes of both sectors. While in public sector the political situation and the politics of the actual ruling government are important, for private sector competitors, technological developments and political stability are main focus.

For application as indicator and guidance for decision making, public value has to be measured in numeric values, to be comparable to former similar situations, as reference or as inter-organizational-benchmark. In case of risk management, the main focus for this consideration is the deviation of the numeric value of public value by decisions. In the case of decisions for not-mandatory tasks under uncertainty, potential deviations in a desired and not desired way are indicators for the decision maker. Regularly desired results will increase public value; undesired results will reduce public value. For a working application a model and a formula for calculating the outcomes are necessary. The following table shows a possible spectrum of variables considering the final quantity and have to be part of the formula to describe the effects of a decision on public value:

Table 3 Deviation of current public value status by decisions to make
Source: by author

Balance of affected spheres over a specific period of time		
Positive effects	**Negative effects**	**Period:**
Affected persons in numbers	Affected/ not affected persons in numbers	Measurement of changesover a certain periodof time
Steady utility and grade of utility	Steady disutility and grade of disutility	
Temporarily utility and grade of utility	Temporarily disutility and grade of disutility	
Side effects for steady utility	Side effects for steady disutility	

35 Moore, M., *Recognizing public value*, Harvard University Press, Cambridge, p. 8, 2013

Side effects for temporarily utility	Side effects for temporarily disutility	
Opportunities	Threats	
As appropriate changing grades of affection	As appropriate changing grades of affection	
Sum of positive effects	**Sum of negative effects**	**Balance of effects**

The table shows and extended the selected influences for the estimation of consequences. It has to be analysed in a given timeframe for a more reliable comparison

The outcomes of public services and products are various and depending on multiple factors from internal and external framework of the citizen; as sum of all activities and outcomes welfare/public value status should be increased. The ratio of input in the meaning of a combination of different resources to output and outcome comes increasingly in focus.

But public value will not only be defined by activities of public sector, but consists also of affections from private sector. The given examples of local society affected persons and the intentional and occasional beneficiaries have to be analysed and calculated, first to get a trend, further to get a comparison of different possible outcomes; caused divergence from a current status in absolute or proportional numbers could be used as indicator and trigger for countermeasures or amplifying activities.

Under conditions of uncertainty the formula to process has to be replenished by the expected probability to get a comparable quantity. Evaluation of potential effects shows the balance in the desired and undesired scenario and will lead to a concrete value taking in consideration the change by the outcomes. As guidance for politics the spread between both, combined with the probability, offers a comprehensive notion of the estimated and expected change in public value. It is comparable with the way of private sector risk management concepts, for example Value-at-Risk (VaR).

The difference lays in the conversion: For private sector economic numeric indicators are used; in contrast for society outcomes, the personal estimations are used in order to show the personal estimated potential ramifications, based on the individual and personal status. According to Olaru et. al. (2013), it is possible by using different methods to assess the impact of various risk categories, including the VaR

under the above mentioned investment projects.[36] For O'Flynn (2007) public value is a reflection of collectively expressed and politically mediated preferences consumed by the citizenry.[37] Traditional it is assumed that political programs are built through deliberation and political integration, involving elected and appointed government officials and other key stakeholders, pursuing sustainable value to the people. Alford and Hughes (2008) mentioned that value is not a net concept; for them it is more a function of benefits created and offered to the society by expenditures of public funds, by public organization in generating those benefits.[38] This model has its limits in measuring the impact of benefits to an individual or to a collective. Each person estimates the grade of benefits by her own situation of life. Each service and product can be evaluated in a personal matter and refers to the individual grade of utility, generating a benefit. A playground in the neighbourhood has a bigger, but also fading over years, benefit for families with kinds, but could generate a bigger disutility for an older person, which is more interested in barrier-free sidewalks, considering the missing infrastructure and the noise generated.

Collective measurement has to consider different aspects to reflect the sum of all effects in case of a decision making:

1. The affected region has to be limited and can be handled by the political and administrative boundaries. In most cases public goods have neither spatial, nor geographical, nor personal limits. It is founded in the character of public goods: A highway could have a big utility for trucks going through Europe; they cannot be excluded from using this transport way, although number and frequency can be steered by an additional toll. Persons in the vicinity of the highway are affected steadily. Evasive actions are almost impossible; in addition affected inhabitants will not become compensated by intensive users for negative restrains, i.e. by noise, pollution, and other factors. A solution like a referendum enhances the ability to take part in a decision; but it bears just as described above the necessity to submit personal interests to the collectively articulated interests and has to be prepared using a formalized timetable.
2. Public value can be produced in an area of conflict. A gain in utility for one person will at least lead to a constant status of utility for a person with divergent preferences. Analogue to the absolute affection of a person, gradual differ-

---

[36] Olaru, M./ Sandru, M.,/ Pirnea, C., *Monte Carlo method application for environmental risks impact assess ment in the investment projects*, Procedia – Social and Behavioral Sciences, Vol. 109, January, pp. 940 – 943

[37] O'Flynn, J., *From new public management to public value: paradigmatic change and managerial implications*, The Australian Journal of Public Administration, Vol. 66, No. 3, p. 358, 2007

[38] Alford, J.& Hughes, O., *Public value pragmatism as the next phase of public management*, The American Review of Public Administration, Vol. 38, No. 2, p. 132, 2008

ences exists. Persons living in the near of the planned highway have a higher impact by noise and pollution that persons in the wider area although both are part of the municipality. According to Hansson (2002) is the utility of a mixture of potential outcomes equal to the utility outcome that actually materializes. By applying a moral discourse an action-guidance could be expelled.[39]

3. Identification of potential outcomes, their deviations and, for both, indicators for change in public value as quantifying part. Public value is therefore to handle as current status represented by a numeric indicator, similar to comparison of the status and ranking analysing the educational system.

But measuring the deviation in public value as outcome of efforts by public administration compared to the input, determined by personal, material and financial resources can be one perspective.

Production efficiency could be measured in the comparison to private sector organization, producing and selling similar products. For example: Winter services are provided by public employees, but also by private organizations or persons. In the case of outsourcing, as Diefenbach complains, only a small fraction of former services are carried out; the former very extensive provided winter service to clean streets, places, and sidewalks is reduced to main streets; some of the services are re-delegated to the citizens. Further outsourcing ignores the function of a public good: It could be used by everyone and without reducing another ones use. The privatization of British Rail led to a thinning of tracks and lines; some smaller villages and regions were complete cut off by efficiency considerations: With few passengers trains will not run profitable, as result, parts of these non-profitable services are re-delegated to government.

For measuring the efficiency of public works public value can be used as dimensionless value, based on individual estimation of cause and effects; focus to a monetary ratio between output and input will dilute the traditional and legal task of public sector organizations. In 1991 Hood argued that NPM has and will damage public service while being ineffective in its ability to deliver on its central claim to lower costs per units of service.[40] The proof will be difficult, especially caused by claimed peculiarities in each public administration.

Public sector performance measurement could be described as to measure the situation of achieving established and ordered goals. After the introduction of tools of NPM the instrument of measurement and evaluation of public services and products is inevitable, but it is seldom used. Indexes like financial returns, market shares,

39 Hansson, S., *Seven Myths of Risk*, Royal Institute of Technology, Stockholm, 2000
40 Hood, C., *A public management for all seasons*, Public Administration, Vol. 69, Spring, p. 3-19, 1991

and performance measures for executives' compensation are not relevant for the public sector. This current condition is based on a position of almost untouchable institution and a function as quasi-monopolist. But the use of double-entry-bookkeeping, currently applied in Germany and Switzerland, offers the ability to measure and to compare productivity, efficiency and effectiveness; Art. 91 d Basic Law for Germany offers explicit the comparison on local level, executed through federal or state level. Aim should be to compare the performance and to improve processes. The use on a personal basis is often neglected and legally prohibited. In the interviews conducted the majority of the surveyed administrations sees the refusal on union level as serious brake pad for comparison. Without any comparable values as orientation an isolated view prevents essential improvements and optimizing of processes. Lindblom has made a notable statement already in 1959 and promoted the system in a "Science of Muddling through".[41] He complained about processes, inefficiencies, and consequence-regardless management. Recently some authors have taken the topic of performance measurement and incentive for public administration to demonstrate effects of the use.[42] The general rejection of the public administration to be assessed by numeric values is currently one of the important distinctions between public and private sector. A slow-moving convergence is notable; evaluation methods, for example benchmarks or balanced-scorecards are currently initiated and introduced; for an inter-communal comparison, but also for public-private organizational comparison.

As pointed out above measurement of managerial performance is limited. The ratio of input to output becomes a topic for the future. Variances of efficiency and effectiveness are currently unusual for the public sector. As the research von Van der Waal (2008) proved, profitability and efficiency are not priority; more the accountability for each person in a decisive function is in focus[43]; therefore to avoid negative results by a wrong decision or to deviate from legal guidelines. Confirmed by the interview focus of the annual planning is to stay on the budgetary and political targets. Deviation from the expected growth and development trajectory leads to further use of resources and a worse proportion of outcome to input. In general a high grade of

---

41 Lindblom, C., *The science of "muddling through"*, Public Administration Review, Vol. 19, No. 2, Spring, pp. 79- 88, 1958

42 For example: Greiling, D., *Performance measurement - a driver for increasing the efficiency of public services?*, Protestant University of applied sciences, Darmstadt, 2005; Propper, C. & Wilson, D., *Use and Usefulness of Performance Measures in the Public Sector*, Oxford Review of Economic Policy, No. 19 (2), pp. 250-267, 2003; Van Thiel, S.& Leeuw, F., *The performance paradox in the public sector*, Public Performance and Management Review, Vol. 25, No. 3, March, pp. 267 – 281, 2002

43 Van der Wal, Z./ de Graaf, G./ Lasthuizen, K., *What's valued most? Similarities and differences between the organizational values of the public and private sector*, Public Administration, Vol. 86, No. 2, 2008

efficiency closes the circle as an indicator of social responsibility during execution of established processes.
The main question remains: Which indicators show efficiency and effectiveness of public service performance. Economic indicators as essential numbers for investors are insufficient; likewise non-economic factors play an important role. This work will later introduce public value as substitute for measurement of public sector efforts and satisfaction results for citizens.

1. 1. 4. Provision of public goods and services and the responsibility

The grade of responsibility of organizations could be cleared by the differences between the products and services they provide to customers: First and most important is the objective of sustainable provision of public goods for the citizenry. Therefore accountability and responsibility for the mandatory tasks are founded on legal basement: public administration has to cope with all cases, based on voluntarily duties, duties without instruction and duties with concrete instruction. Øvretveit (2005) mentioned that in an abstract way public service and product quality has to meet those most in need of the service, executed on available resources and at lowest cost.[44] Limited available resources made it evident: After more than ten years of introduction focus of politics and administration is on input, to distribute the expected material and financial resources to meet most of the legal and political requirements respective expectations. That leads to a providing services and products within the range of available resources, partly regardless of the outcomes to citizens. But the budget is often overstretched by different causes. One significant number resulting is the debt level of the different administrative levels: The aggregated debt level of German public administration was 2,058 Trillion € at the end of June 2013[45]. That means 82% of the Gross Domestic Product (GDP).

The OECD used in 2001 four dimension of accountability: Basement is the transparency of governmental actions, which include the ability to ensure that actions are exposed to public scrutiny. Second level is the accessibility which contents that everybody can obtain information and utilize services at anytime and anywhere. Third level of accountability is responsiveness: The government is expected to be open to new ideas, demands and needs of all citizens. The forth is the inclusiveness in

---

[44] Øvretveit, J., *Public service quality improvement*, in Ferlie, E., Lynn, L.E. jr., Pollitt, C., (eds.), „The Oxford handbook of public management", Oxford University Press, Oxford, pp. 537-562, 2005
[45] Frankfurter Allgemeine Zeitung. 26.06.2013

the meaning that the government has to ensure the broadest base or participation of all citizens.[46]

Denhardt and Denhardt found out three different categories which could be used to distinct public from private goods and services. Further these categories have direct influence to define deviations from an expected quality.[47] They suggest that these three, ambiguity, pluralistic decision making, and visibility, have effects to the awareness of citizens and to any kind of responsibility to the citizenry as sovereign.

Ambiguity is therefore used in the meaning that the performance of a manager or decision-maker is seldom measured. Other results could be found, for example European approaches come to extensive and representative results.[48] It is remarkable that leads to the conclusion that the unit's contribution to the overall success or result has no priority.[49] Saving or losing money is not an important criterion. As trustee and distributor of public funds an orientation to stay within the given budget should be highest priority. Van der Wal (2008) confirmed that mention.[50]

Further pluralistic decision making covers the direct assignment of origin, execution and responsibility for process, for outputs and later outcomes. The involvement of different groups and individuals leads to a different awareness and evaluation of the quality, and utility of public products and services.[51] In addition public organizations operate within a much greater visibility of the manufacturing process, the perception of utility in the meaning of benefits, utility or other intentions, based on personal and material advantages. Customers in private sector expect to get the best possible deal and result from the business. The public and the press tend to compare intended targets and objectives with the reached effect to individual and collective use und utility function. In these cases the kind of measurement and an index should be used for comparison and transparency. But they also use a not transparent or more singular evaluation of the outcomes.

---

46 Van Dooren, W./ de Caluwe, C./ Lonti, Z., *How to measure public performance*, Public Performance & Management Review, Vol. 35, No. 3, p. 501, 2012

47 Denhardt, R. & Denhardt, J., *Public administration: An action orientation*, Thomson Wadworth, Belmont, p. 5, 2009

48 Profiroiu, M.C./ Tapardel, A./ Mihăescu, C., *Performance analysis of the Romanian public Administration,* Transylvanian Review of Administrative Sciences, 40 E, pp. 183 – 200, 2013

49 Van Thiel, S.& Leeuw, F., *The performance paradox in the public sector*, Public Performance and Management Review, Vol. 25, No. 3, March, pp. 267 – 281, 2002

50 Van der Wal, Z./ de Graaf, G./ Lasthuizen, K., *What's valued most? Similarities and differences between the organizational values of the public and private sector*, Public Administration, Vol. 86, No. 2, p. 471, 2008

51 Blumenthal, 1966 cited by Denhardt, R. & Denhardt, J., *Public administration: An action orientation*, Thomson Wadworth, Belmont, p. 6, 2009

As long as the range, the grade of absorption and quality of public services and goods is determined by the political discussion and legal framework, direct participation and responsibility remain absent.

1. 1. 5. The role and importance of public administration for the local and global economy

While globalization is in progress, new technologies support to realize a just-in-time communication and almost exchange of goods and services, global players grew. But because of the more and more complex duties of the municipalities, the increase expectations of the society to provide a mesh of public services and products, the volume of public sector increases, too. The following graph shows the ratio of government expenditures to gross national product. The median of the EU is 48.1, while the range is from high 50ies to low 30ies. These absolute values give the impression of national product compared to consumption by public organizations. There are different estimations and research results considering the optimal ratio. A presentation of areas of public spending and the output and outcomes will enlighten the offered spectrum to the citizens:

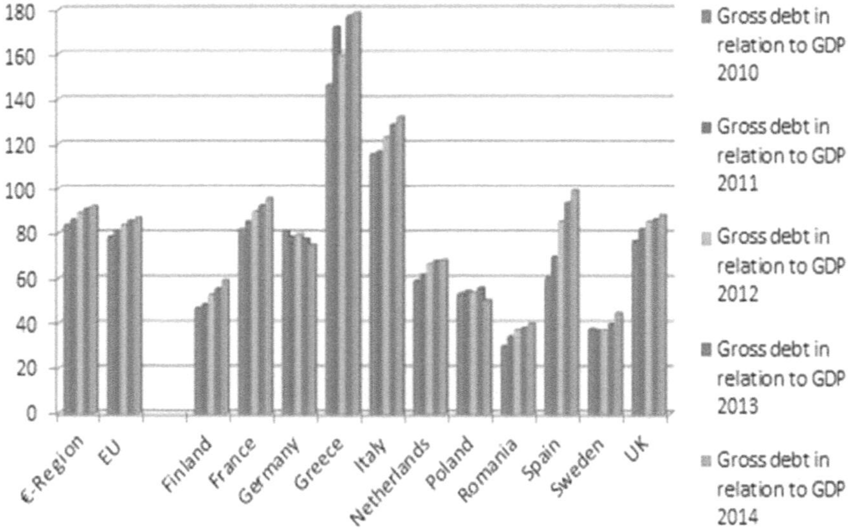

Figure 9: Ratio of governmental expenditure to GDP
Source: http://de.statista.com/statistik/daten/studie/6769/umfrage/staatsquoten-der-eu-laender, retrieved 15.03.2016

As seen the states of various countries lead to the conclusion that without rigorous measures the ratio and the debt level is not to steer. Decrease in public spending is linked with public value. Challenging for all governmental level is to stabilize the expenditure, better to reduce but also stabilize current level of welfare, based on public products and services. Concerning the ratio the possible consequences of decisions under no certainty and the outcomes to public value to the people becomes more impressive. Among others, Rainey complains about the steady increase of this ratio. As to see in the figure the share of governmental spending in ratio to GDP increased over the last five years and represents the influence to domestic economy.

1.2. Considerations about different values in provisioning of services in public administration

1. 2. 1. Corporate social responsibility as objective of public administration

The Cambridge Dictionary of Philosophy (2009) defines the term responsibility as follows: "A condition that relates an agent to actions of, and consequences connected to, that agent, and is always necessary and sometimes sufficient for the appropriateness of certain kinds of appraisal of that agent."[52]

The dictionary describes three different views:

- Role responsibility: Common duties are directly link with that function, for example for execution of those duties. Causal responsibility concerning events including, but not limited to human actions which cause other events, could be subsidized in this description.
- Liability responsibility: This is applied as practices of praise and blame, with the need of constrains, including intention, knowledge, and recklessness toward consequences or outcomes in consuming the utility of the product or service; further absence of mistake, accident, and inevitability of choice.
- Capacity responsibility: Practices of praise and blame assume a level of intellectual and emotional capability.[53]

Both morality and law embody and respect these distinctions. By enabling the law institutionalizes and formalizes the distinction, but also possible consequences.

---

[52] Audi, R. (ed.), *The Cambridge dictionary of philosophy*, Cambridge University Press, Cambridge, p. 794,2009

[53] Ebd., p. 794

The Oxford Dictionary of Philosophy (2008) calls it people's responsibility: Each person is, within personal limits, accountable for thing they do or initiate. Failure to discharge a responsibility leads to some censure or penalty.[54] As one result of research, Van der Wal et al. (2008) confirmed, that for public managers accounting is highest ranked.[55]

In the legal and hierarchical environment of public administration, acting is formalized and determined; that's why public managers seldom bear a high grade responsibility in the meaning to be responsible to execute a duty or provide a service. Remarkably the German Insolvency Order opens an exit in a case of catastrophic mismanagement; at least in the relationship to third persons the consequences to bear were excluded (German Insolvency Order, §12).

Public sector organizations in Germany are traditionally based on the fundamentals of the Weberian model of bureaucracy and hierarchical system[56]; the execution follows the principle of equality, "sine ira et studio" (without anger and fondness). Public servants have to execute their duties without any preferences.[57] Cases are handled by determined processes as basic principles for execution of the function, derivation for an improved outcome are limited. The full autonomy is disturbed by dependencies to regional and federal government, considering resources, duties and objectives and the execution of governmental programs.

Participation in success is seldom used, although the public sector collective wage agreement of 2005 offers an entry (Tarifvertrag Öffentlicher Dienst (TVÖD) § 18). Qualitative and quantitative objectives could be rewarded with a minor monetary compensation. However, the general model without the possibility of personal rewards, praise and blame, and sanctions remains. In the case of Public Private Partnership (PPP) Projects, Forrer (2010) suggests to define and distribute responsibilities to all parties in the partnership/relationship.[58] Therefore accountability has to be established by the relationship created and obligations and requirements divided by both government and the private partner.

In the case of a public good the consumer/ customer has no choice; the provided quality of service is not exchangeable by a market. Moss (2002) argued that

---

54 Blackburn, S. (ed.), *Oxford dictionary of philosophy*, Oxford University Press, Oxford, 2008

55 Van der Wal, Z./ de Graaf, G./ Lasthuizen, K., *What's valued most? Similarities and differences between the organizational values of the public and private sector*, Public Administration, Vol. 86, No. 2, 2008

56 Weber, M., *Wirtschaft und Gesellschaft*, Zweitausendeins, Frankfurt, 2008, orig. 1922

57 Pečarič, M., *Personal establishment and accomplishment of public service values*, Transylvanian Review of Administrative Sciences, 38 E, p. 129, 2013

58 Forrer, J. et al., *Public – private partnerships and the public accountability question*, Public Administration Review, May-June, pp. 478, 2010

results of building bridges or enforcing the law system show different qualities.[59] Specifications and intended outcomes are discussed beforehand, all alternatives are described, all legal and formal requirements, and the process of providing are determined; as one results to make the production easier and to limit a personal and functional responsibility. Benefits or utilities can be very different to individuals; in addition, citizens can hold an individual public value that is not comparable with a self-interested private value.[60]

With his provocative assumption of "organized irresponsibility" Banner summarized the personal involvement in a process in public administration, from the initial point to a final evaluation of output and outcome of the activities. [61]

In this context Bovens present the two different models for accountability in the public sector. It is based on the Westminster Model, applied the Anglo-Saxon states, in which public managers are only accountable to their direct superiors in the chain of command. This model is applied in the United Kingdom, but limited transferable to other European countries also.

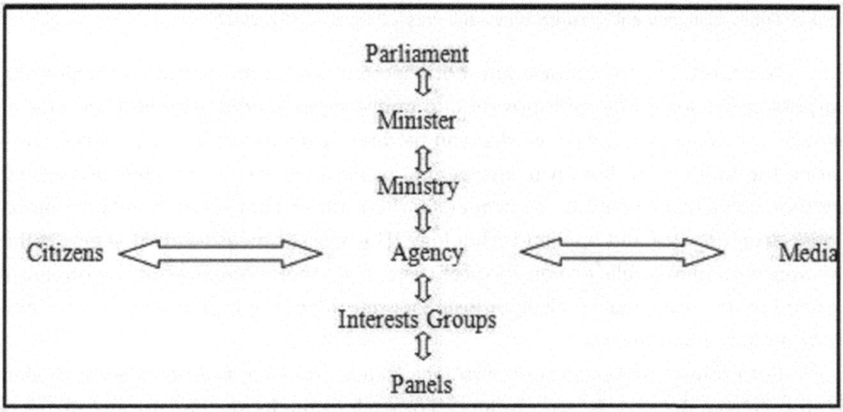

Figure 10: Horizontal accountability in the Westminster Model
Source: Bovens, M., *Public Accountability*, in Ferlie, E./ Lynn, L./ Pollitt, C. (eds.), "The Oxford Handbook of Public Management", Oxford University Press, Oxford, p. 197, 2007

59 Moss, D., When all else fails – Government as the ultimate risk manager, Harvard University Press, Cambridge, 2002

60 Bozeman, B., *Public value and public interest*, Georgetown University Press, Washington, p. 132, 2007

61 Banner, G., *Von der Behörde zum Dienstleistungsunternehmen: Die Kommunen brauchen ein neues Steuerungsmodell*, Verwaltungsführung, Organisation, Personalführung, 1, pp. 6-11, 1991

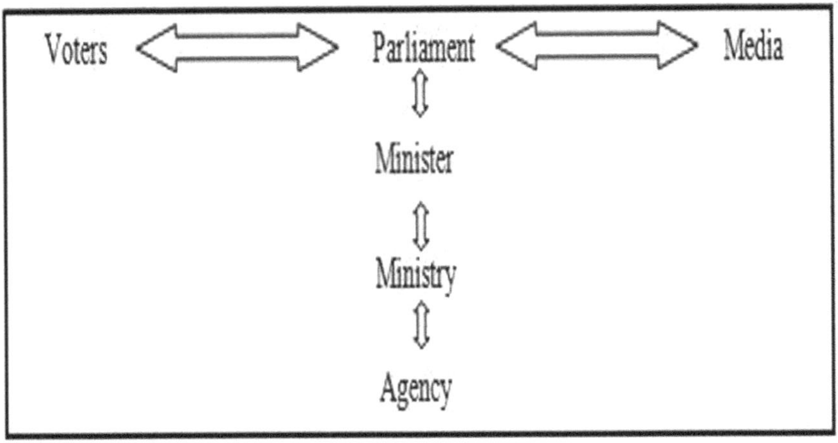

Figure 11: Vertical accountability in the Westminster Model
Source: Bovens, M., *Public Accountability*, in Ferlie, E./ Lynn, L./ Pollitt, C. (eds.), "The Oxford Handbook of Public Management", Oxford University Press, Oxford, p. 197, 2007

Denhardt and Denhardt argue both sectors can be distinct by examining the purpose to be served by both private and public organizations: The performance of individual managers and each worker can be directly measured in benchmarks, comparing the unit's contribution to the overall profit as monetary number of success; another benchmark could be a comparison with other companies, similar in directions, structure size and applied technology. This kind of measurement seems to be not appropriate in public or non-for-profit agencies. Their objectives of the organization are more ambiguous; making or losing money in not the important factor or indicator for success or failure.[62]

Both private and public organizations create, produce, and provide a wide and deep spectrum of services and products. For each of the items the customer expects a certain and specific utility or benefit, independent whether the service or good has to be purchased or it's for free. The monetary value, prevailing for private goods, expressed in units of the currency, is equalized with a personal increased benefit. Thus the providing organizations are responsible for their products and services, both for free or for a transfer price. The customer purchases an increased value, in material or immaterial aspects, and has therefore a legitimate claim for a proportional compen-

[62] Denhardt, R. & Denhardt, J., *Public administration: An action orientation*, Thomson Wadworth, Belmont, p. 6, 2009

sation, this model of "utility for return service" works. But it is different in governmental agencies on federal, state or local level. Øvretveit (2005) describes the public sector as less competitive and culturally different in many facets.[63] On the one hand the increase of utility is different to the citizens, based on the grade of affection; on the other hand the citizen is locked in the formalism of administration and unable to use evasive action. Most mandatory products are protected by the legal framework and are declared statutory tasks. The responsibility for provision lies at the local administration, but the range and quality of provided goods is legally or politically determined. The values for fulfilling the mandatory and voluntarily tasks in public administration play an important role, as Van der Wal et al stated in 2008.[64] The ambivalent function of the citizens as funder, as customer, client, and consumer is peculiar and challenges the execution and the intentionally taken responsibility for development, production, provision and quality check.[65] In addition the political programs and streams complicate a stringent and linear execution.[66] But the consumption of public goods and services and the orientation not to harm in a physical, but also in a material or immaterial way, complement the view by the public administration. To get performance indicators, to get an estimation of increased value, and the grade of impact for an individual or a group of individuals, have to be analysed. Responses to products are deliberate more comprehensive than for similar private produced, offered and purchased goods.[67] Law codifies and institutionalizes responsibility; hence the Oxford Dictionary of Philosophy described the inability to discharge a responsibility as a direct way to become liable to some censure or penalty.[68]

The question remains behind the results why public managers are so aware of accountability, especially in an environment neither within direct competition nor limited marketization and almost fixed determined process and decision-strings. In the case of Germany the public sector is dispersed all over Germany, in federal, state and local agencies. The execution of tasks is based on Weber's model of bureaucracy, combined with essences of Wilson and the scientific management by Taylor.[69] Among other regulations, the public servant should act without anger and fondness, and

---

63 Øvretveit, J., *Public service quality improvement*, in Ferlie, E., Lynn, L.E. jr., Pollitt, C., (eds.), „The Oxford handbook of public management", Oxford University Press, Oxford, pp. 537-562, 2005

64 Van der Wal, Z./ de Graaf, G./ Lasthuizen, K., *What's valued most? Similarities and differences between the organizational values of the public and private sector*, Public Administration, Vol. 86, No. 2, 2008

65 Schedler, K.& Proeller, I., *New Public Management*, Haupt, Berne, p. 102, 2006

66 O'Flynn, J., *From new public management to public value: paradigmatic change and managerial implications*, The Australian Journal of Public Administration, 66 (3), p. 355, 2007

67 Bodemann, M. & Olaru, M., *Responsibility to customers in the context of public value management – a german case study"*, Amfiteatru economic, Vol XVI (35), pp. 171 -186, 2014

68 Blackburn, S. (ed.), *Oxford dictionary of philosophy*, Oxford University Press, Oxford, 2008

69 Weber, M., *Wirtschaft und Gesellschaft*, Zweitausendeins, Frankfurt, 2008, orig. 1922

without any preferences.[70] Basic principles are clear and precise described steps within the production process, outputs and outcomes are actually regarded secondary. Incentives to increase the autonomy and the responsibility for each individual public servant are realized in 2005 with the actual collective wage agreement as pointed out above. This contract offers at least a small amount to reward in the case of fulfilling predetermined objectives in a contract between the principal and the agent, as individual or as group. But the application and the formalized way to introduce and maintain the application made it difficult to use this possibility as motivation or steering instrument. In the case of public good the citizen, as customer, client, and consumer, has to accept the provided quality and content and intended functionality. Because of the political discussion and legal formulation of rules for provision beforehand, all expected results and outcomes are discussed and alternatives weighted. The degree of scrutiny has a greater extend compared to private organizations caused by the differences related to sources of funding. Remaining responsibility lies therefore not by producing an increase of utility or welfare, but to follow the legal and formal aspects. Bozeman states that benefit or utility are different to individuals; the self-interest private value is seldom identical to the public value, if this term could be evaluated.[71]

Important factor for evaluation of utility and benefits, created or destroyed by public actions, is a virtual contract between the citizen and the governmental agency, responsible for provision of direct or indirect consumed public goods and services. A contract, based directly or indirectly on a legal framework, establishes a relationship with bidirectional duties for both partners. On the one side properties, specifications of a product, and the kind of use are agreed between both parties, the individual grade of utility depends on the effective and efficient use of the good or service. Depending on the different abilities and the status quo of utility the scale of increase utility or benefits can differ. The provision itself inflicts a challenge for the manager to set the correct priorities, to keep within the given budget and to meet the demands and expectations of politicians and employees as argued by Øvretveit (2005).[72] Pečarič (2013) considers that the activities, determined or free handled, of public employees could have influence on citizen. They are influenced in their thinking, feelings and behaviour and vice versa.[73]

---

[70] Pečarič, M., *Personal establishment and accomplishment of public service values*, Transylvanian Review of Administrative Sciences, 38 E, p. 129, 2013

[71] Bozeman, B., *Public values and public interest: counterbalancing economic individualism*, Georgetown University Press, Washington D.C., p.132, 2007

[72] Øvretveit, J., *Public service quality improvement*, in Ferlie, E., Lynn, L.E. jr., Pollitt, C., (eds.), „The Oxford handbook of public management", Oxford University Press, Oxford, pp. 537- 562, 2005

[73] Pečarič, M., *Personal establishment and accomplishment of public service values*, Transylvanian Review of Administrative Sciences, 38 E, p. 128, 2013

In opposite to the arguments above and combined with the notion of efficiency and effectiveness based on the clear structure and precise described processes Roger (1998) and Walsh and Rowling (1995) found that bureaucracy leads just as to some undesired but inevitable effects; i.e. resource wastage and budget maximization in the pursuit of increase and stabilization of own position, power, status and ease of management.[74] That leads to an ambivalent view to accountability. By using bureaucracy Weber intended to take away any accountability to the public manager, he should only be held accountable to follow rules and regulation.

However, the legal framework for public administration in general and in Germany in particular reduces the functional and personal liabilities. Alford and Hughes describe the status as processes determined, each eventuality is covered by detailed instructions; on the opposite side deviation from the given path and creativity in the pursuit of opportunities or adoptions for peculiar case are almost excluded.[75] As result public sector processes are not designed to make decision under risk as a matter of volatility in the expected outcomes, risk appetite is not core element, although risk taking contains several success factors.

Consequently a personal accountability is excluded, although avoiding any explanations to stakeholders is ranked first. The relationship between provision of products and services is based on a clear distinction and separation of personal involvement. To go into detail the question remains who will be responsible in the case of an mislead project management or in case of increasing debt levels for local administration, especially in the case of caused delays for collateral projects or services. For vivid risk awareness hierarchical structures and identified risk bearers have to be selected and determined.

The German Insolvency Order (InsO) excludes any kind of insolvency for public sector organizations. Behind this protection a guarantee is hidden for execution and provision of mandatory tasks. From a financial perspective it is assumed that any fail to keeping the expenditure within the given budget will be compensated by the next higher governmental hierarchical level.

The ongoing crisis in Greece shows similar outcomes of an overstretching of financial resources for a long time. Without a stringent political course change the challenges for Greece as state and society will crush any political initiative and incentives for entrepreneurs, businesses and the citizens. Any kind of personal and institutional accountability has to be strengthened in the future to avoid similar scenarios in

---

[74] Cited by O'Flynn, J., *From new public management to public value: paradigmatic change and managerial implications*, The Australian Journal of Public Administration, 66 (3), p. 355, 2007

[75] Alford, J.& Hughes, O., *Public value pragmatism as the next phase of public management*, The American Review of Public Administration, 38 (2), pp. 130 - 148, 2008

Europe, but demonstrates the distinction considering the accountability between private and public sector.

Existence and grade of responsibility of organizations are one method to clear a distinction between private and public provided goods. Direct accountability to citizens is more or less substituted by the objective of sustainable provision of mandatory services and goods to the citizens. Their accountability and responsibility is based on laws and regulations. Outputs should serve the most in need of these services by available resources at lowest costs.[76]

The current discussion all over Europe makes it evident: Provision of these products and services are dependent on the financial and personal framework the politics offer. By analyzing the risk factors a clear distinction can be made to show these differences: Internal risk factors can be influenced by public administration, exogenous risk factors are out of direct influence and determined by politics, economic developments, and the legal and societal framework. In most cases quality of services is therefore not based in pursuit to meet the expectations of the citizens, but is actually oriented on the input, the calculative amount of money to spend in the current year. Citizens' and customers' expectations can differ, but lead not to an instantaneous claim of responsibility. Introducing the term public value Moore argues that public administration is a value creating system. For improving the quality of living of individuals in a collective life the government provided with funds and assets.[77]

The presented list by Burgi contains a mixture of execution and cooperation between federal, state and local level. The range of duties and embedded position of a local administration shows that they are not in the position and provided with a grade of freedom as an entrepreneur. Most of the given examples could be provided by private corporations; challenging is the combination and to meet the expectations of the citizens. A house in the vicinity of the fire station could be reached very fast, but apartment areas in the periphery of a city are subject to the same criteria, but the effort to keep the timelines is disparate more difficult.

The spectrum of municipal duties is combined with a peculiar kind of decision making, evaluating the resources for the input, the expected output and outcome of public provided goods, independent from the real execution by the public administration. For Denhardt and Denhardt the following categories support the distinction of

---

[76] Øvretveit, J., *Public service quality improvement*, in Ferlie, E., Lynn, L.E. jr., Pollitt, C., (eds.), „The Oxford handbook of public management", Oxford University Press, Oxford, pp. 537 -562, 2005

[77] Benington, J. & Moore, M.(eds.), *Public Value - Theory and practice*, Palgrave Macmillan, Basingstoke, p. 92, 2011

private and public goods and services.[78] They argue that ambiguity, pluralistic decision making and visibility have an enormous effects to the responsibility of public administration to the citizens. It reflects the direct line to the citizens as groups as sovereign. Profiroiu et al. (2013) argue by the term of ambiguity that the performance of a manager or decision-maker is increasingly measured; European approaches come to extensive and representative results.[79] Considering individual or collective consumer responsibility Van Thiel and Leeuw stated in 2002 that the unit's contribution to the overall success or better profit has no priority.[80] From a managerial standpoint making or losing money and thereby missing the task, to use the trusted money and to maximize the effects to the people, is missed, because that's not a crucial criterion for success. The research by Van Thiel and Leeuw confirmed that the highest priority in private sector is producing demanded products in pursuit of profit for shareholders and interests of stakeholders; in public sector priority is to stay in budget and fulfill the legal objectives. Decision-making and influence from different pressure group undermine an expected responsibility. Many different interest group and individuals with diffuse notions and expectation which objectives are to reach by activities lead to a wide span of quality of public goods and services; because of the different grade of usefulness the evaluation of them is also diffuse.[81] Especially this grade of measurement will be applied in the later presented substitute for economic values of results in the case of decisions under uncertainty.

Given by law public organizations operate with a much greater visibility of the production manufacturing process. The ability of perception, and the resulting utility of a good in the meaning of benefits, utility and other intentions are legally intended and politically demanded, but absorbed and used in different ways and grade as Bodemann and Olaru (2014) mentioned.[82] Meynhardt (2013) argues that mistrust in leading elites, the dynamic medial processing and the increase of complexity forces public administration to focus to customer responsibility.[83] Although the consumer responsibility is in focus by public managers, the exclusion of choice and the grade of affection determine the peculiar position of a citizen. The public and press tend to

---

[78] Denhardt, R. & Denhardt, J., *Public administration: An action orientation*, Thomson Wadworth, Belmont, p. 5, 2009

[79] Profiroiu, M.C./ Tapardel, A./ Mihăescu, C., *Performance analysis of the Romanian public administration,* Transylvanian Review of Administrative Sciences, 40 E, pp. 183 – 200, 2013

[80] Van Thiel, S. & Leeuw, F., *The performance paradox in the public sector*, Public Performance & Management Review, 25 (3), pp. 267 – 281, 2002

[81] Denhardt, R. & Denhardt, J., *Public administration: An action orientation*, Thomson Wadworth, Belmont, p. 6, 2009

[82] Bodemann, M. & Olaru, M., *Responsibility to customers in the context of public value management – a german case study"*, Amfiteatru economic, Vol XVI (35), pp. 171 -186, 2014

[83] Meynhardt, T., *Public Value Scorecard*, OrganisationsEntwicklung, No. 4, p. 79, 2013

compare the intended objectives with the realized effects, to individuals and to groups of individuals. Consumer responsibility has different grades because of the different grade of use and the resulting utility for the user. By initiating the political process from the idea to the realization and provision to the citizen and the following evaluation of quality is determined by the legal framework; in the case of political programs the local public administration is only in an executive function responsibility is thereby limited and transferred, at least in the intended utility function and outcomes to the citizens. A direct responsibility to the sceptical public is rare in such cases, because of the blurring of political, administrative, and technical responsibility.

A contract establishes a relationship with bidirectional duties. The buyer will have to pay the price, the producer, supplier, or seller will have to provide the product holding the promised specifications. Each consumer has his individual intentions to use the properties and to reach a scale of utility; public sector organizations provide a broad variety of products and services, most of them are legally demanded and have therefore a limited utility, for example the passport, which is used only in special cases, like international journeys or in case of personal identification; enhancement of personal benefit is relatively limited. With new technologies the personal identity card can be used for other purposes, for example to provide a digital certificate for business via the internet or information about medical treatment. These additional functions increase the utility. Question remains whether the utility justifies the price to pay.

However, it becomes clear the economic use of resources is secondary in the pursuit to execute of legal duties to reach political objectives. Main goal remain to fulfil the obligatory tasks.

The legal objective to offer public goods makes the discrepancy and supports to distinguish private and public provided goods obvious. Public goods are thereby defined as jointly consumed, determined by non–rivalness between customer/consumer and are considered as remedies for market failure as Alford and Hughes point out (2008).[84] In addition because of non-excludability a citizen could not be excluded from the benefits or use of the good. In contrast private goods are based on the property of excludability. In the case of public provided goods wide-spread expectations by citizens lead to different expectation of output and outcome. Intended utility and quality are discussed, often on political and public level.

In the hierarchical structure, with citizenry as sovereign in a representative democracy, execution of governmental programs is the ruling order of public admin-

[84] Alford, J.& Hughes, O., *Public value pragmatism as the next phase of public management*, The American Review of Public Administration, Vol. 38, No. 2, p. 132, 2008

istration and organizations. O'Flynn states the focus of private sector is efficiency, quality, scrutiny and reliability; in public sector these characteristics are extended by accountability and public preferences.[85] For Pečarič other rankings of values occur.[86]

All estimations in common is that public sector organizations have to deal with a wider spectrum of accountability and responsibility because of bureaucratic structures, diffuse interests, and grade of absorption by the citizen, although the lifespan of a product is significantly longer than in private sector. Often changes are triggered by technological developments demand from citizens to increase efficiency, i.e. correspondence with public administration via the internet instead of hardcopies.

Van der Wal (2008) proves that responsibility on hierarchical or even personal level is hard to define for public organization.[87] The intended "non-responsibility" is confirmed by Alford and Hughes (2008).[88] They found that "in public services the procedure manuals become even longer with the method for dealing with every conceivable contingency spelled out in great detail. Once this was laid the task of the public official was purely administrative."

This research presents the highest ranking for values for managers in private organization and public organizations: The results depict the differences between both, especially because the manager on upper level are asked. For public organizations accountability is ranked first. In contrast when managers in the private sector were interviewed, they ranked profitability and accountability as the most important values, social-justice as the least important. Based on aims of the public sector to such things as democracy, accountability, equity and probity are highly valued in a public sector milieu, the managers there tend understand their responsibilities differently.

The explanations above considering the existence guarantee of the organization, the virtual unlimited resources and the impersonal involvement in the organization are amplified by the following tables.

Table 4 Descriptive statistics for actual values in the public and private sector in order of importance

[85] O'Flynn, J., *From new public management to public value: paradigmatic change and managerial implications*, The Australian Journal of Public Administration, Vol. 66, No. 3, p. 360, 2007

[86] Pečarič, M., ebd. p. 131

[87] Van der Wal, Z./ de Graaf, G./ Lasthuizen, K., *What's valued most? Similarities and differences between the organizational values of the public and private sector*, Public Administration, Vol. 86, No. 2, 2008

[88] Alford, J.& Hughes, O., *Public value pragmatism as the next phase of public management*, The American Review of Public Administration, Vol. 38, No. 2, p. 138, 2008

Source: Van der Wal, Z./ de Graaf, G./ Lasthuizen, K., *What's valued most? Similarities and differences between the organizational values of the public and private sector*, Public Administration, Vol. 86, No. 2, p. 473, 2008

Ranking	Public sector	Private sector
1.	Accountability	Profitability
2.	Lawfulness	Accountability
3.	Incorruptibility	Reliability
4.	Expertise	Effectiveness
5.	Reliability	Expertise
6.	Effectiveness	Efficiency
7.	Impartiality	Honesty
8.	Efficiency	Innovativeness
9.	Transparency	Incorruptibility
10.	Serviceability	Dedication

The assumed entrepreneur characteristics are not ranked higher in the most important values; while combining lower important characteristics, for example serviceability, effectiveness or efficiency, the ideas of Weber and Taylor are reflected by the given answers. Priority is given to the execution of and accountability to given orders and processes, without an effort to improve the results or outcomes.

Van der Wal et al. gives the managers a prepared definition of accountability: For this evaluation accountability is used for act to willingly to justify and explain actions to the relevant stakeholders. Remarkable are the results when the managers are asked to prioritize the "should" values applied in the execution.

The next table presents answers, the managers gave, asked for "Should be values". That gave the managers the opportunity to present their tendencies if authority and time would allow focusing to other characteristics and aspects than the currently applied ones:

Table 5 Descriptive statistics for should be values in the public and private sector in order of importance
Source: Van der Wal, Z./ de Graaf, G./ Lasthuizen, K., *What's valued most? Similarities and differences between the organizational values of the public and private sector*, Public Administration, Vol. 86, No. 2, p. 475, 2008)

Ranking:	Public sector:	Difference:	Private sector:	Difference:
1.	Accountability	0	Profitability	0
2.	Effectiveness	+5	Accountability	0
3.	Incorruptibility	0	Expertise	+2
4.	Reliability	+1	Reliability	-1
5.	Lawfulness	-3	Effectivness	-1

6.	Expertise	-2	Honesty	+1
7.	Efficiency	+1	Impartiality	+10
8.	Transparency	+1	Efficiency	-2
9.	Impartiality	-2	Innovativeness	-1
10.	Serviceability	0	Incorruptibility	-1

In public sector the given values ranked 1- 10 (Top 10) are still the same in the meaning of "Should be values"; for the private sector impartiality, in the meaning of act with pre-judice or bias toward a specific group interests, is regarded as a more important value and climbs 10 places; dedication is no more ranked in the first ten.

The ranking scheme is the same as in preceded table. Effectiveness is considered to be neglected and should be more important, while the lawfulness of execution is ranked -3. Van der Wal, who gave the addressed manager the following definition: Effectiveness = act to achieve the desired results.[89] That leads to the assumption that both effectiveness and efficiency is not regarded as one of the most important values in both sectors; one fact that will influence the countermeasures in the context of risk management and the outcomes of developments.

Independent of personal intentions the general legal framework for public administration in Germany reduces liability and therefore a personal involvement both in terms of content and in terms of personal or functional responsibility. Using the model of bureaucracy Alford and Hughes (2008) extended the irresponsibility by exclusion of creativity and deviations in pursuit of opportunities caused by detailed determined process steps and instructions. Opportunities in the meaning to gain more than regularly to expect could contribute to a better ratio between output and input.[90] Incentives to seek for such results are actually rare.

As pointed out above the German Insolvency Order excludes per definition any kind of insolvency and consequences for public sector organization; especially if they are necessary to keep the legal and administrative system intact. Extensions of a given budget will be compensated by the next hierarchical level, from local to federal authorities, regardless of consequences for following years.[91]

This net is comfortable, but not unlimited, especially because in the case if external conditions are not steerable. The results prove another reality as examples from Switzerland or the USA showed: A smaller public administration in Switzerland,

89 Van der Wal, Z./ de Graaf, G./ Lasthuizen, K., *What's valued most? Similarities and differences between the organizational values of the public and private sector*, Public Administration, Vol. 86, No. 2, p. 470, 2008

90 Alford, J.& Hughes, O., *Public value pragmatism as the next phase of public management*, The American Review of Public Administration, Vol. 38, No. 2, 2008

91 Bodemann, M. & Olaru, M., *Responsibility to customers in the context of public value management – a german case study*, Amfiteatru economic, Vol XVI (35), pp. 171 -186

the municipality of Leukerbad, has declared bankruptcy after occurrence of insolvency and was later handled comparable to private businesses.[92] Also the State of California (USA) got a financial shortage for a period of time during the financial crisis in 2008. A popular legend of unlimited resources for public sector and an extended safety for all contractors was swept away by these published examples of mismanagement. Increasing social welfare commitments mean more responsibilities for managers in the public administration. But more than half of the chief financial officers of the public administrations, interviewed during the field research, feared that financial and personnel resources at their command might not be commensurate with their increased responsibilities.[93] Identified distinctions lead to a conversion of indices to measure success of public administration. Change in public value will be one indicator.

1. 2. 2. Recent scientific approaches to public value

Each individual has an own notion of best performance and undergoes the use and utility of provided goods in a personal way. Individuals will judge the use of taxes and fees as money spent by government on collective goods at the expense of private consumption.

Provision and consumption of public or private provided products and services creates or destroys also social utility. A balance of utility and disutility is based on collective or individual evaluations. Those judgements are most rational and subjective, but will also lead to an articulated will of a bigger or less big part of the society.

One fundamental question remains within all of the considerations of public value: Is public value only a product of governmental action, executed by public administration and other public sector organizations? Providing a legal framework is the legitimate domain of government within the society. This means boundaries and freedom to act both as business and as private. The membership and the different views have effects to the estimation of the current situation. It remains whether the distinction between public and private value is fixed; or are these value concepts semi-permeable in the meaning that private activities will influence the public value and vice versa. To evaluate public value as an abstract, numeric value, private contri-

---

[92] Rehfeld, D., *Rating von Kommunen*, in Stephan, G. & Meurer, E.(eds.), „Rechnungswesen und Controlling", Haufe, Stuttgart, 2005

[93] Results from the first field research conducted from 2009 - 2012. The research results are augmented by a survey of Kienbaum in 2009 in: *Innovative Verwaltung*, 1-2/2010, p. 21: The research covered 45 big cities in Germany. More than half of them confirmed that the trade tax incomes decreased in 2009 between 15- 25 %. In addition the social aids costs increased by 79% of the examined cities.

butions could not be excluded, i.e. a private park, open to the public, can increase the public value for the persons who are interested to use the park. Combining the possibilities by legal framework through mandatory tasks, to improve or at least to maintain public value, is an issue of government, but the expanded notion that others contribute to public value is realistic. For example voluntary associations, private persons and organization bring in their part of public value and will be estimated as elementary factors for public value, in the meaning of contribution to the quality of life for the citizens. They create utility and consumer satisfaction within the given framework. Public value is hence a function of private and public efforts.

The current financial situation, privatisation, and embedding in the political system lead inevitable to a discussion about performance in public administration and about increase of effectiveness and efficiency by the use of public funded resources. Ostrom and Ostrom (1971) stated that good administration "...will be hierarchically ordered in a system of grades ranks subject to political direction by heads of departments at the center of government."[94] That focus to a devotional execution of political programs could slow down modernizing public administration and highlighting the prevailing notions of this sector.

For a better understanding, the term 'value' and the combination with 'public' is the pivot for application of potential changes in public value through decision-making. Referring to economic indicators for success, the performance of an organization or enterprise is assessed and judged by the value-added statement.[95] This statement shows how much wealth - in the meaning of value for the people added - has been created by the organization or enterprise, in contrast how much has been destroyed. The value added is thereby a product of the collective use of capital, employees, know- how and other resources. This declaration of success is typically made for a specific period of time.

For the concrete application, Oakley et al. (2006) suggest that public value can be used as an indicator of how government should analyse and respond to the changing environment and tendencies of public opinion - as identified by polling and other measurements and types of consumer market researches.[96] They regard public value as a possibility to evaluate the output, expressed as a signal and request of satisfying public demand. The OECD adds that "...public management arrangements deliver not

---

94 Ostrom, V. & Ostrom, E., *Public choice: a different approach to the study of public administration*, Public Administration Review, Vol. 31, No. 2, pp. 203 -216, 1971

95 Law, J. (ed.), *Oxford dictionary of business and management*, Oxford University Press, Oxford, p. 577, 2009

96 Oakley, K./ Naylor, R./ Lee, D., *Giving them what they want: the construction of the public in „public value"*, CREST Media Change & Social Change Conference, Sept 2006, Oxford University, 2006

only public services; they also ensure deeper governance values."[97] Society, politics, and economy are therefore common tasks for politicians, entrepreneurs, electorate and public administration as executives for political programs.

Value added, according to the Oxford Dictionary of Economics, means: "The total sales of a firm less purchases of inputs from other firms. What is left is available for wages of its employees and the profits of its owners."[98] In addition the Oxford Dictionary of Philosophy offers another definition of value: "To acknowledge some feature of things as a value is to take it into account in decision making."[99] Value as a term is split by the Cambridge Dictionary of Philosophy; it highlights the two attempts of value: The thing/objective has an intrinsic value; it is worth of something in the assessment of an individual. Second attempt is to apply the concept of "fittingness" or "appropriateness" to it, certain kinds of emotions and desires.[100] For applicability in decision-making, or at least as orientation for decision-maker in public sector, a combination of several definitions with their concepts behind them represents the best appropriate one. For Kelly et al. (2002) services, outcomes, and trust are the main blocks public value is consistent of. They argue that application of NPM is an interstation on the transition from a traditional public administrative work to the public value paradigm.[101] Thus NPM is forced by the premise that management techniques from private sector are in general applicable and appropriate for public sector. O'Flynn (2007) comes to similar results: Public administration is one paradigm change from the classical administration in the sense of implementation of political master plan; next step was the NPM paradigm as pursuit of results and efficiency gains by contracts and delegation of authority and accountability.[102] Currently public value paradigm is advocate of politics rather than input. Pečarič (2013) confirms that the public administration has to make value judgments, but must be also responsive to articulated or collected community needs.[103]

O'Flynn (2007) concentrates to the distinction to the current way of running the public sector and tendencies of the ongoing reforms. The transformation of the

---

[97] O'Flynn, J., *From new public management to public value: paradigmatic change and managerial implications*, The Australian Journal of Public Administration, Vol. 66, No. 3, p. 358, 2007

[98] Black, J./ Hashimzade, N./ Myles, G.(eds.), *Oxford Dictionary of Economics*, 3rd edition, Oxford University Press, Oxford, p. 474, 2009

[99] Blackburn, S. (ed.), *Oxford Dictionary of Philosophy*, Oxford University Press, Oxford, p. 377, 2008

[100] Audi, R. (ed.), *The Cambridge dictionary of philosophy*, Cambridge University Press, Cambridge, p. 948, 2009

[101] Kelly, G./ Mulgan, G./ Muers, S., *Creating public value*, Strategy Unit, Cabinet Office, London, 2002

[102] O'Flynn, J., *From new public management to public value: paradigmatic change and managerial Implications*, The Australian Journal of Public Administration, Vol. 66, No. 3, p. 360, 2007

[103] Pečarič, M, *Personal establishment and accomplishment of public service values*. Transylvanian Review of Administrative Sciences, 38 E, pp. 125 – 143, 2013

organization and the application of paradigms also for a risk management are obvious: For example the collective preferences as expression of public interest, instead of the former modelling of individual preferences by politicians or by polls. While the former model was built on the legitimacy of public activities without any efforts to legitimate the delegated authority and executive power, the model in pursuit of public value based on the steady task to legitimate the authority and to create and confirm public trust in the public administration activities.

For public risk management the preferences play the important role in the case of a decision. Without any knowledge of grade of affection and expected deviation by the decision, the essentials of risk management, probability and range of consequences, could not integrated as one part of the equation.

Carl Menger puts this already in 1892 in the following way: "Economic value is the importance which concrete goods, or quantity of goods, receive for use from the fact that we are conscious of being dependent on our disposal over them for the satisfaction of our wants."[104] Using that definition public value depends on individual appraisal to a situation while estimating the framework and services given by the government, measured on all levels and their grade or ability to create utility or benefit. Similar observation are named by Benington and Moore (2011): They mentioned that the role of the government, represented through all public sector hierarchies, is not limited to the role of rule-setter and service provider, but to contribute to public value in all public spheres: political, economic, social, and cultural.[105]

Moore developed in the nineties of the last century the strategic triangle of public value: First, he considered the legalization of activities to provide some form of output; second, the operational capacity to create and provide those services and products; and third, the outcomes resulting from the provision. All of the three are dependent among each other as the Figure 1 shows.

Public value can be interpreted to depend and rely upon the politically-mediated expression of collectively determined and articulated preferences. That means what the citizenry, individuals or group of, determined and expressed as valuable. The bandwidth of personal estimation of a current situation spread from an egoistic point of view to a collective view with a pronounced public spirit. Following table draws one possible spectrum of interests and personal evaluation.

Table 6: Categories of outcome-estimation
Source: developed by author analyzing the different models of estimation of public activities

---

[104] Menger, C., *Principles of economics*, Ludwig-von-Mises-Institute, Auburn, p. 18, 1976
[105] Benington, J. & Moore, M.(eds.), *Public Value - Theory and practice*, Palgrave Macmillan, Basingstoke, p. 5, 2011

Focus:	Individual interests	Individual interests	Collective interests	Collective interests
Point of evaluation:	Subjective evaluation	Objective evaluation	Subjective evaluation	Objective evaluation
Category:	Individualism/ egoism	Limited individualism	Limited sense of community	Sense of Community

Each individual has an own notion of best performance and undergoes use and utility of provided goods in unique ways. Spending taxes is thereby a structural and systematic reduction of personal utility. Provided utility of public or private produced products and services creates or reduces also social or personal utility. A balance of utility and disutility is based on collective or individual evaluations. Those judgments are most rational and subjective, but will also lead to an articulated will of a bigger or less big part of the society. A positive net result of added and reduced public value is the target of applying public value.

Bozeman claims that public value is based on the providing normative consensus about

- the rights, benefits, prerogatives to which citizens should be entitled
- obligations of citizens to society, state and one another
- principles on which governments and policies should be based on[106]

The individual should be enabled to hold public values different from their own self-interested private value. Without the orientation to the community as seen above a general basement for analysis of public value and the consequences in the case of decisions is missing. Individual estimation of public value entitles citizens to address their meaning.

1.3. The dilemma of diffuse personal absorption of utility in the context of public services

The conditions and specification to provide public goods differ from regional and local peculiarities. The provide goods tends more and more to focus to the social

[106] Bozeman, B., *Public values and public interest: counterbalancing economic individualism*, Georgetown University Press, Washington D.C., 2007

department, depending on law given duties and politics. But parallel bigger projects for infrastructure and preventive measures dominate the administrative work and the financial volume. The shares of an individual are therefore depending on each individual state. A wide spectrum of personal characteristics forms the conclusion and prediction about the expected intensity of affection and the ability to absorb.

Beneath others, the following characteristics play an important role addressing the change in welfare and will later integrated in the measurement of the public value model:

1. Personal framework
    a. gender
    b. age
    c. marital status
    d. employment status
    e. geographic status of living area
    f. financial status
    g. volume of spent taxes and fees
    h. personal dependency to this good
    i. personal limitations by the product
2. General influence
    a. former affection
    b. composition with other public affections
    c. compensation
    d. number of potential users
3. Kind of affection
    a. direct / indirect affection
    b. unique, steady or frequent affection
    c. active / passive participation in the outcomes
    d. grade of participation
    e. expected gain in utility
    f. expected loss of utility by delay of stop of other measures
    g. known alternatives
    h. free / additional tuition for use

The individual utilization or benefit from goods and services are primarily based on individual estimation of complex environment. This is also relevant for the estimation and evaluation of uncertain future states. For example the effects of an appropriate waste water canalization to prevent floods in a housing area: Persons who live in the upper regions, far away from the threat of combined heavy rain and flooding by river have less benefit from the system as persons who live in the vicinity of the river. Remarkably in the ranking of the expected uncertain influences the climate change is ranked secondarily; the same worked out the analysis of the yearly annual statements: Although the frequency and severity of weather phenomena is increasing, precautionary measures of reserves for compensation are currently not in focus. However, neglected weather phenomena offer a valid statistical basement for reference class models. This model will be introduced by the integration of risk management.

Different to the private sector the diminishing effect cannot be controlled by the citizens, the public good is provided to serve as many citizens as needed and possible. The goals themselves are particularly vague and intangible compared to business firms, as Rainey (2009) argues.[107]

The effects to each citizen have to be measured instead of converting terms from business as sales and profits.

Collecting and processing of the different estimations of possible developments after a decision under no certainty means the main challenge for public management. Persons will vocalize within their individual status, as part of a community with a more egoistic point of view, oriented at the model of an economic actor, who neither intends to promote the public interest nor know how much he is promoting it. His main effort is to create greatest value pursuing his own interests.

Frequently he promotes the society more effectively than when he really intends to promote it, as Adam Smith (1776) describes his observervations.

[107] Rainey, H., *Understanding and managing public organization*, John Wiley & Sons, San Francisco, 2009

2. Today's development of applicability of business behavior in public administration

2.1. General approaches for increasing efficiency in public sector

Following Christensen et al. (2007) public administration is based on these traditional characteristics:

i. political steering from hierarchical, federal to local level
ii. central organization with some satellite
iii. political representative
iv. transparency and publicity of genesis of decisions, intended outcomes and execution
v. accountability
vi. impartiality and equal treatment
vii. professional independence
viii. political loyalty and neutrality[108]

New models and tools for the public administration, like the NPM, have started an organizational and procedural reengineering, or better a rethinking of the way the public ad-ministrations manage their internal processes to get desired results efficiently. Not only formal adapted models, which are supported by the government, traditional rules, and management techniques were derived and transferred to the public sector; to show the possibility to a more effective use of resources.[109] The NPM claims to be a combination of necessary public administration instruments and behaviour, but with an entrepreneurial perspective and competitive aspects. The combination of both types of attitudes should create a more effective and efficient public administration with the focus on the output and outcome, equipped with appropriate instruments, for more transparency and competition between public administrations of the same size and with similar duties. In Germany the new accounting standard for public administration has proved that for example the planned competition and comparison were avoided by the freedom of choice. Critical to the expected effects by NPM are Grimmer (2004) or Kegelmann (2007), positive aspects are worked out by Bogumil et al. (2007).[110]

[110] Grimmer , K., *Offentliche Verwaltung in Deutschland*, Verlag für Sozialwissenschaften, Wiesbaden, 2004, Kegelmann, J., *New Public Management*, Verlag für Sozialwissenschaften, Wiesbaden, 2007, Bogumil, J. et al., A., *Zehn Jahre Neues Steuerungsmodell*, edition sigma, Berlin, 2007

M. Bodemann, *Management in Public Administration*,
Sustainable Management, Wertschöpfung und Effizienz,
https://doi.org/10.1007/978-3-658-22687-9_3

In the aftermath of the introduction phase of NPM and the first estimations, other tools appear to support the steady reform and optimization of service provisioning; i.e. quality management, Balanced Score Card (BSC), performance management and open government are regarded as successors of NPM. As next step of more transparency and comparability the basic rules of double-entry-accounting are in focus: the so called IPSAS, International Public Sector Accounting Standards, currently applied by the EU in Brussels. These standards can lead to a convergence and a better comparability, in mid- and long-terms to a better application of the reference class model. All tools will support the progress and the results, but are based on the estimation and evaluation of hard facts, indicators which are able to reflect the performance. Measurement of indicators, their contribution and limits of application will be discussed in this chapter.

2.2. Concepts of New Public Management (NPM)

2. 2. 1. Basic principles of New Public Management

Trigger of reform the long-standing practices in public administration were the forecast of more and more complex duties, decreasing amount of resources and increase of sceptics, presented by mass media and the public. NPM is therefore regarded as key to a better provision of public services and products and signal that public sector is aware of the changing environment and future challenges.

Schaedler and Proeller (2006) introduced five premises which represent central assumptions and notion on which NPM is based on:

a) Optimized conception of human being, i.e. intrinsic motivated, responsible, complex man, seeking of tasks he is able to identify with
b) State and public administration are necessary
c) Problem is efficiency and effectiveness, not legality or legitimation
d) Rational public management is possible
e) Competition leads to more efficiency and effectiveness than planning and controlling
f) Politics and administration are both capable of learning[111]

NPM is based on the assumption that within limits characters and tools from private sector could be transferred and thereby contribute to reach a higher level of

[111] Schedler, K.& Proeller, I., *New Public Management*, Haupt, Berne, p. 56, 2006

effectiveness and efficiency in public sector. O'Flynn (2007) presents the determining characters as follows:[112]

- result and managerial responsibility
- economic principles
- modern management theory and practices
- service delivery

Managerial aspects include the following positions:

- Clearly defined expected results and services of the different divisions
- Steering using contracts and definition of objectives
- Supporting centralized control and monitoring functions
- Accrual and double entry accounting including resource monitoring
- Decentralized resources responsibility
- Application and maintaining is a long-lasting task, advantages and disavantages have to be weighed up after a certain period of time.

Among other reasons Mussari stated the following drivers for a reform of public administration:

- Private service as an alternative to public services
- Difficulty for tax-payers to understand the relationship between taxes paid and the level of services offered
- Progressing return to market mechanism for growing number of public services
- Loosing of institutional conditions which artificially guarantee the survival of the organization [113]

Hood (1991) gives the following four objectives, combined with the introduction and application of New Public Management:

- NPM attempts to slow down or even reverse government growth; measured in terms of public spending and staffing
- NPM shifts towards more privatisation and quasi-privatisation. Further it shifts away from a core government institution, renewed emphasis on "subsidiarity" in service production and provision

---

[112] O'Flynn, J., *From new public management to public value: paradigmatic change and managerial implications*, The Australian Journal of Public Administration, Vol. 66, No. 3, p. 361, 2007

[113] Mussari, R., *Autonomy, responsibility and new public management,* Conference on New Public Management in International Perspective, St. Gallen, 1996

- NPM focusses on more automation, especially in the branch of IT, in production and distribution of public goods and services
- NPM on international level focussed increasingly on general issues, for example decision styles and inter-governmental cooperation; increasingly breaking with the traditional specialism on local to country level[114]

The reforming and restructuring of public administration is continuously based and triggered by increasing financial problems. By the shorten periods between economic crises in Europe and over the world and the acceptance of awareness of increasing scarce goods by public managers and politics the former input focus is successive replaced by the output awareness. On the long run, under consideration of legal priority to increase welfare and public value, focus is directed to the outcomes of decisions and activities. Differences are recognizable in the process of accepting and applying new management tools. For example in Australia and New Zealand the government continued to retreat form the welfare state model. The private sector was address to bring in new or substitutes for public services and to act as partner for not-profit organizations to deliver these services.[115]

At the beginning of the 21st century the government in North Rhine-Westphalia has decided to build up the finance regulations, similar to the private sector. The "Kameralistik", in a wider view similar to cash-accounting, which excludes for example depreciations or assets accounting, was replaced in 2005 - 2009 by the double-entry-accounting. For the former cameralistics important point was to spend all planned budget for projects or operational work. If a department has saved money, the budget for the next year was reduced just by the amount. Saving in the meaning of stay below the budget has for the department undesired consequences, so the system focussed on consuming and not economizing the spending.

This new kind of double-entry-accounting is oriented towards the regulations of the German Commercial Code (HGB) and includes also a consolidated financial statement. Later results of these statements will be used by the empirical part to prove the risk awareness in general and the focus to endogenous and exogenous risks in particular. Annual reports become a more valid basis after the years of introduction and give a better impression of the current financial status and expected corridors of development; the reports allow further an inter-organizational comparison of costs for public services and products, while prices for services are mostly standard-

[114] Hood, C., *A public management for all seasons*, Public Administration, Vol. 69, Spring, p. 3-19, 1991
[115] Sleave, P., *Public Management Reforms in Australia and New Zealand*, Public Management Review, Vol. 10. Issue 3, pp. 453 – 465, 2008

ized: A first step for financial control and competition in between governmental agencies and trigger to leave the input-orientation for a more output and outcome orientation.

Visualizing the finances in a more transparent way was only one tool suggested by the wave of NPM. NPM tries, as explained, to convert and adapt private sector management tools for application in public sector. Contracts, agreed and measurable aims, and the participation in corporate success are only some examples of assumed tools of the NPM; the German version was called New Steering Model (NSM).

The movement of NPM focused to adopt or at least imitate applied managerial and accounting practices from the private sector.[116] NPM as model prioritize the cost-efficiency rather than to transport or enshrine governmental goals or objectives. Outcomes in the meaning of measurement of impact to public value are noted secondary. Symbol for this beginning transformation and change can be downsizing public services and products. These measures are accepted as intended results for better transparency and verification of better performance. For Blankart (2011) Germany used the opportunity in the context of reunification in 1989: Already existing autonomous organizations are demerged from the public sector to act as entrepreneur, provisioning marketable or market-oriented services and products. Main issue for NPM is to demerge more of these organizations and transform greater segments of public sector to private organizations.[117]

The following table illustrate the differences in the two paradigms prepared to be applied in past and in future public administrations. In the context of consumer responsibility it gives the impression of responsibility given to politicians and public managers to initiate, prepare and to provide. Both paradigms are presented in a pure model structure; in reality, differences, caused by size, objectives, integration in governmental structure, and historic roots exist, so a more idealistic model structure is shown:

Table 7 Paradigms of public management

Source: O'Flynn, J., From new public management to public value: paradigmatic change and managerial implications, The Australian Journal of Public Administration, Vol. 66, No. 3, p. 361, 2007

	New Public Management	**Public Value Management**
Characterization	post-bureaucratic; competitive	post-competitive

[116] Kuhlmann, S./ Bogumil, J./ Grohs, S., *Evaluation administrating modernization in German local governments: success or failure of the "New Steering Model"?,* Public Administration Review, Sept.-Oct., pp. 851-863, 2008

[117] Blankart, C., *Öffentliche Finanzen in der Demokratie*, Vahlen, Munich, p. 558, 2011

	government	
Dominant focus	results	relationships
Managerial tools	active agreed performance targets	Multiple goals including responding to citizen/user preferences, renewing mandate and trust through quality service, steering network
Definition of the Public interest	individual preferences are aggregated	collective preferences are expressed
Performance objective	management of input and output to ensure economy and responsiveness to customers	multiple objectives are pursued including service outputs, satisfaction, outcomes, trust and legitimacy
Dominant model of accountability	upward accountability via performance contracts; outwards to customers via market mechanism	multiple accountability systems including citizens as overseers of government, customers as user and taxpayers as funders
Preferred system of delivery	private sector or tightly defined arms lengths public agency	menu of alternatives selected pragmatically

Compared to the public sector the consequences for private organization in the case of not-satisfying results, based on quality and quantity of the offered products and services, can be disastrous: The private organization faces a decrease in turnover and selling, combined with a decrease of market shares, reduced or destroyed reputation; combined with a short notice of threat of existence of the organization, at least of the branch or production chain. Analyzing and respecting the customer's interest and the public power in the case of missing the quality standards is one of the most important tasks from the board of directors to the operation level. Missing of expectations by customers or losing the focus on budgeting threat the existence of an organization.[118] Diefenbach (2009) goes further: He complains about the products and services provided. Powerful stakeholders take initiative and influence to design them for affluent customers who are willing and able to pay for them, in the environment of NPM in defined setting of factual or artificially created market-mechanisms.[119] Every part of the production chain is combined with a direct responsibility, in functional and personal aspects. Especially in the case of products which could endanger a person's health negative information and publicity will lead immediately to severe consequences, hitting the reputation as one of the markets most important values.

---

[118] Levitt, T., *Marketing-Kurzsichtigkeit*, Harvard Business manager, Edition 02/2012, pp. 67–81, orig.1960

[119] Diefenbach, T., *New public management in public sector organizations – the dark side of managerialistic 'enlightment'*, Public Administration, Vol. 87, No. 4, 2009, pp. 897

In contrast public organization acts in a more stable and untouchable sphere. As pointed out above, institutions that execute mandatory task and political programs are secured by the constitution; in the case of risk awareness and measurement of consequences concrete models are necessary to depict the chain processes and consequences to be controlled by politicians and public managers. If one wants to describe the term responsibility for the provision and outcomes of products and services the different objectives of both private and public organization have to be taken into consideration. Main duties have priority, first to fulfill the mandatory tasks, second to execute political programs, often tied together. The financing of the execution to support the constitutional task of improving public value by provision of benefits contribute to a stable culture of distance to personal and functional responsibility as Bodemann and Olaru (2014) argue.[120]

A customer in the case of public products and services is also the sponsor; paying fees and taxes gives each citizen the position of a stake - and shareholder. To comply with the expectations of the citizens, a contribution to the increase of welfare or at least to maintain an infrastructure for private activities to improve welfare, investments are necessary. A research submitted from 2009 - 2012 in a selected number of public administrations in Germany shows, that investment backlogs are typical. The following table summarizes the results for investment backlogs. Especially investments in buildings and infrastructure are given by 2 out of 5.

Table 8 Investment backlogs in the public administration in Germany in %
Source: result of the field research conducted by author from 2009 - 2012

No.	Type of backlog	Percentage
1	Buildings	39.13 %
2	Infrastructure	39.13 %
3	Personnel development	17.39 %
4	Others	4.35 %

Convergence with private sector managerial characteristics will increase functional and personal responsibility. These first steps have to be accompanied with a model of participation, within certain limits, on the positive effects and results. Without that kind of participation, the complained organized irresponsibility remains.

[120] Bodemann, M. & Olaru, M., *Responsibility to customers in the context of public value management – a german case study"*, Amfiteatru economic, Vol XVI (35), p. 180, 2014

Concrete measurement and evaluation of results and outcomes could be helpful to create a peculiar customer-responsibility.

2. 2. 2. First evaluation after practical use in public sector

Since 30 years public sector organizations are under external pressure and also triggered by internal emphasis of becoming more efficient. The development of tools emerged to replace the traditional system, which was regraded to be not sufficient and adequate to cope with present and future tasks. Among others, the NPM ideas are based on the notion that government can be treated as if it were a business. Some measures paid off, some less. Mussari argued already in 1996, that the fear or error and the legal consequences were so strong that many public activities are paralysed or significantly decelerated. That corresponds with the results of Van der Wal et al. (2008) considering the values of public managers. Mussari also stressed to the later repeated ideas for improved financial reporting. For effective application indicators are needed and cash accounting has to be replied by double-entry-accounting with a consolidated balance sheet.[121]

At the beginning the notion of convergence of both sectors was strong, now there is an increased sceptism about. Summarizing the current results with the notion at the beginning, the principles of NPM have positive and negative effects to structures and processes of a public administration. Formalizing leads to more bureaucracy and slower speed of providing the expected results. It also brings more irresponsibility, delegating responsibility to the process. On the other hand, privatization, delegation of authority to lower levels, and using instruments to make administration more transparent and comparative can lead to an increased awareness, considering the output and outcome. Especially any kind of entrepreneurial approach is hard to implement; political programs, parliamentary decisions, and the steady observation and scrutiny by citizen prevents this kind of acting.

According to Diefenbach (2009) the negative effects of applied NPM tool box equalize the positive effects. He complains about the additional workload for routine processes, monitoring and internal and external communication.[122] Already in 2005 Kirkpatrick et al. come to the conclusion that the efforts to change created a large amount of costs, human and financial resources, but effects to quality of service

[121] Mussari, R., *Autonomy, responsibility and new public management*, Conference on New Public Management in International Perspective, St. Gallen, 1996

[122] Diefenbach, T., *New public management in public sector organizations – the dark side of managerialistic 'enlightment'*, Public Administration, Vol. 87, No. 4, p. 904, 2009

stayed away.[123] Kuhlmann (2006) argued from a political point of view: She found out that on political level no interest is created on precise targets and measurable objective which are necessary for any kind of performance measurement and following improvement.[124] Further the separation of politics and admin, as Wilson 1889 demanded, could be a main hindrance for effective use of NPM tools. Caused by reelection periods and personal interest in power and authority only a limited interest in transparency and verifiability of decisions and execution exists.[125] Related to the assumed main objective to increase, Peter Steane (2008) comes to the conclusion that for Australia and New Zealand the governments have continued to retread from the traditional welfare state model.[126] This estimation is mainly based on the increase grade of privatization and the effects to the delivering of services to the citizens. But he point to a future challenge, western states will have to cope with: Responses to the demography will force government to realign the provision of services and infrastructure, requiring new forms of collaboration and partnerships.

Pollitt and Bouchaert (2011) name their estimation of public management reforms "through a glass darkly", although they are convinced that performance will continue a central concern for many theorists and practitioners the result are more a "slippery concept".[127] They criticize the use as indicator for progress the Government effectiveness Score (World Bank Indicator). Composition of the sources and the definition of used terms are in doubt and to general to present a reliable state of the examined states. But as indicator of development they could be of use to see a trend:

---

123 Kirkpatrick, I./Ackroyd, S./ Walker, R., *The New Managerialism and Public Service Professions*. Palgrave Macmillan, New York, in Diefenbach, T. *New public management in public sector organizations – the dark side of managerialistic'enlightment'*, Public Administration, Vol. 87, No. 4, p. 905, 2009

124 Kuhlmann, S., *Hat das "Neue Steuerungsmodell" versagt? Lehren aus der "Ökonomisierung" von Politik und Verwaltung*, Verwaltung und Management, No. 3, p. 150, 2006

125 ebd. p. 151

126 Steane, P., *Public Management Reforms in Australia and New Zealand*, Public Management Review, Vol. 10. Issue 3, pp. 453 – 465, 2008

127 Pollitt, C.& Bouckaert, G., *Public management reform*, 3rd edition; Oxford University Press, New York, p. 129, 2011

Table 9 Government effectiveness score (World Bank Governance Indicators)
Source: Pollitt, C. & Bouckaert, G., *Public management reform*, 3rd edition; Oxford University Press, New York, p. 128, 2011

Australia	1.66	1.82	1.80
Belgium	2.01	1.99	1.36
Canada	1.93	2.09	1.93
Finland	2.11	2.21	1.95
France	1.79	1.81	1.54
Germany	1.85	1.81	1.85
Italy	0.88	0.93	0.39
Netherlands	2.29	2.09	1.86
New Zealand	2.16	1.81	1.76
Sweden	2.19	2.07	1.99
UK	2.04	1.93	1.74
USA	2.22	1.82	1.65

One basic idea is the introduction of delegation of authority and decentralization. But Mongkol (2011) comes to the conclusion, that the expected results are perverted by the application of NPM: For him NPM may lead to centralized decision making by public clerks, rather than to encourage decentralization through the organization as expected.[128]

He further argues that because of the complex objectives, and a more dynamic and turbulent political environment the public sector could not simply adopt private sector management tools.

Shad and Malik found that although they regard NPM as a failure, public manager use the experiences, tools and ideas behind NPM.[129]

For Germany the first evaluation take place since 2005. After some practical experiences, but also based on a limited number of public organizations scholars and practioners are mixed in their statements about intended and reached results of NPM. For Germany the derivate New Steering Model (NSM) was created to underline the small differences between NPM and the German application.[130]. In 2007 Bogumil et al. found that the level of introduction the different tools of NSM. Kuhlmann,

[128] Mongkol, K., *The critical review of New Public Management model and its criticisms*, Research Journal of Business Management, 5(1), pp. 36, 2011
[129] Shad, H./ Malik, A., *NPM is dead, long live NPM: The strategic shift in public sector discourse*, University of Hertfordshire Business School Working Paper, 2012, https://uhra.herts.ac.uk/dspace/handle/2299/5549
[130] The author is aware that there are differences between both models and tools. Results of researches are intentionally regarded as equal. -

Bogumil and Grohs (2008) state that only a minority implemented and maintained organized reform activities according to the elements of NSM.[131]

Table 10 Implementation of NSM elements
Source: Adapted from Bogumil, J./ Grohs, S./ Kuhlmann, S./ Ohm, Anna, *Zehn Jahre Neues Steuerungsmodell*, edition sigma, Berlin, p. 40, 2007

NSM elements	Entirely implemented, in %
New department structure	43,6
Strategic steering units	25,9
Decentralized/ operative controlling units	10,9
Internal service centers	23,9
Abolishing levels of hierarchy	34,5
Decentralized management of resources	33,1
New budgeting procedures	33,1
Output analyses (definition of products)	29,0
Cost and activity accounting	12,7
Reporting	22,1
Contracts between top management and services	24,3
Contracts between politics and administration	14,8
Quality management	13,9
One-stop agencies	57,5
Customer surveys	54,7
Citizens' charters/ services guarantees	7,1

Reichard came in 2004 to similar conclusions: He identified that the three streams improvement to services functions, improvement in participation opportunities, and improved opportunities for civil collaborations has moved the local German administration towards a greater citizen focus.[132]

Kegelmann (2007) pointed to the constraints faced by municipal administration even while seeking to implement the New Public Management (NPM) approach: Hierarchical structures dominate the public sector, where everything is focused on files, on sanctions enunciated clearly in writing.[133] The bureaucrats are all supposed

[131] Kuhlmann, S./ Bogumil, J./ Grohs, S., *Evaluation administrating modernization in German local governments: success or failure of the "New Steering Model"?*, in "Public Administration Review", Sept.-Oct., p. 854, 2008
[132] Reichard, C., *The New Steering Model and the Citizen*, Deutsches Institut für Urbanistik, 2004
[133] Kegelmann, J., *New Public Management*, Verlag für Sozialwissenschaften, Wiesbaden, p. 36, 2007

to strive to react similarly in similar situations and based on clearly laid down guidelines.[134]

Bogomil states 2006 that NPM has strengthened the role and influence of the citizen; public administration acts more like a service provider. But he also states that loss of control caused by decentralization and privatization is also one result.[135]

After ten years of introduction and maintenance of the new system researches present a very different evaluation of the success of the application. For example Banner (1991) is convinced that the double entry accounting based local budget, a spin-off of the NSM, is giving a new boast to the implementation of basic NSM elements. He points to single-line lump-sum budget, targeting, indicators performance contracts, and cost accounting.[136] Others, like Kuhlmann, Bogumil and Grohs (2008) come to a more different result in the realization. They notice even hints of a renaissance of the traditional Weberian bureaucratic model. Restrictions and the grade of mandatory tasks are indicated to limit the ability of the public administration, to plan and act strategically. The new collection of rules and regulations imposed specific substantive duties on the local administration and anticipates a vivid risk management system; Diefenbach sees more disadvantages and developments in directions NPM was created to change. For him NPM ignores, reduces, damages, or even destroys many traditional values, for example impartiality, social equality, integrity, or equity. He fears for the fundaments of public value, like citizenship, representation, neutrality, welfare and social justice, substituted by cost orientation.[137] But he also observed that critical aspects of public administration are amplified by NPM, for example increase in bureaucracy, formal requirements, more complex relations between the centre and the periphery.[138]

From a more abstract point of view Holtkamp argued in 2008, that the optimistic assumptions of human behaviour are in contrast to the historic assumption of increase of budget and power seeking public managers and politicians. For him NSM is more a failure in Germany. Expected outcomes of output orientation and lean management became illustrious. Further, the governmental sector expanded and implementation of NSW resulted in a more giant apparatus.[139] Contrary to the evalu-

[134] ebd. p. 49

[135] Bogumil, J., *Administrative modernization and the logic of politics*, German Journal of Urban Studies, No. 45, 2006

[136] Banner, G., *Von der Behörde zum Dienstleistungsunternehmen: Die Kommunen brauchen ein neues Steuerungsmodell*, Verwaltungsführung, Organisation, Personalführung, 1, pp. 6-11, 1991

[137] Diefenbach, T., *New public management in public sector organizations – the dark side of managerialistic 'enlightment'*, Public Administration, Vol. 87, No. 4, p. 895, 2009

[138] Ebd. p. 899

[139] Holtkamp, L., *Das Scheitern des Neuen Steuerungsmodells*, dms-der moderne Staat, No. 2, p. 439, 2008

ation by Holtkamp, other researchers come to more positive results. Banner (2008) sees the necessity of change to service- and citizen-oriented organization. He is sceptical about the assumptions of Holtkamp and demands more empirical proof for failure or success. Banner notice advantages in the development of targets, indicators and performance contracts, first steps out of vague notion about results to more measurable numbers.[140] Andrews and Van der Walle (2013) offers a spectrum to measure the effects of NPM. They use a matrix consistent of measurable quantitative indicators combined with expected characteristics how to manage the duties:

Table 11 NPM practices and citizens' perceptions of efficiency, responsiveness, equity and effectiveness as evaluation-matrix

Source: Andrews, R./ Van der Walle, S., New public management and citizens' perception of local service efficiency, responsiveness, equity and effectiveness, Public Management Review, 15 (5) pp. 762 – 783, 2013

Variables	**efficiency**	**responsiveness**	**equity**	**effectiveness**
Public-private relationships				
Performance management				
Entrepreneurial strategy				
Customer focus				
Capital charges				
Temporary staff				
Controls				
Deprivation				
Age diversity				
Ethnic diversity				
Social class diversity				
Population				
Population density				
District council				

As discussed, indicators for performance measurement are hard to define and values to get.

140 Banner, G., Logik des Scheitern oder Scheitern an der Logik, dms-der moderne staat, No.2, pp. 447 – 455, 2008

2.3. Deduction of performance indicators

2. 3. 1. Performance ratio in public sector

Scarce goods have a different meaning for the public administration. The OECD stated in the economic survey of Germany in 2010, that additional consolidation effort will be needed in subsequent years to meet the convergence criteria of the EU and to provide a direction to reduce the yearly added debt level. But it also announces that the balanced structural budget of the federal "Länder" (states) could be reached in a certain timeframe. That meant the debt level for each citizen will increase in the next years. Similar effects will be recognizable at local level.[141] So being economic is interpreted in another way than the private sector; target of a balanced annual report by expenses and revenues. That implies not necessary to invest or to build up reserves. By reviewing the annual financial status often a gap is left: It is obvious that the provided services are either to expensive produced or the quantity of provided services cannot be compensated by public funds. In both cases a dynamic change in management to heal this imbalance is needed.

Woodrow Wilson pointed out way back in November 1889 that the object of an administrative study is first to discover what the government can properly and successful do and secondly, how it could do these proper things with the utmost possible efficiency and at least possible cost, either of money, of energy or other resources.[142] The provision of public services at minimum cost should be the main focus of the municipality. As discussed above trigger for reform in public sector are changes in external and internal environment, public scrutiny and the political acceptance of necessity of change. Measurement of hard facts and presenting the results are often regarded as remedy, for public sector this topic will be handled very sensible though reactions not necessary follow. Simon (1946) made recommendations for analysing and improving administrative efficiency:

- Administration efficiency is increased by a specialization of the task among the group
- Administrative efficiency is increased by arranging the members of the group in a determinate hierarchy of authority
- Administrative efficiency is measured by limiting the span of control at any point in the hierarchy for a small number

---

141 OECD, *Economic Survey of Germany*, www.oecd.org, retrieved on 26.03.2010

142 Wilson, W., *The study of administration*, Political Science Quarterly, Vol. 2, No. 2, pp. 197–222, 1887

Administrative efficiency is measured by grouping the workers, for purposes of control, according to

- Purpose
- Process
- Client or
- Place[143]

But all the explanations circle around the dominating value: What determines efficiency and how to measure the output of public administration? For a private sector product, the specifications generate a utility the customer is searching for or is assumed to search for, purchasing and consuming this product creates a benefit for the individual or a group. In some case the vendor offers a more convenient living or influence by protecting environment; tools to add the primary objective of profit maximization.

Mihaiu et al. (2010) draw a comparison of the transformation process to illustrate the differences in measurement of efficiency in private and public sector.

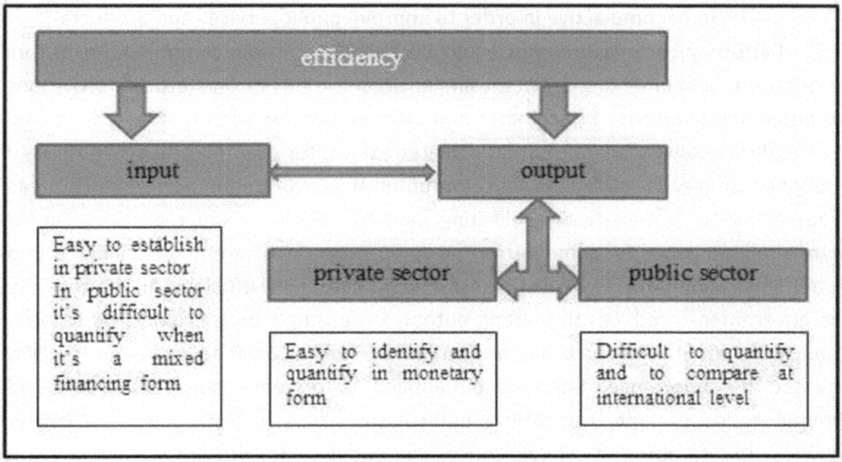

Figure 12: Determining the efficiency indicator
Source: Mihaiu D./ Opreana, A./ Cristescu, M., Efficiency, effectiveness and performance of the public sector, Romanian Journal of Economic Forecasting, 4/2010, p. 134

The OECD distincts two different levels for performance management: Output as result of production and distribution processes with the limit that public sector

[143] Simon, H., *The proverbs of administration*, Public Administration Review, Vol. 6, No. 1, pp. 53-67, 1946

mostly non-market goods provides; a certain market value is therefore hard to define and usually unknown. Outcome defined as long-term-effects of programmes, directed to capture the various dimension of society values and indicated in terms of welfare.[144]

In general efficiency is calculated by the relation between input to output or costs to benefits. The measurement, for example for a machine, what produces a great amount of standardized products, based on estimation of cost, estimation of proceeds generated revenues and the comparison of both. Especially for public sector organizations investigating measurement the role of the measurement and indicator system has to be defined and limits argued. Nakamura (2010) stress that following targets and indicators create a framework:

- to control
- to improve accountability
- to compare organizations' performance
- to influence behaviour
- to become active in order to improve public services and products[145]

Performance measurement could be based on absolute numbers in historic comparison, benchmarking between similar organizations or on statutory provisions; for public sector internal benchmarks and external benchmarks are thinkable, including the direct comparison of market-oriented goods, for example the provisioning of energy or surgery in a hospital. Van Dooren et al. (2000) define performance measurement as "... systematically collecting data by observing and registering performance-related issues for some performance purposes."[146]Thereby especially for public administration it has to be distinguish the pure technical efficiency in the case that the government produces the wrong output; for example an efficient production of guns versus an efficient production of bread. Already in 2000 advocates of the NSM stressed the importance of defined and applied performance indicators; after an additional period of time, the reform enthusiasm seems to slow down.[147] Manzoor (2004) points to different schools concerning public sector efficiency: First, the supporter of traditional public bureaucracy, based on Weber: For Weber this kind of organization is a form of efficient organization. In contrast argue the critics of bureau-

---

[144] Mandl, U./ Dierx, A./ Ilzkovitz, F., *The effectiveness and efficiency of public spending*, European Commission, Economic Papers 301, p. 6, 2008

[145] Micheli, P. & Neely, A., *Performance management in the public sector in England: Searching for the golden thread*, Public Administration Review, July/ August, p. 598, 2010

[146] Van Dooren, W./ Bouckaert, G./ Halligan, J., *Performance management in the public sector*, Routledge, Oxon, p.5, 2010

[147] ashold & Bogumil cited in Van Dooren, W./ Bouckaert, G./ Halligan, J., *Performance management in the public sector,* Routledge, Oxon, p.7, 2010

cracy that there is a lack of efficiency "...in pursuing multiple value-based goals in a democratic system."[148]

Alfonso et al. introduced 2006 public sector performance efficiency indicators. They split the spectrum of public production and provisioning in different branches and micro- and macroeconomic areas; including administrative, education, health, income distribution, economic stability and economic performance outcomes.[149] Van Dooren et al. (2012) add that the indicators will be used by journalists, aid organizations, or potential investors to evaluate the current and future situation for their own decisions. Further, analogue to private sector, evaluation of indicators hold the government accountable.[150] Output, based on processes, determines the overall objective of public administration outcome and delivers through processes also the intended or not intended output and outcome on political. Via this way, political programmes and their long terms impacts can be measured and evaluated.

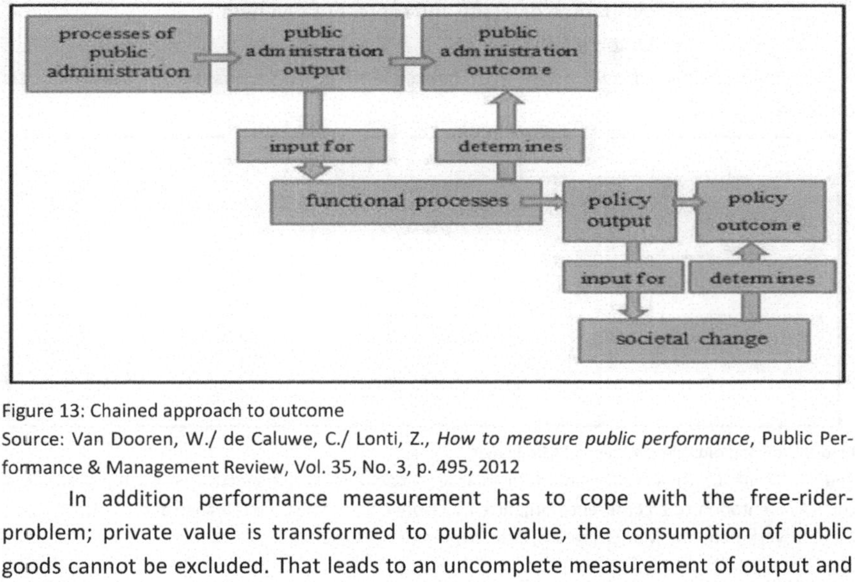

Figure 13: Chained approach to outcome

Source: Van Dooren, W./ de Caluwe, C./ Lonti, Z., *How to measure public performance*, Public Performance & Management Review, Vol. 35, No. 3, p. 495, 2012

In addition performance measurement has to cope with the free-rider-problem; private value is transformed to public value, the consumption of public goods cannot be excluded. That leads to an uncomplete measurement of output and outcome.

---

148 Manzoor, A., *A look at efficiency in public administration: Past and future*, in „Sage Open", October-December, pp. 1-5, 2014

149 Afonso, A./ Schuknecht, L./ Tanzi, Vito, Public Sector Efficiency – Evidence for new EU Member States and emerging markets, European Central Bank Working Paper Series, No. 581, p.5, January 2006,

150 Van Dooren, W./ de Caluwe, C./ Lonti, Z., *How to measure public performance*, Public Performance & Management Review, Vol. 35, No. 3, p. 489, 2012

To increase the efficiency Van Dooren et al. suggest that the following elements should be optimized:

- Product: matching of resources and tasks, given by the public through the politicians to administration. Based on economical, efficiency, and effectiveness values
- Procedural: contribution in keeping the government fair and honest
- Regime: success in maintaining the public sector robust and resilient[151]

Beneath others Currestine et al. (2007) come to the conclusion that there are institutional drivers of efficiency in the public sector:

- Increasing the scale of operations
- Functional and political decentralization
- Human resource management practices
- Ownership , competition, and agentification
- Workforce diversity and representativeness
- Union's role [152]

Pollitt (2004) draws a circle of causes and effects considering performance measurement:

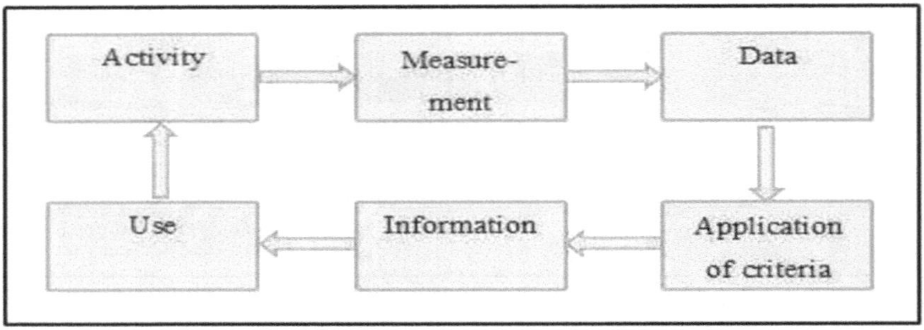

Figure 14: Unavoidable choices in PMS design
Source: Pollitt, C.; Governance and performance. A comparative perspective on contemporary Europe, Presentation to a conference organized by Norwegian Ministry of Finance and the Ministry of Local Government and Modernization, Oslo, September 24th , 2014

This circle is applicable for every kind of organization. As earlier discussed, political streams and measurement of results, or even success of political programs, are seldom intended. During the introduction of NPM-tools in Germany, several

[151] Van Dooren, W./ de Caluwe, C./ Lonti, Z., *How to measure public performance*, Public Performance & Management Review, Vol. 35, No. 3, p. 493, 2012
[152] Curristine, T./ Lonti, Z./ Journard, I., Improving public sector efficiency- challenges and opportunities, OECD Journal of Budgeting, Vol. 7, No. 1, p. 6, 2007

options for local public administration were given to evaluate their assets for the first balance sheet. Comparison and the following benchmark remain hard to realize because of the artificially created special status. Without proven and prescribed standard-values performance measurement will lead to internal improvements, without any comparison best practices will not contribute to more efficiency in using all kinds of resources. The Governance Institute of Australia (2015) suggests introducing key performance indicators (KPI), which can be used internally, but also available to the public.[153] Applying a measurement system has to keep in mind, that the ratio of input and output can be soon calculated, while outcome measurement is both hard to execute and staggered. As benchmark and incentive to support integrity in seeking ways for better performance different models are possible; some ratios and numbers exist, also applicable as KPI, others are in the introduction phase. By applying some score level important point is what is measured and evaluated and which indicators are used. As discussed earlier the ratio between output to input or outcome to input, or outcome to income are possible ways. For comparison market-oriented products and services are easier to measure. For example the provision of energy, based on a basic price and load-dependent energy prices are easier to calculate and to compare that the provision of public safety.

Research results show that there are several dependencies between micro- and macro-level indicators. For example high fiscal capacity and a high degree of party fragmentation contributes in Norway to low efficiency, further that centralized hierarchical budgetary procedures are associated with low efficiency.[154] These results can be state-oriented; a transferability has to be proved. Output ratio can be direct dependent to revenues. Borge et al. (2008) argue that there is a positive relationship between aggregate output and local government revenue; local governments with low revenues are able to provide less output to citizens than their neighbors with higher revenues. But volume of output is not guarantor for political or socio-economic intended outcomes.

2. 3. 2. Remaining public sector indicators

Researches concerning performance management cover different views and motives; important guide is the future role of measurement and the expected and intended function. Objectives and indicators can be used for controlling local service

[153] Governance Institute of Australia, Good Governance Guide, www.governanceinstitute.com.au
[154] Borge, L./ Falch, T./ Toymo, P., Public sector efficiency: the roles of political and budgetary institutions, fiscal capacity, and democratic participation, Public Choice, No. 136, pp. 475 – 495, 2008

delivery, comparing organization's performance or improve the quality of public services and products.[155] The design of measurement systems and the determination of indicators and their value have direct influence to results, conclusions and following activities.

Measurement and evaluation of performance have to be based on indicators which are appropriate to present the intended values. By indicators conclusion are possible to evaluate the performance of an organization in an isolated view or by benchmark with comparable organizations. De Groot searched for an evaluation by using various indicators, including quality of staff, level of absenteeism or client satisfaction.[156] On a macro-level the OECD uses indirect measurement to evaluate performance in the different branches of the public sector; for the health care sectors the average length of stay for all conditions, for the justice sector the number of days of trial length of first instance and trial cost, for the educational sectors mathematic scores and spending per student. Especially the last one enlightens performance differences very clear: For example in Luxembourg the cumulative spending per student in Dollar was in 2009 175.000, the PISA score was 492; in comparison to New Zealand, where the spending per student was below 75.000 Dollars, the result in PISA though 520.

Overall a report from the OECD (2013) focused to the following sectors to measure, while others are possible:

- Health care
- Justice
- Education
- Tax administration

Mihaiu et al. used a score composed by seven elements:

- administrative
- education
- health
- public infrastructure
- distribution
- stability
- economic performance

[155] Micheli, P. & Neely, A., *Performance management in the public sector in England: Searching for the golden thread*, Public Administration Review, July/ August, p. 598, 2010

[156] deGroot, H., *Performance management and cost-effectiveness of public services: empirical evidence from Dutch municipalities*, Annual Conference of the European Group of Public Administration, Bucharest, September 7-10, 2011

Each of the indicators based on several sub-indicators. The values are transferred in a table on Musgrave and opportunity indicators. Each individual state could be classified in high, medium, and low performer. For each state the change over time can be used as indicator.

On the case of results the World Bank describes effectiveness as capturing perceptions of the quality of public serves and the degree of its independence from political pressures, the quality of policy formulation and implementation, and the credibility of the government's commitment to such policies.

The following graph shows the developments in governance effectiveness in selected states. The World Bank offers data from more than 200 states around the world. The selected states represent especially the countries in which the modernization of public sector was initiated and states which present a remarkable development considering effectiveness. Finland and Sweden claim the top states during the 18 year period while France values decrease steadily since 2004. Germany has high and lows in each election period, minimum in 2004.

The values range from approximately -2.5 (weak) to 2.5 (strong) governance performance) as limiting factor by the World Bank.

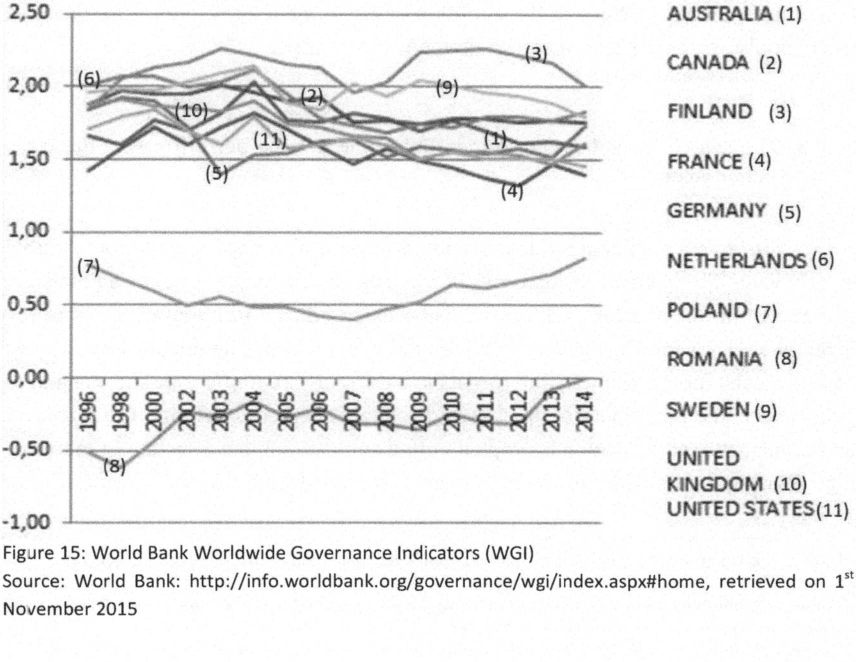

Figure 15: World Bank Worldwide Governance Indicators (WGI)
Source: World Bank: http://info.worldbank.org/governance/wgi/index.aspx#home, retrieved on 1st November 2015

Some authors criticise the use of effectiveness because of the general approach and not further defined used terms.[157] It shows that the measurement of effectiveness combined with outcomes to individuals are very complex; to measure and to process the later introduced term of public value will amplify the challenges for public administration.

Measurement of performance in public sectors remains a topic for the future, but it is needed as threshold and reference for developing and improving activities by public sector. It further serves as prove of willingness and effectiveness of citizen involvement and to stabilize the confidence of citizens in the local to federal government. Multiple market failures are one reason for public service provision; that lead to the limit that classic microeconomic theories will not function. Greiling (2005) argued that scepticisms are existent and eligible based on the target for public bureaucracies to meet external institutional expectation rather than to be in a technical sense efficient.[158] With clear determined long-term goals including desired outcomes, greater discretion for service providers, more and reliable information about performance and a system of incentives to meet user's needs and expectations results of performance measurement can contribute to increase welfare. Especially desired outcomes will be important to the adoption of public value as reference for value at risk in public sector decision-and management-processes.

2. 3. 3. The search for indicators to measure public service performance - the term public value

After twenty years of modelling and adopting the ideas of Mark Moore considering a value fitting best for outcomes of services and products of public administration the term public value is discussed to be invented as appropriate substitute for economic results for the society.[159] Outcomes of dams, street-lighting or public order could be used for the chances and threats in a decision situation for public managers; politicians could participate to analyse and validate their assumptions. The technical and organizational realisation by implementing and maintaining a system of monitoring receiving-points and the processing of gathered data becomes an outstanding

---

157 Pollitt, C.& Bouckaert, G., *Public management reform*, 3rd edition; Oxford University Press, New York, p. 129, 2011

158 Greiling, D., *Performance measurement - a driver for increasing the efficiency of public services?,* Protestant University of applied sciences, Darmstadt, p. 13, 2005

159 Moore, M., *Creating public value: strategic management in government*, Harvard University Press, Cam bridge, 1995

challenge, but lead to a better understanding in the case of a decision to make. Utility for the society and the individual could be better brought to an order to fulfill the statutory task of increasing welfare. In addition integration of probability and dependencies of various risk factors is one topic on content management and processing. For a vivid public management missing or special data could be compensated by applying a reference class model.

Based on the models describes above the meaning of utility needs to be extensive discussed, to understand the different complexity for decision under uncertainty and risks in the public administration.

To reduce the object to a general topic for all municipalities the restoration of a dam is discussed. The dam has the function to protect the residential area if snow melting and rain raises the level of a nearby river. Persons affected by the consequences of a flood are residents in this specific, but local limited area. Measurements and processing of the water level over the last 50 years leads to a probability of 25% each year, under normal forthcoming climate conditions. The distribution over the examined term was normal; no significant change is recognizable. In the case of initiative by the public administration the expected damages, expressed in quantified and qualified values is necessary. But there will be different damage bearer, for example the residents, especially those without appropriate insurances; all businesses are settled in this residential area and the municipality as local limiting factor in the case that they aren't prepared and fulfilled their obligations to protect the residents.

But in addition to these direct physical losses, expressed in monetary values, other ramification could be possible, for example political responsibility in the case a modern dam could have protected the area; consequences in the meaning of inflow of new residents if the activities by the public administration were intentionally stopped or few settlements of new businesses caused by the assumption that this omission was causal for damages. On the long run from an outside view that could lead to a negative interpretation of the ability and capability of the public administration to protect residents, businesses and infrastructure.

On the other hand among numeric values of damage and a potential liability for omissions a subjective estimation of chances and threats for results of decisions under uncertainty seems to be important. Because of the majority of unique projects in the public administration, the term risk, in the meaning of known probability and estimated threat or loss, is hard to use.

To describe the system of the market of public sponsored goods and services is difficult, the partial monopoly and the local dependency for specific goods lead to the superficial conclusion, that risk and uncertain developments are absence for the public administration. But the accountability to the public and the limits of scarce goods remains. As Frank J. Goodnow in 1900 pointed out "...in transacting its business the government's objective is not usually the acquisition of gain but the furtherance of the welfare of the community."[160]

In the case of building new streets, bridges or other infrastructural building the projects are based on public functions and decisions. Funds are collected directly or indirectly by the public administration, for specific services, but as well as based on tax legislation and therefore steering policy. Because of their collective financing the residents or citizens have an individual interest for return on these compulsory investments. The subjective estimation of the investment in infrastructural buildings and installations is different from the private sector markets. A customer pays for goods and service and gets a product which should have the promised and offered specifications. The customer has nothing to share; he is able to decide how much he saves and how much of his capital he spends for consumption, as Hall and Jennings (2008) state: "Consumers have the ability to choose. Consumers have option, not the obligation, to participate."[161] The customer chooses that product what creates for him the highest level of utility, considering the cost-benefit-relationship of the specific good and the depending on the funds he is able and willing to spend. Acceptance of the price is than the indicator of the personal estimated value of utility.

Providing public goods, especially infrastructure, means to decide in the pursuit of maximization of collective public interest and utility; this combined with unknown possible outcomes of the projects. Signals for demand or higher demand for an already existing product could be the constant fully occupied section of highways or public transport that operates permanent with full or over full capacity. But for the political point of view every mainstream, initiated by interest groups or by isolated persons, could find the way to be accepted as a necessary demand; that's a parallel from the private sector where high potential customers have direct or indirect influence and access to the design and specifications of a product, whereby the private sector is able to select and to concentrate to a specific target groups. The public sector has to focus to objectives represented by the majority of the citizens or residents; in the worst case to handle a puzzle of interests. Although, as explained above, Diefenbach (2009) argued, through NPM the trend toward realization of targets and requirements of most influential stakeholder is increased.[162]

---

[160] Goodnow, F., *Politics and administration: A study in government*, Macmillan, New York, 1900, p. 10

[161] Hall, J. & Jennings, E., *Taking Chances: Evaluating Risk as a Guide to Better use of Best Practices*, Public Administration Review, July/August 2008, p. 706

[162] Diefenbach, T., *New public management in public sector organizations – the dark side of managerialistic 'enlightment'*, Public Administration, Vol. 87, No. 4, 2009, pp. 896

Awareness and acceptance of utility of the products is far different from specific investments for only a selected number of potential users. Quality of service and, in the case of uncertain future developments, closer examination of utility composes a fragmented picture: More users, instead of customers, participating actively or passively from the provided service and products, lead to a higher sum of utility. But this interpretation has its limitations: If the personal utility is restricted by other customers, the utility decreases. The following figure showed the decrease of additional quantity, to be applied for public value. Additional streets will not add benefits to citizens in a linear function.

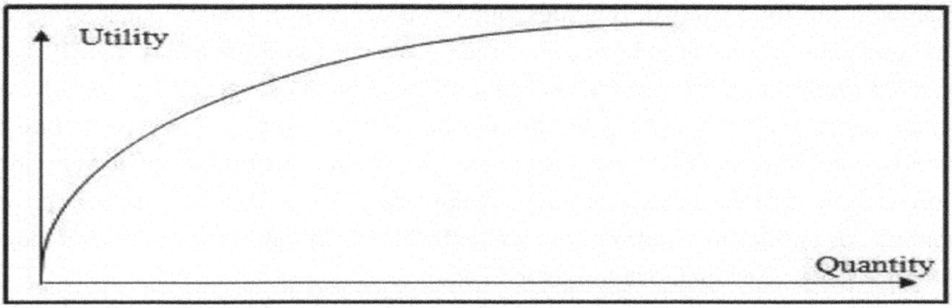

Figure 16: Frontier function between quantity and utility
Source: by author

Initial point for an aggregate utility function is a discussion about building a new public road. The new road has a higher utility for a single car than for hundred cars using the road simultaneously. The lonely driver goes as fast as it is allowed or technical possible. In the case of hundred cars, everybody has to pay more attention; the possibility of a traffic jam is higher. Each additional car has an additional utility, but the additional utility is decreasing and can turn downwards

Selective objectives, concentrated to a small customer group have less utility than to focus to projects targeted to the majority of citizens and a higher grade of utility in sum. But what kind and meaning of utility has to be recognized managing objectives and assessing uncertain situations?

In the case of public administration the estimation of utility further developments depends on the different interest groups or singular interests introduced in the decision process. Utility is in this consideration a delivery of a positive effect or development, for example improved functionality. Burden could be additional material or financial effects in the case of an undesired development. However these effects are easier to calculate by monetary values, regardless of their influence to the public value.

Furthermore the administration has to report to the local parliament and to check the expenses and to guarantee the expected time frame, the estimated and expected functionality of the projects. These quantified and qualified specifications could be measured to analyze the grade of utility for the individual citizen. From the managerial point of view they have no direct influence to the measurement and delivery of utility; they have also not to bear any negative ramification in the case of loss; for example time or additional expenses for a specific project. As function the loss of reputation could be a trigger but the past has proven that especially in larger projects, time and cost are exceeded. Publicly discussed examples were some notable examples, but the results of the questionnaire prove that in smaller public projects cost and time are hardly obeyed. Inadequate planning and managing lead to not planned expenses and make services and products more expensive, similar to private sector; for example if a highway section was delayed caused by poor planning. Direct ramifications were internally compensated, but on a more global point of view the citizens have to take additional costs, limited benefits or delayed availability. As pointed out uncertainty leads not consequently to risk; in this case the decision maker has, in general, no negative results to bear.

Citizens are liable to taxes. With this steady renewed investment they often deduce a demand to the state, on local level to the public administration. For their payment they expect an appropriate service and improvement of quality of life in return. Utility in the private meaning is the delivery of a positive and desired effect. For example a public good spends utility to all persons who wants to participate; most people or businesses were depending on. Examples are health care, modern infrastructure, public transport or connections to highways and railroads, and, as new part, a broad bandwidth for internet connections; for the local area playgrounds, parking lots or street services in the wintertime. These objectives are codified by law and regulations, some can be delegated to private vendors, and others have to be executed by the public organization. The responsibility to customer is then to act to realize all these duties.

The utility is estimated by a higher grade the more use of the public service is done by the citizen. For some projects contrary meanings raised, triggered by economic, ecologic and political reasons. The utility and the personal positive or negative effects are hard to estimate or to measure. Criterions have to be precise, subjective interests will influence the results. Partly violent demonstrations against the project Stuttgart 21, a new complex train station project in the city Stuttgart in Germany, were a good example for split public meaning and a switching of majorities and uncertainties for the project to be finalized.

Citizens are therefore differently affected, depending on their interests and personal relevance, political intentions and economic and ecologic positions. The idea behind is the local authorities are called upon to provide such services and utilities in the best interest of the local community, as Wollmann (2002) defines the main objective.[163] Managerial challenge for the politicians as directors is to analyze and to exploit political interests under consideration of economic conditions and premises; depending on the relation of revenues and expenses in the public budget. Larger projects often have an important official stand: Benefits, opportunity costs in the meaning of unrealized or delayed projects and the created utility are discussed, especially in current times; desolate financial status become acute thresholds for public projects; false or inadequate planning in the last years left gaps in being prepared for regularly tasks. Political decisions follow often the desired re-election; measurable results and benefits for the citizens were of higher value than plans for sustainable and steered developments. Decisions under uncertainty have for the politicians, especially the mayor, priority. In the case of failure and mismanagement his reputation will decrease.

Intended utility is part of the estimation for the politicians of results for future developments. Variances in time, cost and estimated benefits will be delegated to the politicians, at least to the local parliament which has to decide the project. Re-election and the desired and measurable positive effects of change are tied together.

Most complex part to measure is the value and the utility for the society of different projects and the effects in the case of failure: Uncertainty for results in social aids, uncertainty in projects of youth protection or ecological projects. More it is a societal development to fulfil, but sufficient data are missing because of the rapid changing environment.

The dilemma for the public administration is long terms of return. Public funds invested, for example for additional street workers, for protection plans of beaches, or to establishing a new playground, will pay off after years. Sustainable benefits and the positive effects for individuals will pay off after decades only. In private sector benefits of products and goods could be measured more easily and prompt.

In the use of provided goods and services the customer faces a dichotomy: On the one hand the municipality acts like a quasi-monopolist with the constraints to accept the dominance of the public administration. On the other hand the customer is free to participate in the provided areas; his personal benefit and usability of the

[163] Wollmann, H., *German local government under the impact of NPM modernization and new direct democratic citizen rights*, Proceedings of „International Conference on Reforming local government", Stuttgart, Sept. 26th, p. 5, 2002

good depend on his peculiar situation. In the case of risk management, each failure to gain something, as the opposite part of loss, has following consequences: The customer has to participate in the compensation, through fees or direct and indirect taxes. The compensation has to be paid by all and sometimes by following generations. Arrow/Lind (1970) suggests in the case of public investments that government should ignore uncertainty in evaluating public investments.[164] Contrary were the intentions of strategic management for public administration: Main objective is to create awareness and a tool for objective assessment and evaluation of desired situation under considering the societal development.

2.4. Specific features of public sector as distinctive characteristics

Management in general can be distinguished in two ways: As functional level in an organization or as steering and monitoring activities.[165] The Oxford Dictionary of Economics described three different meanings of management:

- The role of making decision in an organization
- The people who decide
- The academic function that analyses the decision-making role[166]

The roots of the discipline go back approximately 200 years. But the function of management and the linked areas of study are a product of the developments in the twentieth century. Implied in the word management is to put in scarce materials and business goods to the best possible use and with intention maximizing profits.[167]

According to Henri Fayol, the basic functions and elements of management are the following:[168]

- Planning: Setting objectives, strategies, policies, programs and proce dures.
- Organizing: Jobs need to be organized within sections or departments; so authority needs to be delegated.
- Commanding: The ability to give instructions to subordinates to carry out tasks, to make decisions and to take responsibilities.

[164] Arrow, K. / Lind, R., *Uncertainty and the Evaluation of Public Investment Decisions*, American Economic Review, June 1970 (60), p. 367

[165] Schierenbeck, H., *Grundzüge der Betriebswirtschaftslehre*, Oldenbourg, Munich, p. 81, 1993

[166] Black, J./ Hashimzade, N./ Myles, G.(eds.), Oxford Dictionary of Economics, 3rd edition, Oxford University Press, Oxford, p. 276, 2009

[167] Wöhe, G., *Einführung in die Allgemeine Betriebswirtschaftslehre*, Franz Vahlen, Munich, p. 19, 2002

[168] Hall, D. et al. (eds.), *Business Studies*, Causeway Press Ltd. Harlow, p. 442, 2007

- Coordinating: Bringing together the activities of all the people within the business. The hired individuals or employees and groups of employees will have their own goals, which may be different from those of the business and also vary from person to person. To bring together the production results, "just in time"; in big and global companies, it is a decisive function of management.
- Controlling: Measurement, analysis and interpretation of activities and the necessary correction of those activities of individuals or groups; to make sure that their performance fits within the plan.

Drucker (2007) uses another, but similar description of activities a manager has to carry out:

- Setting objectives: Goals in each area of objectives. The separation of management from ownership in most publicly traded firms creates in addition potential conflict. The conflict of interests between what seems to be good for business and what is good for the manager for his self-interest;[169] objectives and especially estimation of risks and the results can differ, depending on the personal targets of a manager and a neutral or objective analysis of the situation.
- Organizing: Analyzing activities, decisions and relations needed.
- Motivation and communication: Convincing the individuals that reaching a common goal will lead to personal satisfaction
- Measurement: Orientation to targets and yardsticks and milestones
- Developing people: Personal planning and promotion of key players[170]

Without the ability to set objectives, a person cannot be an effective and efficient manager. The focus is directed to middle and long term objectives and the ways to reach the desired results. The variety of tasks, in management in general and risk management particularly, have to be performed in cooperation, synchronization and communication. Without these three important factors an efficient management and also risk management is impossible. The Stanford Encyclopaedia enlightens the

---

[169] Damodaran, A., *Strategic risk taking*, Wharton School Publishing, Upper Saddle River, p. 9, 2008

[170] Drucker, P., *Management Challenges for the 21th Century*, Butterworth-Heinemann, Oxford, reprinted edition, p. xi, 2007

bandwidth by definition of risk management as a major interdisciplinary field of research with links to epistemology, philosophy of science, ethics and the philosophy of economics.[171]

Governmental management, same as local administration, are subject to closer scrutiny by legislation oversight groups or even judicial order. That is the result of the societal position of the administration: Financed by all tax- and fee-payers, directed by legal framework, legal objectives and duties and politics; controlled by politics and internal and external interest groups. Residents who are subject to tax legislation have at least the right to analyse the proportion of investment and individual and collective benefit. A control function is indirectly executed by such groups or committees.

Private sector organisations face control by public accountants or other control committees. But those groups do not control the forwarded execution of the business with the leading management level. Planning, development and fulfilment is subject of the managers, including measure of performance of singular projects and activities, as well as the development of the business as player on the market. Control authorities which are placed by partnership agreements have not external legal-control function.

Neustadt (1979) confirmed the presentation of results by Dunlop, reducing his distinction to areas, consisting of

- time horizon
- authority over the enterprise
- career system
- media relations
- performance measurement
- implementation[172]

Especially his observation concerning time horizon, authority over an enterprise, and performance measurements are very similar, but based on the circumstances of the 70ies of the last century. A convergence of both sectors could be an explanation of further similarities. Neustadt explains that the time horizon could be one essential distinction; in addition a trigger for decision is not unusual re-election campaigns. But measurement of results of decisions in private sector is not more a matter of decades. Especially the stock-exchanged listed companies use periodical

---

[171] Zalta, E. (ed.), *Stanford Encyclopaedia of Philosophy,* Stanford University, Stanford, available online: http://plato.stanford.edu/, 2011

[172] Neustadt, R., *Public management and corporate executives*, proceedings of the National Academy of Public Administration's Panel on Presidential Management, October 7-8, 1979

reports to convince investors and use this instrument for short-term analysis. Globalization and dynamic reactions by the market, based on a variety of suppliers, better communication ways and melting advantages for the industrialized nations contribute to a more dynamic environment with shorter terms of measurements.

The authority over an enterprise could be a difference between both sectors, too: Neustadt argues the focus of the private executive is to set goals, shift structures, procedures and personnel to suit the execution of tasks, to monitor results and to renew operational decisions.[173] For him the decisive factor is the authority of the board to appoint and fire executives. In the public sector electorate decide over the value of results, for example concerning the last election term of a mayor. The local parliaments are also subject to be judged by their results to influence the administrative work and set of objectives. Especially in the case of risk, majorities are to attack easier than in the case of consensus. Parties and other interest groups have influence to voters and follow their own interests. From a managerial point of view voters have to be convinced to be served well by politics and policies; they want to see personal benefits and be part of the results. But consideration of awareness and utility of products and services is different. Some of the residents have only singular contacts to the public administration, other need the support, personal or indirect through projects or offers. Awareness of personal effects and the used resources is very diffuse and part of political work to convey residents to the valuable services the administration offers to the residents. Thus individual interests are channelled by politicians and interest groups. The more influence the higher the pressure to the mayor and the main managerial level. Performance of the public administration is partly monitored by the society members; they judge the results, individually or collectively. They judge at least in part by what the residents or citizens think and expect and be aware of what will happen to their own life, the personal benefit of public investments and the local quality to live.

Contrary to business: There the virtue of profit is legitimately; offering of products that attracts customers necessary, as Drucker (2008) worked out.[174] Remarkably, for him management is not only focused to business and private sector, more it has to become the governing organ of all institutions of modern society. Convergence of both sectors is therefore predictable, from the point of view by Drucker. On the private market a customer is able to decide which good or service to buy; specifications and expected utility are known and pursued. In the public sector con-

---

173 Allison, G., *Public and private management: Are they fundamentally alike in all unimportant respects*, Proceedings of Public Management Research Conference, November 1979, Washington D.C., p. 20, 1979

174 Drucker, P., *Management*, rev. edit., Collins, New York, p. 97, 2008

tinuous payment of taxes and selected fees create not directly and not even a personal utility. Neustadt explains the difference between both sectors further with example of performance measurements and values which could be used to indicate positive or negative developments. While in private business the general aim is to make profit, in public sector other virtues are in focus. Remarkably Drucker criticizes the singular direction to make profit as objective for a business; for him maximizing profit is irrelevant; but otherwise without making profit a business will have a limited life span. For public administration objectivity, fairness and societal usefulness are important characteristics, partly forced by the legal framework, partly implemented by the individual political programs. In the interviews associated with the field research the addressed persons complain that centralization, the budgetary constraints and the lack of delegated authority and responsibility contribute to be less effective and efficient. More individual freedom to act in the next lower hierarchical level, responsibility by heads of subordinate departments and further delegated responsibility is not wide spread in the public sector in all three countries examined. The later discussed fundamentals of NPM content this delegation of authority.

While in business functions of management profitability is ranked very high, each department and lower sections and units are able to contribute to reach a higher grade of productivity, efficiency and effectiveness. The hierarchical structure of a public administration implies the possibility to react by objectives, to projects and initiatives in the context of desired political and societal targets and objectives. Steering and control of a public administration is made difficult by the rigid system of structures, personal development and different influential interest groups. Impacts to the institution of public administration or personal consequences are unlikely, as long as constitutional and legal guaranties exist. For managing uncertain situations in the public administration this system has special effects.

As discussed above, it should be borne in mind that the framework of management structure in public service will not be the same as managing services in the private sector. Pollitt summarizes the fundamentals the recent public sector reforms:

a) Modern business techniques will eliminate waste and lower public spending
b) Standards will be set for public services and better information will be provided to the citizens
c) Evidence-based policy partnerships and e-government
d) Enhanced responsiveness to customers and businesses

For proof of results shares of public expenses as part of GDP are used.[175]

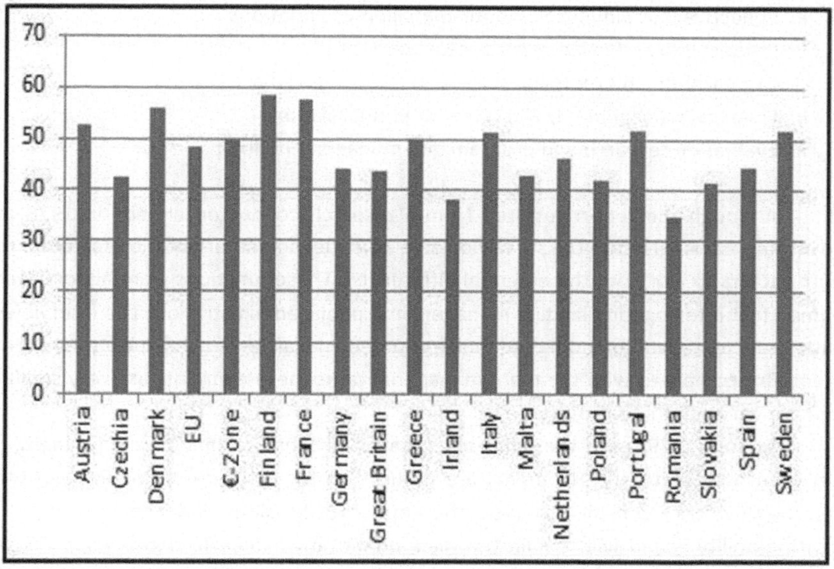

Figure 17: Public spending 2014 in comparison to GDP in %
Source: http://de.statista.com/statistik/daten/studie/6769/umfrage/staatsquoten-der-eu-laender, retrieved 23.03.2016

Measuring the other branches of public sector, worldwide recognized indicators are used to compare progress or in use as benchmark; e.g. illiteracy, number of graduates from higher education, people below poverty level, or average income level.

When business, run by an individual, turns into an organization, it requires for its own survival different structures and different principles, always depending on the product and services the company produces or provides. Market conditions generally determine the way a company is managed.[176]

The Mushkin Report (1978) offers an elementary list of public management elements:

---

175 Pollitt, C., *40 years of public management reform – what we have learned, what have we forgotten*, 40th Anniversary Conference "40 years of policy and politics" , 19.09.2012, University of Bristol, UK
176 Drucker, P., *Management*, rev. edit., Collins, New York, p. 2, 2008

- ➢ Personal management
- ➢ Work force planning
- ➢ Collective bargaining and labour-management relations
- ➢ Productivity and performance measurement
- ➢ Organization and reorganization
- ➢ Financial management/ intergovernmental relations
- ➢ Evaluation research and program and management audit

Although the report resulted from a research conducted already in 1978 at governmental level in the U.S., it could serve as guideline and orientation to compare both sectors to work out the essential differences. Those functions were almost ever named first interrogating leading managers in a public administration. The interviews with representatives of public administrations on local level confirmed this statement. But compared with the main managerial tasks these elements are very similar and not very helpful to distinct.

Allison (1979) used the point of a treatise of John T. Dunlop to draw the line between both sectors.[177] His points are reduced to focus to the distinction and the factors what are important to show the impact to decisions under uncertainty. Financing ability is and will remain the main quantitative value to detect gaps in risk management, for example insufficient resources for projects or for compensation of undesired results of decisions.

The list of arguments for a clear and precise distinction of private and public sector organizations is long, a diffuse status is created. A long-term comparison, conducted by Rainey at al. in 2000 comes to the following conclusion: The more recent researches and studies confirm that the boundaries between both sectors are diminishing and former integral differences irrelevant.[178] Reports from Steel and Warner (1990) and DeSantis and Durst (1996) found higher levels of general work satisfaction in the public sector.[179] But they also report a lower work satisfaction from specific areas; e.g. frustration with promotion, autonomy in the job and supervision. Based on the legal framework and processes political intervention is also criticized. Remarkable

---

177 Dunlop, J., *Public Management*, draft of an unpublished paper and proposal, Summer 1979, cited by: Allison, G., *Public and Private Management: Are they fundamentally alike in all unimportant respects*, Proceedings of Public Management Research Conference, November 1979, Washington D.C., 1979

178 Rainey, H. & Bozeman, B., *Comparing public and private organisations: empirical research and the power of the a priori*, Journal of Public Administration Research and Theory, 10 (2), p. 459, 2000

179 Steel, B. & Warner, R., *Job Satisfaction Among early Labor Force Participants: Unexpected Outcomes in Public and Private Sector Comparison*, Review of Public Personnel Administration, Issue 10, pp. 4-22, 1990; DeSantis, V./ Durst, S., *Comparing Job Satisfaction Among Public and Private Sector Employees*, American Review of Public Administration, Issue 26, pp. 327 – 343, 1996

for the general risk awareness and anticipation of social welfare as main objective of the public administration are the results of values of the work direction: Public managers place for higher value on public service, in the meaning of work that is directed to be beneficial to others and the society. Rainey and Bozeman (2000) named in addition self-sacrifice, responsibility and integrity.[180]

Recently published researches close incidentally the gap between both sectors, at least based in the former essential analyses on the basic criterion. Novell (2009) asked managers in both sectors to evaluate the emphasis of their daily work and challenges; interestingly are results of the five most-time consuming activities, five most prevalent problems at work and five conditions receiving the most attention from supervision:

Table 12 Comparison of public and private sector considering operations
Source: Novell, G., *Public vs. Private Managers: A new perspective*, Journal of Business & Economics Research, Vol. 7, No. 3, p.3, 2009

Most consuming activities				
	Public organization		**Private organization**	
	rank	%	rank	%
Dealing with superiors	1	24	1	26
Developing new ideas for improving productivity	2	21	2	23
Doing paperwork	3	21	3	21
Most prevalent problems at work				
	rank	%	rank	%
Labour shortages	1	23	4	15
Equipment breakdown	2	12	1	18
Low quality work	4	10	2	17
Conditions receiving most attention from superiors				
	rank	%	rank	%
Relationship with customers	1	30	4	29
Quality of work	2	25	1	34
Keeping expenses in line	4	23	2	34

180 Rainey, H. & Bozeman, B., *Comparing public and private organisations: empirical research and the power of the a priori*, Journal of Public Administration Research and Theory, 10 (2), p. 460, 2000

The general conditions, organizational structure and legal environment have an essential influence for the numeric assessment. But the result shows the tendency that there is a blurring of both sectors.

This research fully confirms the withering criticism of Banner that the public administration is based on an "organized non-responsibility." In a system where tasks and goals are laid down as also the guidelines to reach the goals, there is little incentive for individual initiatives and an awareness of threats and chances.

NPM demands more and more decentralized accountability, enabling managers to respond to a changing environment without waiting for the cue from their political masters, to accept and handle chances and threats as dynamic factors of a quasi-entrepreneurial environment and act accordingly to the goals. When clothed with necessary authority, managers down the line will be able to take a holistic view of the risks in the meaning without treating them as isolated events. Management by delegation will introduce the subordinate levels in a more entrepreneurial behavior and pave the way for greater all around efficiency –optimizing processes and reducing wastage of resources, men and material even while implementing the strategies mapped out. But the first results of the introduction of key elements of the NPM in Germany have exposed the limitations of the new style.[181]

2.5. New approaches using non-monetary unit measurement – public value as reference

The value theory is concerned with the nature of value and with what kinds of things are regarded to have a value and the measurement conditions for ordinal scale or other benchmarks. For example the research of Bogumil et al. (2007) shows despite the change in customer orientation of the administration since NPM, there is virtually no change in the number of complaints or litigations. [182]

Material and non-materials can therefore have

- aesthetic
- ethical
- epistemic values.

---

[181] Bogumil, J./Grohs, S./ Kuhlmann, S./ Ohm, Anna, et al.: Zehn Jahre Neues Steuerungsmodell, edition sigma, Berlin, p. 71, 2007

[182] Audi, R. (ed.), The Cambridge dictionary *of philosophy*, Cambridge University Press, Cambridge, p. 949, 2009

But the theory combines the general value with the expression or measurement and therefore comparability with others by desire of the consumers of the things or services. For the later identification of persons affected and to be asked for estimation of consequences of decisions, value theory offers the range of main forms of the worth of something:

- intrinsic
- instrumental
- inherent
- relational value.

Considerations about outcomes to interests and values will support the path for regaining responsiveness; this will further contribute to faster orientation and better guidance, with focus on society, on fulfilling fundamental objectives and increasing the welfare of the citizen. Kahnemann and Knetsch (1992) use a different approach: They compare the evaluation of provided public services and goods with the estimation of private goods. But they also criticize that the willingness to pay (WTP) for public goods is not comparable to the economic value of the goods.[183] All of the thoughts of public value are directed to the common sense that public value can be defined and measured; this value is created by several players, including government, executive departments, and organizations for the realization of political programs. Main focus for influence to the term of public value is the notion of public goods and services as non-rivalrous and non-excludable. Public value refers thereby to public goods, the public interest and choice or the public domain.

Gomez and Meynhardt (2009) call public value the social net product. They summarize among others, the future challenges for private and public actors in contributing to welfare in general:

- thoughts recognizing global business and network,
- capital markets,
- transparency for medias,
- internet communication changing societal expectations,
- real social imbalances and following the increased sensibility - considering climate, natural environment
- protection of species.[184]

[183] Kahneman, D. & Knetsch, J., *Valueing public goods: the purchase of moral satisfaction*, Journal of Environ mental Economics and Management, No. 22, pp. 57-70, 1992

[184] Gomez, P. & Meynhardt, T., *Public Value: Gesellschaftliche Wertschöpfung im Fokus der Führung*, in Seiler, S. (ed.), „Führung neu denken – Im Spannungsfeld zwischen Erfolg, Moral und Komplexität", Orell Fuessli,

For private cooperation they suggest the following table for origins of objectives, their threats and the possible measurement of results respective outcomes. Different interests by position and expectations lead to an individual approach to products and services and to the provider.

Table 13 Value benchmark for private corporations
Source: Gomez, P. & Meynhardt, T., *Public Value: Gesellschaftliche Wertschöpfung im Fokus der Führung*, in Seiler, S. (ed.), „Führung neu denken – Im Spannungsfeld zwischen Erfolg, Moral und Komplexität", Orell Fuessli, Zurich, p. 130, 2009

	Shareholder value	**Stakeholder value**	**Corporate social responsibility**	**Customer value**
Focus	Increase of welfare for shareholders	Focus to interest groups	Recognizing of other, minor interest groups	Focus to customer/ consumer satisfaction
Danger	Financial value domination	Too strong heterogeneous expectations	No relevance for core business	Super-elevation of customer satisfaction
Result	One-dimensional views, qualitative evaluation	Unsatisfiability of expectations	Loss of credibility	Neglecting social effects
Valuation standard	Instrumentally, material	Political-social	Ethical, moral	Hedonistic, aesthetic

All of them mean an obvious value for the society, articulated in the political environment. Combining the different approaches to public value, the following definition builds up a bracket for further considerations:

Value as a term, what is being evaluated by the citizenry, can be influenced in both increase and decrease by the government through services, products, laws regulations and other actions. Public value is individually or collectively articulated through politics or through referendums concerning certain decisions to make. Using expected changes in public value can lead to better estimation of outcomes of political and administrative decisions under no certainty. But public value can also be influenced by third parties, private persons, organization, weather, socio-economic developments; these factors are out of control of governmental influence. The theoretical aspects show the complex area; the later developed model compresses all indi-

Zurich, p. 131, 2009

vidual considerations in simple mathematical formulas. For analysis, each of the aspects has to be combined with a scale for valid and comparable results.

3. Considerations of risk and developments of risk management in a global economy

3.1. Specifying the elements of risk

a) Certainty

In general certainty is assumed when developments statistically or based of experience are sure or mathematical proven; a deviation would be out of any evidence or coincidence, for example the sunrise each day, time delayed or over the globe, or a certain fatality while jumping without a parachute from an airplane.

For risk management certain developments are comfortable to handle, because it is assumed from a psychological and epistemic point of view that a decision-maker has no doubt that p (probability), as a proposition, is true. Unger criticises this approach: For him psychological certainty is required for knowledge, but he also claimed that no person is ever certain of anything or hardly anything.[185] Another approach is to divide certainty in three classes:

- moral certainty
- metaphysical certainty
- logic certainty

On a philosophical standpoint certainty is not an absolute term. The Oxford Dictionary of Philosophy put it as follows: "We take a proposition to be certain when we have no doubt about its truth."[186] A philosophical argument for no absolute certainty is that a possibility of upsetting events remains. In addition an objective certainty is in doubt. This approach is similar de Finetti, who is sceptical about risk in general.[187] For practical use of risk management and in combination with the model of Knight the distinction of certainty - risk - uncertainty will be followed, in which certainty is regarded as assumption that a development or an event is sufficient "certain" or a deviation will be out of any known likelihood. For risk management and decision-making in operational use certainty plays a secondary role. Following Finetti, Einstein and Hawkins, all data of all atoms have to be simultaneously processed to get a situation of 100%. But the question remains whether computers calculate in a certain way.

---

[185] Audi, R. (ed.), *The Cambridge dictionary of philosophy*, Cambridge University Press, Cambridge, p. 129, 2009

[186] Blackburn, S. (ed.), *Oxford Dictionary of Philosophy*, Oxford University Press, Oxford, 2008, p. 57

[187] De Finetti, B., *Theory of probability*, John-Wiley & Sons, London, 1974, p. x

M. Bodemann, *Management in Public Administration*,
Sustainable Management, Wertschöpfung und Effizienz,
https://doi.org/10.1007/978-3-658-22687-9_4

b) Risk

The Oxford Dictionary of Economics defines risk as following: Risk is "...a form of uncertainty where, while the actual outcome of an action is not known, probabilities can be assigned to each of the possible outcomes. This permits application of the expected utility function to represent preferences over alternatives. The variance of the distribution of possible outcomes is frequently used as a measure of risk, particularly in the financial theory."[188] In this context of risk the following main characteristics are to involve:

- action
- uncertainty
- outcome
- utility
- preferences
- alternatives
- distribution

All these characteristics to define risk, especially the characters concerning utility, preferences, and alternatives will dominate the thoughts about implementing public value as indicator for outcomes.

Risk is used in the meaning of uncertainty of future developments of current status based on decision-situations. Risk from a subjective and concrete point of view can also mean the threat of undesired variance from predicted path.[189] In addition risk is characterized by the chance of loss or gain, a probability and a magnitude. Loss for example could be expressed by numbers of injuries, property damage or financial losses in monetary terms.[190]

Remarkably risk is intentionally combined with a negative emotion. It stands for not desired development, for personal direct or indirect negative consequences. Coleman points out that risk usually is associated with the downside or bad outcomes, considering both uncertainty of future outcomes and benefits of these outcomes.[191] Also the magnitude has important influence to decisions – a higher risk, whatever one combines with this term – is traditional assumed to become compensated by a higher expected return.

---

[188] Black, J./ Hashimzade, N./ Myles, G.(eds.), *Oxford Dictionary of Economics*, 3rd edition, Oxford University Press, Oxford, p. 394, 2009

[189] Brühweiler, B., *Risikomanagement als Führungsaufgabe*, Haupt, Berne, p. 23, 2007

[190] Gough, J., *Measuring perceived and acceptable risk: an application of survey approaches*, Centre for Resource Management, University of Canterbury and Lincoln University, Information Paper No. 24, 1991

[191] Coleman, T., A practical guide to risk management, CFA Institute, Amazon distribution, Leipzig, p. 14, 2011

But Coleman (2011) criticises to be risk averse in the meaning, to focus to the downside, ignoring chances and opportunities beneath the risk of loss.[192] Others bring in empirical results to describe the affects handling risk; Alghalith states that risk-averse firms tend to maximize their expected utility of the profit.[193] For him the exploitation of opportunities and gains is a fixed content of management and entrepreneurship. In his perspective financial firms that are effective in manage risk, control downsides and seek for upsides. But risk in general is one component of private and business world, as discussed above. Different approaches confirmed this notion of the combination of certainty, risk and uncertainty. But to get a full overview a deviation is missing:

Philosophers, mathematicians, statisticians, and economists argued that because of the lack of concrete knowledge of the future and a wide spectrum of developments, triggered by events or decisions, risk is a substitute for missing data. In a laboratory, excluded from external influences, complex situations could be simulated. Though a large number of results will guide to a better and better notion what will happen next. Decisions to be made could be done on a verified data basis, the thread of not desired results could be reduced, using data collected by receptors and receivers and processed to simulate future developments as precise as possible; at least to limit and present range and outcomes of possible developments as support to the decision maker. In the case, that it will be possible to place receptors in every possible dynamic position to measure very small tendencies and to process all of these data simultaneously, the status of risk and uncertainty could be limited. Albert Einstein stated to the same assumption, later confirmed by Stephen Hawkins, that the free will deceased to exist as science will explore more biological, chemical and physical processes and their dependency. His famous quote "God does not play dice" shows his conviction that the future is fully determined, but without tools to measure of changes in all atoms the future remains uncertain, at least varies in alternatives.[194] In 1970 De Finetti provoke by his simple statement that probability simply does not exist.[195] He argued that the common contemplation to regard the future as unknown field, where only statistical values and experience allow one to forecast, is based on a subjective view. Summarizing all known, measurable and processing data, could at least limit the range of possible outcomes to a minimum, eventually to only a single path of development. Knight had introduced a similar approach. For him probabilities

---

192 Coleman, T., *A practical guide to risk management*, CFA Institute, Amazon distribution, Leipzig, p. 12, 2011
193 Alghalith, M., *New economics of risk and uncertainty*, Nova Science Publishers, New York, 2007
194 Hawkins, S., *The universe in a nutshell,* Bantam Press, New York, 2001
195 De Finetti, B., *Theory of probability*, John-Wiley & Sons, London, 1974, p. x

depend only on an observer's particular lack of information.[196] Despite his critiques for the intention to define the risk as a concrete and clear bounded term, five different views to risk by Hansson (2000) will demonstrate the spectrum and the different perspectives risk is used, in both theoretical and practical approach. By using his mentions about the term risk and filled with results from the field research a final model of risk in the context of probabilities, uncertainty, event, sources and results can be developed.

As pointed out above, for Hansson risk is always combined with negative or not desired outcome. He used different perspectives to offer a complete picture in terms of time, processes, outcomes and quantification.[197]

1. **"Risk = an unwanted event which may or may not occur"**

   Risk is used not in the meaning to describe a potential gain, nor any description of monetary or non-monetary values to quantify the results. Using this equation describes an event, which is not desired. It has a negative meaning. Hansson does not give the explanation whether the beginning of the event is just happening or already in process; further it remains open whether the event plays a direct role for a development.

2. **"Risk = the cause of an unwanted event which may or may not occur"**

   This is the description of the reason for the event, consequently an event in time before the unwanted event occurs. The reason for the critical incident mentioned above. Risk the reason for a negative result which is not certain.

3. **"Risk = the probability of an unwanted event which may or may not occur"**

   In the model of Frank Knight known probability is one essential condition to distinguish risk from uncertainty. In the model of Hansson probability is used a quantified value to describe a not certain situation. The decision-maker uses probability to evaluate two of more possible alternative states in the future.

4. **"Risk = the statistical expectation value of unwanted events which may or may not occur"**

   From a technical standpoint the expectation value shows the singular view of one event, combined with negative consequences.

5. **"Risk = the fact that a decision is made under conditions of known probabilities"**

   It describes the distinction by Knight that a decision is made under the given and known probabilities of the different possible developments and outcomes. Under missing or only insufficient probabilities the decision is factual made under uncertain-

[196] Knight cited in Holton, G., *Defining Risk*, Financial Analysts Journal, Volume 60, Number 6, 2004

[197] Hansson, S., *Philosophical perspectives on risk*, Delft University, 2002

ty. No expectation corridor could be provided. In this case the steerable future as separated from fully unknown developments. For a declaration of the situation risk is used as an indicator for a situation in which the outcomes and the inherent probabilities are known and limiting the range of possible developments.

One of the more technical notion of the term risk offer Cottin and Döhler.[198] For them risk is a valuable object which is subject to a potential future alteration applying to the determined decision situation or applying to the certain or not specified period of time. Risk management is considering both sides of a situation determined by uncertainty in probability and outcomes, recognizing an opportunity to create value. As result risk can be split by the following comparison:

Table 14 Expectations and translation
Source: by author

	Positive expectation and realization	**Negative expectation and realization**
Business management/ operations	gains	losses
Abstract outcome	opportunity	disadvantage
Sides of risk	chance	threat
Intentional assessment	desired outcomes	undesired outcomes

A synthesis of the premises and the parameters of influence lead to a final model. This model will be used in further explanations and was the basis of the questionnaires distributed and the empirical part conducted. The quantifying definition of engineers which is focused on a numerical value to define acceptable risks is not sufficient to describe a risk for managerial use. As earlier cited the UK Audit Commission (2001) defined a threat, with the circumstances that one event or action could occur. This event will adversely affect the organization's ability to achieve its objectives and to execute successfully its strategies.[199]

---

[198] Cottin, C. & Döhler, S., *Risikoanalyse*, Springer Spektrum, Wiesbaden, 2013

[199] UK Audit Commission, *Worth the risk*, CW Print Group, London, p.7, 2001. Critical note by the author: The word risk is here defined by a threat. This does not correspondent with made explanations of threat, which in the authors mind is a situation which cannot be influenced. But especially the use of thresholds could influence the dimension of the loss, for example at the stock exchange to place a stop-loss-process to avoid higher losses in stocks. Damodaran pointed out in his list of risk definition and the distinction, that in some disciplines, a contrast is drawn between a risk and a threat. For his distinction, a threat is a low-probability event with large negative consequences, where analysts may be unable to assess the probability. A risk, on the other hand, is defined to bea higher probability event, where there is enough information to assess both the probability and the consequences. Damodaran, A., *Strategic risk taking*, Wharton School Publishing, Upper Saddle River, p. 6, 2008

The model begins at the situation the decision-maker is on the starting-point; no valid or processed data are available. By identifying the expected and possible results of a decision based on premises and by comparing with similar situations, with references or by statistical data, the funnel of possible outcomes opens. The range of the funnel is determined by number and grade of affection of events, based on risk factors that can affect the expected path. Positive and negative developments can be linked, but not only symmetrical. By a chain reaction outcomes can be amplified, so the effect to addressed persons or objectives is not a linear or static one. In addition the grade of affection by external events and risk factors varies over the timeline; that means opening and closing of the funnel. Combined with the individual probability this model leads to a complex synthesis of available data; for steady adjustment the data has to be on latest level. Especially the opportunity to make some adjustments, based on the changed environmental conditions seems to be difficult in the public administration, as Table No. 1 and Figure No. 2 show.

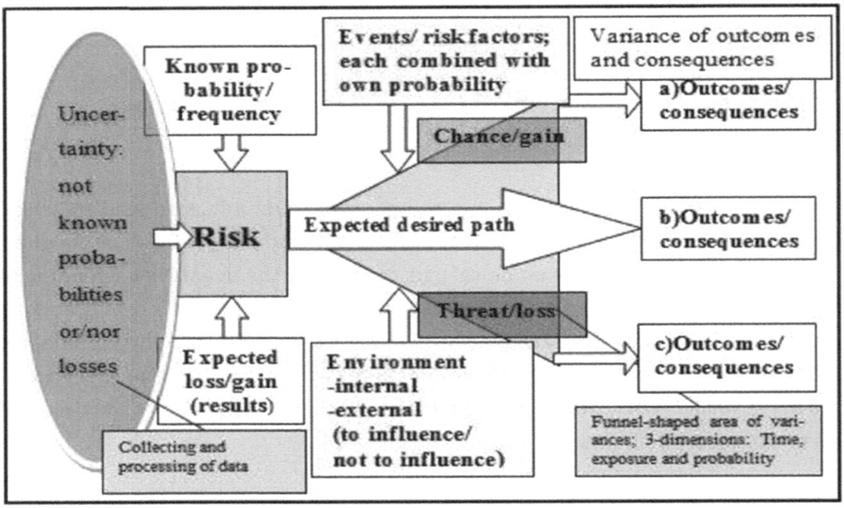

Figure 18: Model of risk: Causal relationship between uncertainty and outcome
Source: by author, based on literature research and interviews. Idea by: Monahan, G., *Enterprise Risk Management*, John Wiley & Sons, Inc., Hoboken, p. 2, 2008, extended by Romeike, F. & Hager, P., Erfolgsfaktor Risiko-Management 2.0, Gabler, Wiesbaden, p. 262, 2009

The assumptions made leads to a common definition of risk, although the challenges for risk management are only superficial integrated:

Definition of risk:

Reason => event/result => positive/ negative effects/positive/ negative deviation from expected results, immanent also the increased or decreased grade of expected efficiency. Results can be defined as outputs or outcomes; outcomes can be defined as increase or decrease of public value in the case of measurement of public sector efficiency. In general deviations cause gains, profits and fewer resources used as well as losses, damages or waste of resources.

c) Uncertainty

To distinct risk and uncertainty a statement of Gough (1988) enlightens the correlation: "Uncertainty does not imply risk if there are no direct consequences to the individual or decision maker. Uncertainty is therefore a necessary condition for risk, but it is not sufficient (....) and reducing uncertainty in a system does not necessarily reduce risk."[200]

In the absence of a definition of certainty, it remains unclear what reflects uncertainty and risk. Contemporary researches by Knight 1921, Keynes and Mises 1928, and Kolmogorow 1933 confirmed but also extend the model of Knight to distinguish between the three conditions:

Knight's separation is used to distinct between different conditions in a decision situation. Risk combines a known probability and an expected gain or loss.

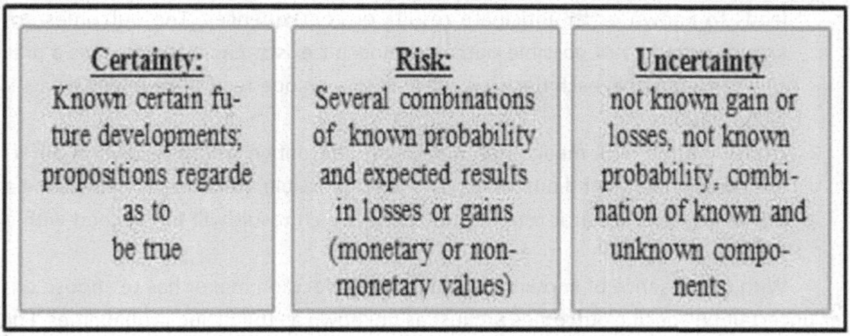

Figure 19: Distinction between certainty and uncertainty
Source: Knight, F., *Risk, Uncertainty and Profit*, reprinted by Dover, New York, 2006, original published by Houghton Mifflin, Boston and New York

[200] Ebd. p. 25

Similar to Knight is the bandwidth between certainty and uncertainty by Marchazina:

Certainty	Uncertainty	
	Risk	Uncertainty
Alternative with maximum of expected value	Multiple expectations	
Predicted and certain results	Objective and subjective known probabilities	Missing probability

Figure 20: Correlation between quantity and utility
Source: Marcharzina, K., *Unternehmensführung*, Gabler, Wiesbaden, p. 595, 2003

That leads to a classification of decisions to make and a comparison with already executed steps to get a better estimation of future ramifications. For a situation under uncertainty other ways to estimate are necessary, although all of results will be remain vague. Combining several considerations and models of risk, the following distinctions are the results:

1. Decision under certainty means that decisions were made under recognized and considered knowledge about the developments. Once made decision leads to known or to anticipate results or consequences. The outcomes are known, a variety of possible outcomes doesn't exists. Each decision has a precise consequence; each decision will lead to a unique result. There will be a 1 x 1 correlation.
2. Decision under risk means that a decision alternative will have several different consequences and outcomes. The set of possible outcomes is known and a probability given. But it remains uncertain which result will be reached with a specific decision.[201]

With the absence of known probabilities the decision maker has to choose under uncertainty; specific outcomes are just as unknown as the fitting probabilities. For Frank Knight this situation is completely to differ from the contemplation of risk.[202]

[201] Gough, J., *Risk and* uncertainty, Information Paper No. 10, Centre for Resource Management, University of Canterbury and Lincoln College, p. 25, 1988
[202] Knight, F., Risk, *Uncertainty and Profit*, reprinted by Dover, New York, 2006, original published by Houghton Mifflin, Boston and New York, 1921

There are a few researches that explain the inaccuracy in forecasts. Flyvberg and COWI Consulting Group tested technical, psychological, and political-economic explanations for inaccuracy in forecasts. Invariably technical explanations dominate the literature on this issue.[203] They proved and explained inaccuracy in terms of unreliable or outdated data and the use of inappropriate forecasting models.[204] Flyvberg (2006) doesn't accept such an explanation and points to the steady improvement seen in gathering data. Despite such an improvement, there is no impact on the accuracy of forecasts.[205]

Flyvberg also attributes inaccuracies to psychological and political factors. Most people tend to judge future events in a more positive light than it is really warranted by actual and recognized experience.[206] The game theory can also explain political decisions to some extent. In many cases, projects in public sector have been accompanied by strategic misrepresentation - cost underestimated and benefits for citizens overestimated. There are indicators that such under- and overestimations are intentionally set to get a political decision. But when things go awry, those responsible seek to take cover under political patronage.

In private firms, increasing costs or the missing benefits for the customers have their own effects, for example reducing the owner's yearly dividend or increasing unsold stocks. Hence in both sectors, any variance from the planned results could prove costly, though in different ways. Dividends will be dropped; necessary investments will be stopped, new stakeholders will be more concerned about the expected development of a business. Flyvberg pointed out that private lenders, shareholders, and stock market analysts would also be hit strongly if their own forecasts prove wrong.[207]

Different models have been proposed for greater accuracy, like the reference class forecast method. In 2005, the American Planning Association (APA) endorsed reference class forecasting and recommended that planners should never rely solely on conventional forecasting techniques:

"APA encourages planners to use reference class forecasting in addition to traditional methods as a way to improve accuracy. The reference class forecasting

[203] Wolke, T., *Risikomanagement*, Oldenbourg, Munich, p. 31, 2007

[204] Vanston, J. & Vanston, L., *Testing the tea leaves: Evaluating the validity of forecasts*, Research-Technology Management, Vol. 47, No. 5, pp. 33-39, 2004

[205] Flyvberg, B., *From Nobel prize to project management: Getting risks right*, Project Management Journal, Vol. 37, No. 3, August, p. 6, 2006

[206] Ebd.

[207] Ebd.

method is beneficial for non-routine projects. Planners should never rely solely on civil engineering technology as a way to generate project forecasts."[208]

Reference class forecasting predicts the outcome of a planned action based on actual outcomes in a reference class of similar actions to that being forecast. The theories behind reference class forecasting were developed by Daniel Kahneman and Amos Tversky.[209] The methodology and data needed for employing reference class forecasting in practice in policy, planning, and management were developed by Bent Flyvbjerg and the COWI Consulting Group in a joint effort. The theoretical work helped Kahneman win the Nobel Prize in Economics. Today, reference class forecasting has found widespread use in practice in both public and private sector policy and management.

Improving the accuracy and reliability of forecasts in projects and for operational work is necessary to cut cost, at least to hold the cost inside a planned and steerable margin. Because of at the beginning unique projects the reference class comparison will contribute to more precise forecasts; for example of a technological leap forward in development. Public project or public-private project are often peculiar, considering motives and expected results. But also in this sector, comparisons of projects will be helpful to increase welfare as ultimate objective to the people.

d) Probability

Few models of risk evaluation use a two-dimensional model, dealing with the status of a risk and ranking it in the context of other risks. The values can be derived from statistics or from subjective judgments by experts, from within or outside the organization and who are familiar with the total environment of the organization. Without knowledge of the complex causal relationship of initiators, following up on risks, threats, resulting from the internal and external environment, a definition of likelihood remains impossible or could lead to incorrect/ invalid or at least less accurate values.

Probability can be used as numeric value for uncertainty, based on historical data base, intentions, visions, experiences. The highest probability is the value of 1. Critical for the top management or those at the operational level to this simple model is to know exactly when an event could occur, as that could help avoiding losses - this is also an important point of Knight's model.[210] He demands a numerical value of

---

[208] The American Planning Association, *APA Article Calls on Planning to Help End Inaccuracies in Public Project Revenue Forecasting*, April 7, 2005

[209] Kahnemann, D./ Tversky, A., *Prospect theory: An analysis of decision under risk*, Econometrica, Vol.47, No. 2, pp. 263-291, March 1979

[210] ebd.

probability, between 0% and 100%. When there is a probability of 100%, the event is realized in the considered time, no uncertainty exists; differences between output and outcomes remain. In addition another scale of probability rating is used.

- Almost certain (but not 100% in the period of examination)
- Likely
- Possible
- Unlikely
- Rare

These descriptions combine numeric values with a qualitative expression. In the case of a rare event the probability is low, just above 0; also certain can be translated to almost 1. For data processing qualitative expressions have to be converted to a range in numeric values. Almost certain, for example, can be expressed with numeric values from 0.8 to 0.99, rare from 0.01 to 0.2. By processing the probability and the expected damages from different expected developments after a decision, simulations can be done. The value of probability has to be adjusted over the observation time; other impact factors could be changed. Threshold passed leads to a higher probability or threatening factors disappear.

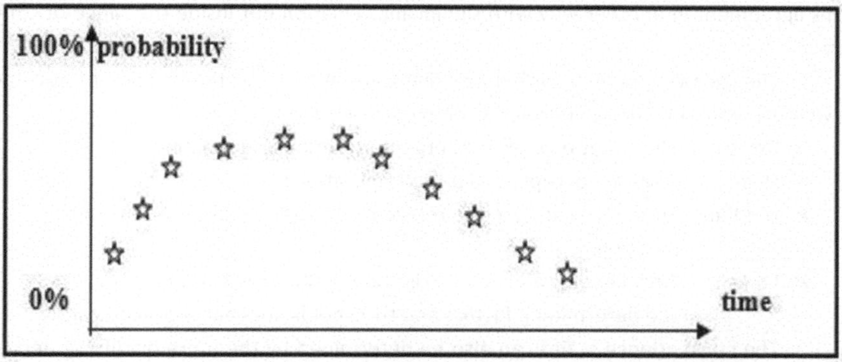

Figure 21: Chance to get wet in a thunderstorm in a certain geographical position depending on time
Source: by author

This figure can be complemented to a three-dimension graph with the grade of wetness as substitute for gain or loss, and a test version will receive during the certain time. Other influences like wind or a changing geographical position of the test-person will increase the complexity of the model and the numbers to process to calculate a valid forecast. Both in private as well as in public sector those models have to deal with multiple dimensions and risk factors to be as well dynamic as the consequences of one decision.

3. 1. 1. Magnitude and coutomes as indicator for achievement of objectives and derivation from status quo

Both values are used in combination to determine a spot in the area of a 2-dimension- model, composed of probability and expected loss. In this model different spots mark the current or expected risk situation of the municipal administration, e.g. for the next fiscal year. This matrix offers only isolated absolute values. The range of negative influence factors, which have priority, is not displayed in proportion to possible compensation budgets. But the advantage is the direct approach to the negative impacts which can be identified clearly by traffic-light model.

With these categories it is possible to fill out a matrix for more transparency to make better decisions; as result to get indicators for ranking and support of the decision maker. A direct real time comparison or a comparison with equal administrations, in size or geographic situation, is neither legal neither demanded nor pursued, on the contrary: Public administrations claim to be very special and have to cope with unique problems; an example is the application of the collective wage agreement: Each administrative district in North Rhine-Westphalia, as state in Germany, manages this agreement in another way with significant deviation but inside the range of contract.

The following ranking with normative translation is another version of qualitative measurement, connected with an activity description:

- Extreme: The situation demands urgent attention and reaction
- High: Risks are accepted as part of operations
- Medium: Situation is assigned to relevant manager for observation and reaction
- Low: Only keeping a watch on risk taking shape will do unless the determining factors and thresholds are changed significantly

The consequence scales can also be determined by the more qualifying depiction:

- Catastrophic
- Major
- Moderate
- Minor
- Insignificant

These qualitative expressions are using the correlation between damage and potential resources for compensation. In this reflection only negative results and consequences are described. Calculation the ratio between estimated loss and for example capital resources or annual budget addresses the awareness of politicians and public managers; benchmarking by the model of capital at risk can present the overall situation in a county or state as geographical bounded entities.

Analogue to probability the potential chances or opportunities have to converted to measurable and valuable terms; this can be monetary values but also decrease of utility and comfort. Further these terms have to be brought in a correlation to a reference value. The loss of € 100.000 has for global players not relevant meaning, for a firm with a yearly budget of € 300.000, this can be catastrophic.

Positive or negative developments are hard to read, especially through yearly changing budget. Comparisons with similar organizations are impossible this way because of the absence of a common denominator; results and advantages are not transferable and one final number to indicate an organization-wide risk status cannot be easily and understandable provided. If the construction of a public building costs about € 1.0 Mio, it might not make much of a difference in a yearly budget of € 500 Mio.. Additional costs can be raised by cutting down on other projects or shifting some money from them for the moment. Thus there is not much of a threat for the organization. But if it is a case of a yearly budget of € 50.0 Mio additional cost of € 1.0 Mio will cause major liquidity problems forcing stoppage of some other, perhaps even more important, projects. Alternative solutions are new loans, but this way delegates the results to an uncertain future.

As discussed above another limiting factor is the timeline and the future expectation of developments. For political decisions could a later realized threat easier to be argued than comparably early threats with low potential losses.

With the additional consideration of the correlation to the yearly budget it is more transparent to initiate effective and efficient measures to evaluate the current state and possible consequences and outcomes. With a third dimension of magnitude or expected loss and gains, beneath time and probability, the risks are more detailed and comparable.

The depicted relationship in the process of initiation of a process until the measurement of its outcomes shows that risk is not based on a single examination. Known and also unknown risk drivers and events can disturb the results. For a better decision the model of risk management should encompass every possibility to influence the outcomes.

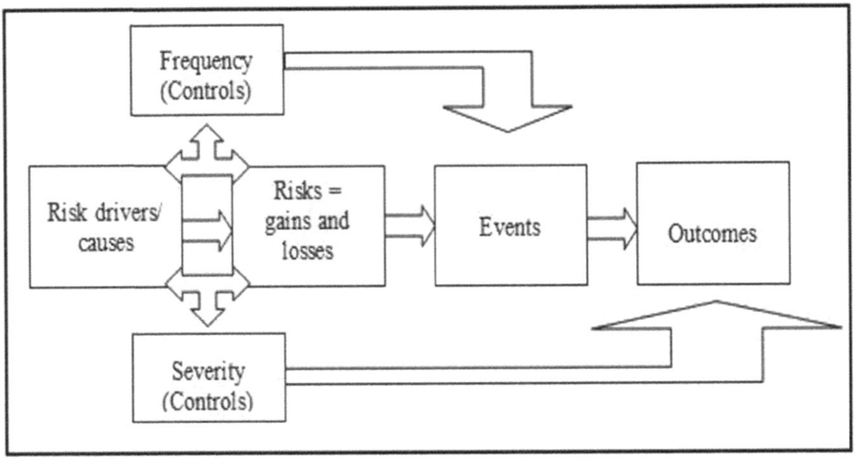

Figure 22: Relationship of risk and outcomes
Source: Monahan, G., *Enterprise risk management*, John Wiley & Sons, Inc., Hoboken, p.8, 2008

As discussed earlier, that means to get all information from every influence sphere and to process this information in an appropriate and not-delayed matter. But that is currently technically not possible; using receptors, collecting and processing of data will give a narrower corridor of possible paths of developments in the future, using the timeline this corridor will be sharpened.

For Knight, ignorance of probability is not compatible with the term risk. From his point of view it is necessary to identify a situation linked with a risk and therefore with uncertainty and a known probability. For any risk management approach a probability is indeed necessary. Ignorance about possible uncertainties ahead could prove costly. The Germany-wide task force for risk management in the public sector[211] deduced that ignorance could turn risk into threat, uncontrollable that takes you off guard and looks inevitable. Any new, unfamiliar technology could also pose uncertainty. Forecasts in such situations become more difficult, sometimes even impossible, especially when precedents are not easily found. Ironically though, both sectors, private and public, have to look for new technologies to flourish, while accepting a higher grade of uncertainty.

The reference class forecasts search for valid and transferable data from the environment. In those cases a calculated probability is hard to find. But perhaps an expectation value is possible. With an expectation value, which is not empirically proven, often intuition is combined. At least intuition has not been proven to deliver

[211] Task force of risk management in the public administration by the KGSt.

results in stock trading. Some stock traders have a natural bias for individual companies or organization, but such intuitive bias has not necessarily fetched better returns. Despite all the data available and past experiences, there is noteworthy improvement in accuracy.[212]

There are some indicators that properly designed private-public-partnerships (PPP) may help to improve the accuracy of cost forecasts.[213] But those projects are often long-term projects. First results have to be proven over years; but, if the partner goes bankrupt, maintenance will be transferred unavoidable back to the local municipality.[214]

3. 1. 2. Integrating probability in decision-development-strings

For the private sector more than one definition of risk management exists, just as different systematic approaches to risk management. As seen in the comparison of risk in private and public sector, the organizational approach is similar, but not identical. Risk management is most successful, when it is initiated and driven by the directors and the chief executives; this is relevant for the private sector, but suits also for the public sector. Public service organizations, such as the municipal or public administration, may vary in sizes, duties, geographical situation and complexity, but they share many features in common with their private sector neighbours. Attempts are numerous to transfer the meaning of the word enterprise to the public administration. It leads to a distorted impression, often used in the context of risk management, with its connotations of commercial, profit seeking activities; thus there is no doubt that the principles and practices of enterprise risk management are also functional as in the private sector than for the public sector.[215] The NPM campaign showed that the transfer of private sector principles is possible and successful, although there will be always peculiarities and principles which have to be adjusted for use in the public sector environment.

From the Australian/New Zealand Standard 4360 is taken the following definition, which will lead to the different steps to determine a sound and successful risk management approach: "Risk management is a systematic application of manage-

[212] National Audit Office 2003, cited in Flyvberg, B./ Holm, M./ Buhl, S., *How (in)accurate Are Demand Fore casts in Public Works Project*, Journal of the American Planning Association, Vol. 71, No. 2, Spring, p. 138, 2005

[213] Critical in general to PPP: Acar, M./ Guo, C./ Yang, K., *Accountability When Hierarchical Authority is Absent* The American Review of Public Administration, Vol. 38, No. 1, March,, p. 3, 2008

[214] Note by the author: Shared responsibility without equilibrium and advantages for the private investor.

[215] Drennan, L. & McConnell, A., *Risk and crisis management in the public sector*, New York, Routledge, New York, p.38, 2007

ment policies to the task of communication, establishing the context, identifying, analysing, evaluating, treating, monitoring and reviewing risks."[216] These different steps declare the risk management process in short.

Summarizing the different factors above the following graph illustrates the status for a decision-maker, assuming that all relevant information are collected and processed properly.

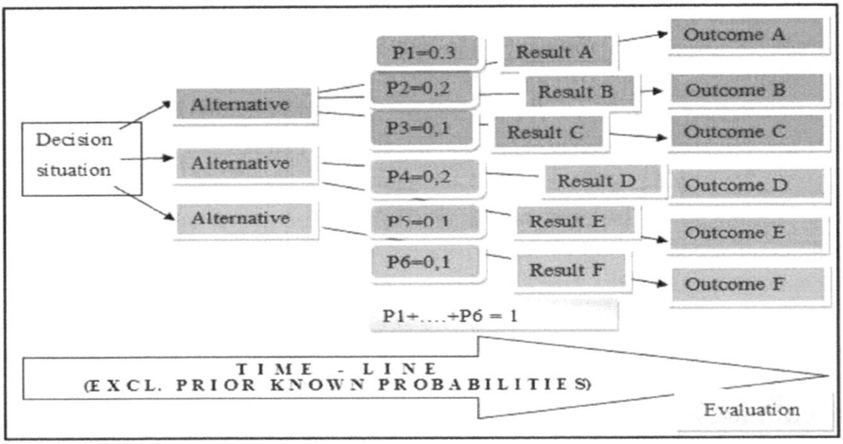

Figure 23: Development over alternatives in time line
Source: by author

This simple decision tree shows different probabilities and potential outcomes. Some of the risk management models focus to the output, the direct result of the decision[217]; but for the long-term examination in the public administration the societal, political and financial outcomes of a decision are relevant values. Not included are influential factors from the in- and outside which could permanent change the values for probability and estimated outcomes.

Most of the models lack of the different sequence of events, considering the probabilities. Threats, occurring only in two years, could be better absorbed, even with higher amplitude of damage, than threats occurring in the next half year, caused by the missing liquidity or not planned budget. So most of the theorists composed their model with an assumed time chronological coincidence of events that could cause a loss or a gain. But there are differences in the priority if the period of time is

[216] AS/NZ Standard 4360: Standards Australia, 2004

[217] For example mathematical models for investment decisions, prepared by Damodaran, A., *Strategic risk taking*, Wharton School Publishing, Upper Saddle River, 2008, p. 309; focus to operational risks by Crouhy, M./ Galai, D. / Mark, R., *The essentials of risk management*, McGraw-Hill, New York, p. 325, 2006

calculated. The given example symbolizes a mathematical model, but lacks on the individual outcome specifications. Replenished by an individual utility the complexity is increased, also in the case of weighing up or subtract positive and negative consequences in the case of realization.

3.2. Specific features of risk management models

3. 2. 1. Evolution of risk management

In recorded human history, risk and survival have been an inseparable combination. The cavemen, for instance, were faced with new or recurring dangers every day, every month and every year, nay every minute of his life. Initially his life was dominated by weather, by animals, predators and the search for food and shelter. For him, as individual human, these were his daily routines, his business: To survive as human being, to compete with weather, other living beings, and together with other human beings, steady and exhausting challenge for a lifetime. It was a short life and full of uncertainties; the search for food and shelter exposed them to physical dangers; from preying animals to poor weather. By stocking food up, the people could reduce considerably the negative consequences of a harsh winter. [218]

Physical risk and reward were linked together strongly. The objectives and goals were focused to survive, later to improve the living conditions and to withstand unplanned weathers, food shortages or threats by other living beings, humans or animals. Distinct investments for actual consume and storage for uncertain future situation were important decisions to made and risk management for their age, but also a simple method of risk management for each person, later for family and groups, combined with the beginning of division of labour and specialization.

The invention of ships and the development of faster routes, paving the way for better and faster transportation of persons and goods, were the next steps in the progress of civilization and globalization. One natural threat was to lose a ship with cargo and sailors by poor weather or by wrong decision on maps by the captain. It was followed, and currently faces a renaissance, the danger to be waylaid by pirates. Trade was one of the firsts step to separate physical harm from economic reward. While the owners were able to limit their physical losses, the sailors, who signed a contract to serve on a ship, were exposed to thunderstorms, malnutrition, disease

[218] Bernstein, P., *Against of The Gods: The remarkable story of risk*, New York, Wiley, 1996 and Erben, F. & Romeike, F., *Allein auf stürmischer See*, Wiley, Weinheim, 2006

and attacks by pirates. The owner was able to decide, weighing the potential benefits and threats by accompanying the transport. Kaplan and Gerrick (1981) combined this later in the approach of evaluation of relative risks and acceptability of risks. In a decision situation one has to weight along with all other costs and benefits in the decision process.[219] Until the industrial age, economic activities often expose those, attracted by economic rewards, to physical risks. A good example is the conquest of the new world by the Italian explorer Christopher Columbus and his crew who set out on their journey knowing full well the risks factors involved, later followed by other explorers: Today scientists and explorers for natural resources, like gas or oil, are same way exposed, whereas they have more information and capabilities to being prepared for or to cope with uncertain developments and events, threatening personal, material or project goals.

First steps measuring and comparing success by numbers and the correlation to risk were made by Fra Luca Bartolomeo de Pacioli (1445 - 1514), an Italian mathematician and Franciscan friar. He was in addition often regarded as the "Father of Accounting" and authored the first book on double-entry accounting. With Candano 1524 and Pascal and Fermat in 1654 followed more detailed mathematical backgrounds and scientific explanation for the probability theory. 1693 John Halley invented tables for the calculation of life expectancies of people; an idea and basis on which economic calculation work with, for example life insurances or retirement insurances. Today, these fundamental statements still have a relevance to the later discussion. Tied with this, the municipal employment conditions and the acquired rights to a pension, which must be provided for, are mentioned. As life expectancy increases, these must be adapted continuously, so that the authorities are not surprised by follow financial obligations when demographic changes and proportions manifest themselves. But, as later seen in the empirical part, the model of pensions in general and the individual adjustments each year are regarded as uncertain factors. Democratic change is one of the identified factors, named by public administration and corroborated as clear and present challenge. Personnel and quality capacity for a steady development of a society are further dominating indicators, the identification of a disproportion is an important indicator for politics and policies to develop and initiate countermeasures.

Bernouilli introduced a paradigm with his utility theory to rational behaviour in 1738. He assumed that animals can comparatively act only out of instinct. In his model the animals cannot asses the environmental conditions and the consequences in the future; they act, based on an actual analysis, instinctively. Not to act in an in-

[219] Kaplan, S. & Gerrick, J., *On the quantitative definition of risk*, Risk Analysis, Vol. 1, No. 1, p. 11, 1981

stinctively way, based on historical data, empirical researches and models for forecasts, is favored in private sector; partly claimed by legal environment, partly applied by management to prevent the firm from surprising events. The still ongoing scientific discussion on economic effects was started with the work "Doctrine of Chances" in 1753 by De Moirre and is still a resilient topic in financial analysis and economic forecasts. Another milestone in the story of the risk research is the book "Risk, Uncertainty and profit" by Frank Knight (1921). His statements concerning uncertainty and risk are still consulted in current risk researches.[220] Briefly, Knight assumes that frequently repeated events with known probabilities do not necessarily enable one to make statements on the future with any certainty. Moreover, only known and fixed probabilities could influence the forecasts and measures. Consequently for Knight they have to be accompanied with a determinable and mathematical flow. However, newer researches offer results which question, enlarge and complete Knight's theory, for example Hansson (2000) and Holton (2004).[221] Especially the philosophical contribution by Holton demonstrates the wide field defining risk as term and the deviations for scientific approaches. In 1937 John Maynard Keynes sought to make use of his examination of the relationship of copper prices to interest rates and thus applying mathematical probabilities to economic connections. Keynes assumed that there remained uncertainties just as economic phenomena, which do not permit any valid forecasts of events. Remarkable after the internet bubble at the beginning of the 21st century, the financial sector points out to every customer, that the developments of the past are not monotonic functions and an indicator for further developments. Public managers currently claimed that insufficient consultation lead to and justify financial operations, eventually to become exculpated from critical decisions.

The literature about risk, risk management and tools for prevention starts with papers in the 50ies of the 20ies century. Main trigger was the attempt of insurance companies to create a valid and reliable basement of prognoses, for example for life-insurances. In the current era of internet, changing technology, globalization and deregulation, the possible variation of future environment is also growing, as word spreads fast on products and services. Deviation from forecasted paths faced by a public administration could be different, but risks in the general meaning of chances and threats are very much there. Not only for insurances but for finances risk management and tools for forecast became popular and needed. Markowitz provides a model of preferences when he introduced his mean-variance portfolio allocation

---

[220] Knight, F., Risk, *Uncertainty and Profit*, reprinted by Dover, New York, 2006, original published by Houghton Mifflin, Boston and New York, 1921

[221] Holton, G., *Defining Risk*, Financial Analyst Journal, Vol. 60, No. 6, p. 19, 2004 or Hansson, S., *Seven Myths of Risk*, Royal Institute of Technology, Stockholm, 2000

framework.[222] Tversky and Fox enlighten risk and the psychological side, combined with decision theory as another theory to manage uncertain prepositions.[223] Concrete specifications to risk management were worked out for the first time by Henry Markowitz 1952, who was later awarded with the Nobel Prize for Economics in 1990 with Merton M. Miller und William F. Sharpe. In his essay "Portfolio Selection", outlining his so-called portfolio theory, he deals with trading in securities, risk diversification and the risks at trade. The overall examination of the environment requires an approach other than focusing on one single share. Not only the potential damage, but the possible yield was included in the risk consideration with the portfolio theory.[224] The following discussion and definition of risk will adapt parts of different models, consistent of chances and threats behind decisions to make and developments to cope with. Other scientists and scholars followed with results of models for markets and uncertain situations, for example George Akerlof with his article about the "Market for Lemons".[225] The portfolio theory was developed further in the sixties and the seventies of the last century. Main emphasis was still the securities trade and insurances. Risk management ideas and models expanded through the manufacturing industry to cover all commercial organizations in the middle of the seventies; the public sector and the not-for-profit sector also took up the idea. The biggest U.S. pension fund, California Public Employees Retirement System, carried out an examination in 1987. This initiative was aimed to check the management of 42 enterprises. Among other fields of interest, the enterprises were consulted on risk provision measures and instruments.[226] Among other fields of interest the enterprises were ask for their own risk provision measures and tools. The "Standard and Poors Stock Index" was adopted as reference of comparison. Aim of the initiative was to strengthen the ownership with rights which, among others, were to be reached by the following measures:

- disclosure and transparency of information
- disclosure and performance orientation of the management salaries
- abolition of poison pills
- questions about control mechanisms

---

[222] Coleman, T., *A practical guide to risk management*, CFA Institute, Amazon distribution, Leipzig, p. 14, 2011

[223] Tversky, A. & Fox, C., *Weighing risk and uncertainty*, Psychological Review, Vol. 102, No. 2, pp. 269 – 283, 1995

[224] Wolke, T., *Risikomanagement*, Oldenbourg, Munich, p. 9, 2007

[225] Akerlof, G., *The Markets for "Lemons": Quality Uncertainty and the Market Mechanism*, The Quarterly Journal of Economics, Vol. 84, No. 3, August, pp. 488 - 500, 1970

[226] Haesler, H. & Gampe I., *Corporate Governance*, 2002, S. 120 cited in Ertl, P. & Steindl, M., *Risikomanagement und Corporate Governance - Entwicklung und Inhalt, Stellenwert und faktische Durchsetzbarkeit* in: Ertl, Peter (ed.), *Risikomanagement und Jahresabschluss*, Linde, Vienna, p. 9, 2006

The enterprises examined and sensitized, using various kinds of risk management, were on an average at least 39% more successfully than those in the "Standard and Poor's 500". As other characteristics, like quality management, risk management has become a substantial value for competition and to penetrate new markets. With regard to contribute to a sustainable existence this instrument was added in the management tool box. The current remodelling of the former Basel II and Basel III shows a constant adoption to developments and demonstrates the seriousness to develop risk management as basement for sustainable existence; main motives for Basel II and recently Basel III were to guarantee an adequate equity capital for banks to avoid break downs and to force banks to check the status and the perspectives of a company based on the annual reporting.

In the last couple of centuries, the advent of financial instruments and markets on the one hand and the growth of leisure business on the other have resulted in a new separation of physical from economic risks. A person, who has strong preferences for options in the technology or biotechnology sector, can be exposed to significant economic risk. But there is no direct threat or physical harm: A bungee-jump contents a high physical and psychological thrill and personal risk, but it is comparatively cheap.

Over the years, more and more integrated and enterprise-wide risk management models were developed. The first idea of the risk management was established in the fifties of the last century. During a North American Insurance Buyers Conference in Chicago in 1957, Prof. Wayne Snyder used for the first time the word risk management in a modern context.[227] Eventually in the nineties, it was recognized and accepted that risk management, on operational level, could lead to considerable improvements in the achievement of economic objectives. In 1994 the Value-at-Risk (VAR) principle appeared. This principle serves as a method of the risk management and is used for supervising and measuring market and interest-rate risks. Most developed areas for risk measurement consider financial risks or substitutes of finances. VAR measures the worst expected loss over given time interval under normal market conditions at a given confidence level. VAR is therefore a monitoring tool, not a forecasting tool. VAR relies on data of the past and can take into account only risks that can be measured quantitatively. It cannot process drastic events or surprises such as political, liquidity, personnel, or regulatory risks.[228] Other principles to make uncertainty transparent by monetary values are "Risk Adjusted Return Of Capital" (RAROC)

[227] Drennan, L. & McConnell, A., *Risk and crisis management in the public sector*, New York, Routledge, New York, p.11, 2007

[228] Barton, T./ Shenkir, W./ Walker, P., *Making Enterprise Risk Management Pay Off*, Prentice Hall, Upper Saddle River, p. 16, 2002

or "Return Of Risk Adjusted Capital" (RORAC). First bi-national risk management standards for public sector in Australia and New Zealand were published in 1995 by the Australian and New Zealand Standards Association, named AS/NZS 4360. Other revisions followed in 1990 and 2004.

Risk management as a function and tool is not new or is necessarily a result of developments in the twentieth century. But the concept became more and more important only after the significant crashes and breakdowns of global players in the 90ies and after the New Market hype at the beginning of the current century. First normative approaches took place in the US during the preparation and execution of the NASA Space missions. For these programs the US-MIL-STD 882 was introduced. Following the introduction of quality management, other norms like FTA (Fault Tree Analysis), ETA (Event Tree Analysis), or the HAZOP (Hazard & Operability) have also begun to use risk management as an essential component. For use in the insurance sector the so called guidelines Solvency I and II were established to take care of the monetary reserves, for credit institutes to measure the risks in the sense of loss for loans or mortgages. To minimize losses the regulations of Basel I - III were introduced.

Risk management shares the same problems and challenges as the leadership of an organization itself, only focus is on situations under not given and known certainty with a variety of different possible developments and results. Hence risk management must be handled integrated in the management processes in general.[229] In comparison with the management functions additional effects will be: Creating and strengthening of risk or uncertain factor awareness of every individual in the company, so that any disruptive action and consequences of all leading activities could be foreseen, identified, and assessed. Even while assessing presumably isolated issues, managers should keep in mind the fallout for the entire company. In result risk management should create a system of information that could become the basis of any long-term decisions, both at the top and at the lower levels of management.

The word "risk management" stands in competition to improving of products and new markets as other objectives of an organization to get sustainable established in a market.[230] The word could also be open to a lot of misinterpretations. The old paradigm, so called silo approach, favoured isolated and distinct risk management for different departments, depending on the functions assigned to them. It was more ad hoc management; acting on a case by case and day-to-day basis, reacting as when

---

[229] Götze, U./ Henselmann, K./ Mikus, B., *Risikomanagement*, Physica, Heidelberg, p. 11, 2001

[230] Girotra, K./ Netessine, S., *How to Build Risk into Your Business Model*, Harvard Business Review, p. 2, May 2011

risk factors or even uncertainty are identified. The focus was directed to the local and timely environment, to the departments, but less to be an integral, enterprise-wide view to bring out the correlation between cause and effect and the correlation to the grade of efficiency of the organization. Mostly the main activities to work on risk were linked with insurable or financial risks.[231] Slywotzky and Drzik see the most successful approach in a comprehensive organization-wide approach, different from the micro-businesses used at the beginning.[232] They suggest an ERM (Enterprise Risk Management), which as tool seeks to integrate available risk management techniques in a comprehensive and integrated organization-wide approach. This more sophisticated new model includes a view of all potential risks in every department and a possible overlapping area of consequences. Perfectly anticipated it is a framework for fully integrated risk management. Only those managers, who create risk awareness, use tools to handle, and strive to be effective, perform better. Awareness is also a wide area to consider, introducing and maintaining risk management. Audi (2009) summarizes that objects to be aware of, can be external and internal, in addition experiences will contribute to distinctive qualities for application of risk management.[233]

Table 15 Schematic overview about risk management paradigms
Source: The Economist Intelligence Unit, written in cooperation with Arthur Andersen & Co.: "Managing business – An integrated Approach", The Economist Intelligence Unit, New York, 1995, p. 15-16, cited in: Barton, T./ Shenkir, W./ Walker, P., *Making Enterprise Risk Management Pay Off*, Prentice Hall, Upper Saddle River, p. 16, 2002, and additions by the author.

Old paradigm	**New paradigm**
1.Fragmented-department view/ function, managing risk independently, involving primarily the accounting treasurer or the internal audit	1.Integrated risk management with senior level oversight, required by different regulations and governance guidelines, for example Basel II and III, SOX, IFRS
2.Isolated view at the operational level, each risk considered isolated	2.Continuous risk management process is an ongoing, sound management process, factoring in potential future uncertain situations and building up extensive information basement
3.Ad hoc response , whenever managers	3. Broadly focused. All business risks and oppor-

[231] Barton, T./ Shenkir, W./ Walker, P., *Making Enterprise Risk Management Pay Off*, Prentice Hall, Upper Saddle River, p. 3, 2002
[232] Slywotzky, A. & Drzik, J., *Countering the biggest risk of all*, in "Harvard Business Review on Managing External Risk", Harvard Business Press, Boston, p. 39, 2009
[233] Audi, R. (ed.), *The Cambridge dictionary of philosophy*, Cambridge University Press, Cambridge, p. 64, 2009

believe there is need to respond	tunities considered
4.Stringent distinction of fields, no coordinated action in case of an unforeseen	

Nowadays organizations readily accept the need for a comprehensive risk management system and the managers in the middle to top level have a key role to apply and maintain such a system. Therefore is risk management seen as a continuous process, which has to be continuously adjusted for standard application. The International Standardization Organization (ISO) has worked out an internationally recognized norm, the ISO 31000 in 2009: "Risk Management. Guidelines and principles and implementation of risk management." It was introduced in 2009 and it is accompanied by the ISO guide 73 "Risk management vocabulary". With regard to the own peculiar targets and objectives for public administration different and additional assumptions are needed with converted solutions, coming from a different kind of risk management approach. Public sectors in Australia and UK have already adopted these standards.

In the USA the SOX has determined standards for an internal control system; in Germany the Accounting Standard No. 5 been extended by the explanations to the appropriate documents from German Commercial Code (HGB) and Publicity Law (PublG), found insufficient in the specifications of the KonTraG for an internal control system. This accounting standard intends to examine possibilities of a negative development in a planning horizon of up to two years. Reports have worked out doubts that risks are managed in a proper way. The reality is often proven to be different: In an examination by the external auditor McKinsey to the Corporate Governance topic the following became evident:

- ✓ Risk Management in general: More than 40% of those companies surveyed confirmed that they whether apply neither have effective processes for identifying, safeguarding and planning their own key risks. Almost 20% had no process at all. As exemplary statement of chief risk officers is quoted: More than 25% of directors with a financial risk perspective affirmed to have some concerns about oversight of the CRO by the board, and 60% have not even observed the nature and importance of this oversight.
- ✓ Independence: Twenty five per cent of the directors doubt whether the subordinated directors were independent.

✓ Understanding own business: Nearly the half of the examined directors acknowledged not having an oversight of the value created. Assessing their colleagues, they stated that half of them perform average or lower.[234]

Beyond national and international laws voluntarily rules are developed to demonstrate the will by the board to secure and stabilize the development of an organization or enterprise. For example the Corporate Governance Codex (CGC), which is expanded and updated every year, recognizes uncertainty factors for the steering and controlling of an enterprise. The CGC gives some suggestions to handle those influences for a stable and controllable development. The CGC has no binding effect, but is accepted and introduced by many global and national players all around the world. For a better fitting, locally used published adoptions of the CGC can be found: For example considering the national peculiarities the German Corporate Governance Codex (GCGC) is introduced.

Increasingly the municipalities are squeezed between the imbalance of the costs of providing basic products and service and flat or declining revenues. Risk management could contribute to avoid these imbalances, if applied appropriately, although their constitutional objective is to provide a so called welfare state.

For initially surveyed public administrations in the three countries in Europe no integrated kind of risk management is neither legally provided nor described nor binding; although communal budget ordinance in all countries content hints to recognized uncertainties for future developments; the latest version from Germany make risks subject of the discussion, neither giving any concrete requirements nor specific standards. But without an appropriate bookkeeping using adequate internal control instruments the public sector will remain unable to seek for deviations from a predicted and intended path. Signals or milestones are hidden behind political discussion and scrutiny as Dunlop already worked out in 1979.[235] In his comparison between public and private management he detailed the differences and described similarities and peculiarities of both sectors considering ten lines of "orthogonal lists of differences." Most of the lines seem to be a reflection of the management in the public sector, but changes are obvious. The NPM tools box contributes to a more awareness, more delegation of responsibility and thus personal interest in uncertain environments and developments and forecasts, not only driven by the legal framework, analogue to private sector standards. But also the NPM gives only hints but no binding guidelines for transparency and comparison and chronological processes.

---

[234] Crouhy, M./ Galai, D. / Mark, R., *The essentials of risk management*, McGraw-Hill, New York, p. 86, 2006

[235] Dunlop, J., *Public Management*, draft of an unpublished paper and proposal, Summer 1979, cited by: Allison, G., *Public and Private Management: Are They Fundamentally Alike In All Unimportant Respects*, Proceedings of Public Management Research Conference, November 1979, Washington D.C., 1979

Technically offered software is able to provide forecasts based on known statistics and selected data. But risk management for public sector has to keep in mind the societal effects and the position of public administration. Selected models of suggested behavior and expected effects are discussed later.

To demonstrate the complex environment the schematic visualisations in Chapter 1 enlighten the peculiarities of the public sector. The exemplary factors of the municipal administration concerning management and risk awareness can be applied in almost every European public government, nonetheless with individual complements.

In line with other management methods assessment is the most important and extensive part of the process. The better choice among other alternatives is based on the results of the risk assessment. Without an extensive analysis and correlation to compensation abilities decisions would tend to be made under uncertainty.

Difficulties considering validity and reliability occur, when

- collected historical data being used are insufficient considering the specific purpose
- estimating obtained is applied to a different test organization
- probability of occurrence is very low
- data collected does not cover sufficient long period[236]

Another term in the context of risk management is risk volume, considering undesired developments, which means the maximum damage resulting from an output. This is often not identical to the possible gain, if the development is positive. Possible ranges could be asymmetric. It is used analogue the expression of range of possible outcome, including the whole range, from desired gains to undesired losses, expressed by their monetary volumes or other measurable and comparable values.

Hampton (2009) provides a comprehensive summary in his extensive definition: "Enterprise risk management is the process of identifying major risks that confront an organization, forecasting the significance of those risks in business processes, addressing the risks in a systematic and coordinated plan, implementing the plan, and holding key individuals responsible for managing critical risks within the scope of their responsibilities."[237] Although there is little agreement in the use of private life and business, this work will prove that this definition can be converted to and applied for public administration risk management, too.

---

[236] Gough, Janet, *Risk and uncertainty*, Information Paper No. 10, Centre for Resource Management, University of Canterbury and Lincoln College, p. 15,1988

[237] Hampton, J., *Enterprise Risk Management*, Amacom, New York, p. 18, 2009

Due to the demands of scientific work, first it has to be identified what determines the expression of risk; next step contrasts risk in the context of public administration, combining the private sector orientation and the peculiar situation of the public sector. So the definition of the word risk is not based on the word or description immanent definition; risk is more defined by the internal and external assumption and influences and the way of looking to reasons, circumstances, utility and ramification in the case of negative development. So risk involves threats to desired outcomes that humans value.[238]

In principle the risk in a narrower view is reduced to future uncertain situation and events, which starting point has to be decided or assessed in the present, based on a more or less valid and precise forecast and desired results of the development.

On the other hand future effects and results must have a direct influence to financial resources or other valued resources of the public administration and therefore direct influence to the overall picture of the execution of mandatory or voluntarily tasks.

As Gough (1988) stated, combined with the peculiar projects in the public sector will lead to a comparison with other projects. Gough posted "...where no historical or experimental data are available, is to use risk comparison procedures. Risk comparison involves attempting to find on equivalent risk which is quantifiable, and applying the same probability of occurrence to the unknown risk."[239] Therefore public sector faces peculiarities which determine the threat framework and unique projects which could cause serious threats for executive duties.

For effective and purposeful application of risk management risk managers must accept that each model will have gaps. Ambitious models cannot include all things for all people; goals should be stated specifically and what the system is intended to accomplish; on the other side managers have to be aware what is intended not to accomplish.

The examined public administrations are currently neither using a professional kind of risk management system nor generally accepted principles. Only one confirmed to have a risk management implemented and applied. The board discusses periodically ongoing changes in the internal and external environments, but there is no structured model of evaluating uncertainties and possible positive and negative effects.

---

[238] Fischhoff, B. & Kadvany, J., *Risk – a very short introduction*, Oxford University Press, New York, 2011

[239] Gough, J., *Risk and uncertainty*, Information Paper No. 10, Centre for Resource Management, University of Canterbury and Lincoln College, p. 25, 1988

3. 2. 2. International risk management standards

a) Requirements by model of Committee of Sponsoring Organizations (COSO)

The COSO (Committee of Sponsoring Organizations) internal control framework consists of a cube. An enterprise's or organization's ability to achieve defined objects is influenced by a variety of internal and external factors. It is a result of the discussions, started in the fifties of the last century, about internal and external controls and management systems. Within the COSO framework, facets of controls and their combinations were defined at the beginning of the 1990s. It was replenished in 2011 with COSO risk guidance. COSO combines the risk management process with organizational levels and managerial functions.

On the front side of the cube the chronology of the risk management is presented, from environmental analysis to the monitoring of developments of decisions. The organizational levels are on the side, while the different stages of planning and execution are framed on the top of the cube.

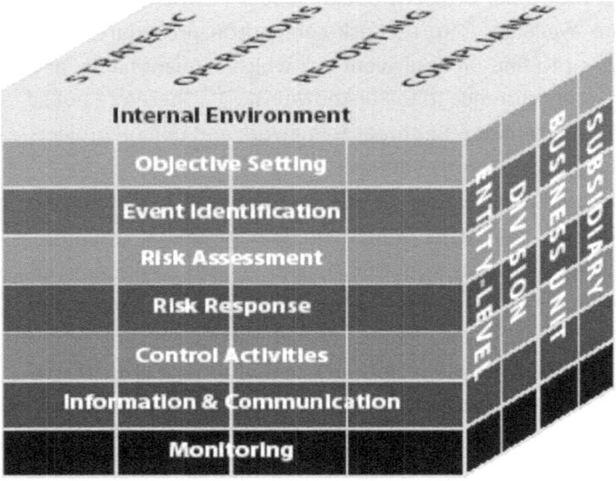

Figure 24: COSO ERM graphic
Source: Tarantino, A., Manager's guide to compliance, Wiley, Hoboken, p. 179, 2006 and https://www.risknet.de/wissen/glossar/coso/0c7640034dcc3ae9de0f7d2e7ddc10ee/?tx_contagged%5Bsource%5D=default&hspart=Lkry&hsimp=yhs-newtab, retrieved 30.05.2016

COSO handles the management of an organization as entrepreneur, seizing opportunities and seeking proactively chances for the organization. For this model factors which can cause negative or positive impacts, are events: Events have to be identified, their consequences to the organizations, the internal and external environment, estimated and measures prepared to cope with them.[240] Similar to COSO, but in a conceptual view without the internal and external environment are ISO 31000 Risk Management or the former used model by UK authorities:

b) Requirements by Norm DIN ISO31000

Risk management is thereby regarded as activity to quantify and qualify uncertain future status by desired and undesired outcomes; to collect and process relevant and valid data to describe potential gain, damage and the probability of the different outcomes. Another more comprehensive function is to indicate a singular risk by numeric and comparable values or to indicate the current or future risk status correlating with the ability to compensate the damages. Risk management itself is determined by environmental complexity and dynamic of processes; both of the influence the decision-maker. From the inside view, for example size, organization, capital stock and legal basis, play important roles. From the outside given legal framework and objectives or unpredictable reactions of competitors to initiatives or new products.

One consequence was to combine all approaches and models to a standardised guideline. The ISO Standard 31000, which was implemented 2009 and overtook such combined role, defines the management process as follows:

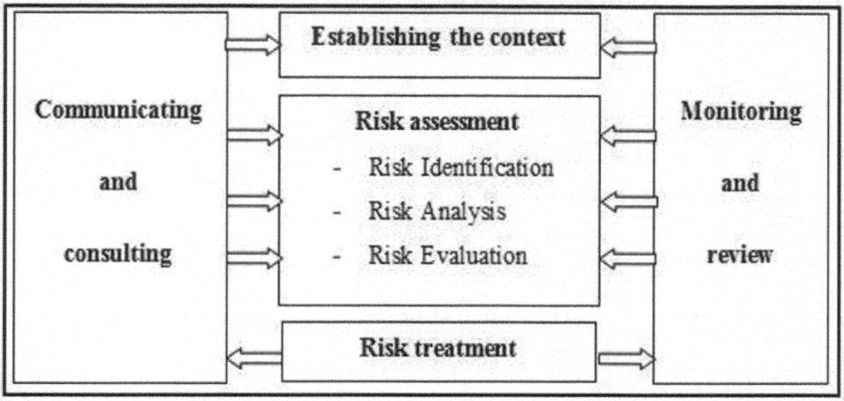

Figure 25: Risk Management ISO Standard 31000
Source: Organizational Framework (ON-R) and Risk Management according to AS/NZ 4360 and new ISO Guide 73 and Principles

---

240 http://www.coso.org/publications.htm, retrieved 10.01.2016

The government in British Columbia in Canada stressed the ISO 31000 as standard for all provincial public sector organizations. This means that this standard is the framework for assessment of risk at the strategic all-of-government level. It provides rules and regulations for business planning, project management and daily business decisions.[241]

For the European Union a recommendation is not yet released to establish a consistent standard, similar to the different accounting systems used. Similar to not yet binding accounting standards, which vary over the member states, a standard for identifying, estimating and evaluating should be determined to get a comparable notion of the current risk status, replenishing other reports.

c) Risk management model of The Association of Insurance and Risk Managers/ The Institute of Risk Management (AIRMIC/IRM, United Kingdom)

In the UK the introduced model and methodology of ISO 31000 is also set as a standard for risk management. Both private and public sector combined favorite the similar handling of risks in organizations.

The model of the AIRMIC/IRM from UK offers a clear and distinctive picture of whatever is required for a functional system in the public sector:

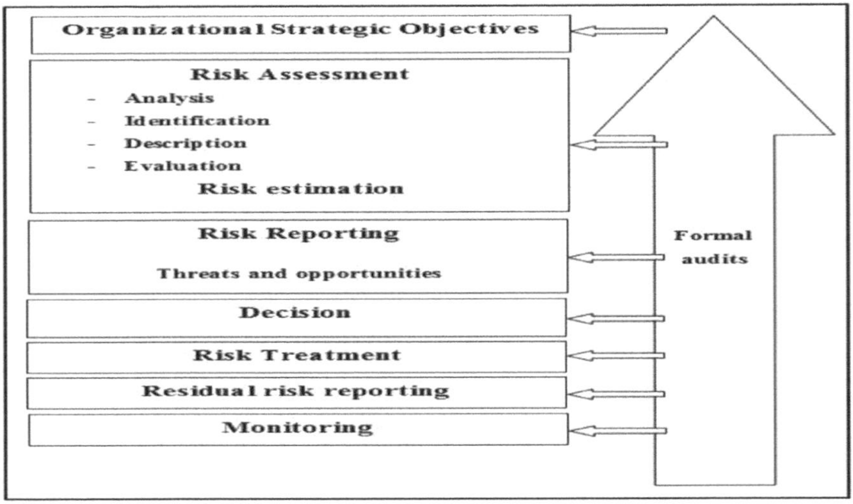

Figure 26: AIRMIC model of risk
Source: Drennan, L. & Mc Connell, A., *Risk and crisis management in the public sector*, Routledge, New York, p.12, 2007

[241] Province of British Columbia, *Risk Management Guideline for the BC public sector,* Province of British Columbia, 2012, p. 8

Also the European Union has developed and published a model of risk management which contains similar steps for managing risks and offering a functional circle to handle risks and the opportunities ahead; the obligations of the management level were extended and a higher dimension introduced to ensure the reliability of the financial reporting with the 8th EU guideline.[242] The scope of the 8th EU guideline is directed at enterprises that are legally required to conduct audits and are subjects in the public interest, for example Chapter 10, Art. 39 - 43. In a wide-ranging interpretation, the guideline determines that public administration must provide risk management as ordered by the EU legislation. A convergence of organizational techniques of private and public sectors thus becomes discernible. Results, presented by the annual reports examined later, are sobering; only a few stated to plan an integrated risk management system. A managerial attention on the issue of public value is not recognizable, because of the missing strategy and comprehensive model for measurable objectives and purposes of public administration.

AIRMIC, ALARM and IRM decided to promote ISO 31000 as framework for risk management in United Kingdom. They offer a table of basic information for understanding and application of risk management for best practice:

Table 16 Detailed risk description
Source: airmic/ alarm/ irm, *A structured approach to Enterprise Risk Management (ERM) and the requirements of ISO 31000*, London, p. 5, 2010

1.	Name or title of risk	Unique identifies or risk index
2.	Scope of risk	Scope of risk and details of possible events, including description of the events, their size, type and number
3.	Nature of risk	Classification or risk, timescale of potential impact and description as hazard, opportunity or uncertainty
4.	Stakeholders	Stakeholder, both internal and external, and their expectations
5.	Risk evaluation	Likelihood and magnitude of event and possible impact or consequences should risk materialise at current level
6.	Loss experience	Previous incidents and prior loss experience of events related to the risk
7.	Risk tolerance, appetite or attitude	Loss potential and anticipated financial impact of the risk Target for control of risk and desired level of performance Risk attitude, appetite, tolerance or limits for the risk
8.	Risk response, treatment and controls	Existing control mechanisms and activities Level of confidence in existing controls Procedures for monitoring and review of risk perfor-

[242] Nayer, M., *Umsetzung der neuen EU-Richtlinien in Hinblick auf Risikomanagement und IKS*, in Ertl, P. (ed.), *Risikomanagement und Jahresabschluss*, Linde, Vienna, p. 39, 2006

		mance
9.	Potential for risk improvement	Potential for cost effective risk improvement Recommendations and deadlines for implementation Responsibility for implementing any improvements
10.	Strategy and policy developments	Responsibility for developing strategy related to the risk responsibility for auditing compliance with controls

3. 2. 3. Exemplary legal references

a) Legal requirements by Gesetz zur Kontrolle und Transparenz - model (Germany)

In addition bankruptcies, crises and fraud should be prevented or early detected in Germany by the application of law of supervision and transparency (Gesetz zur Kontrolle und Transparenz (KonTraG)) of 1998; followed for companies listed at the New York Stock Exchange by the "SOX" (Sarbanes-Oxley-Act) in 2002. KonTraG was the corner-stone of mandatory enterprise-wide risk management for the public limited companies. Distributed over several individual laws and regulations, in combination the KonTraG defines concrete responsibility and accountability for managers to prevent organizations bankruptcies. Aims were increased transparency, reinforcing the role of the board of directors as well as to increase the controlling and observing function. Further it creates an obligation for the directorate to introduce the systematic implementation of a supervisory system in listed enterprises that could help recognize uncertainties and the impacts for the company early or at least earlier than without. The allocation of responsibility by this law went beyond levels known previously. For example § 91 II AktG demands a supervisory system to arrange particularly that the executive board has to take suitable measures, so that developments endangering the continuance of the enterprise could be recognized early. This concept of individual responsibility for the success of an enterprise was thus given the goby. Attempt was to safeguard the firm from disruptions, follow business goals and strengthen corporate values.

For the Banking sector in Germany minimum standards are developed; for example the general requirements for a risk management for banks are:

Table 17 General requirements for risk management for banking industry
Source: Bank-Verlag, Mindestanforderungen an das Risikomanagement, Bank-Verlag, Cologne, 2006

AT 4.1.	Risikotragfähigkeit	Ability to cope with undesired developments
AT 4.2	Strategien	Organizational and risk strategy
AT 4.3.	Internes Kontroll System	Internal control system
AT 4.3.1.	Aufbau- und Ablauforganisa-	Organizational structure / operational struc-

	tion	ture
AT 4.3.2.	Risikosteuerungs- und controllingprozesse	Risk control and steering processes
AT 4.4.	Interne Revision	Internal revision

b) Legal requirements by Sarbanes-Oxley-Act (United States of America)

The need for risk management tools has come to sharp focus after the spectacular collapses at the New Market in 2000 and 2001 and again after the financial crisis in 2008. To strengthen the link between management and accountability in enterprises SOX was released by the American government in 2002. The increased insolvencies and falsifications of the balance sheets of global players, like Enron or Worldcom, led to these specifications for all enterprises, which are listed at the New York Stock Exchange (NYSE). Danger for existence and threat for shareholder-interests, like white-collar fraud, shall be stopped; furthermore a foresighted operative and financial planning should help avoid collapses of corporations and companies. Among other rules it is regulated in the SOX that responsibility for the final examination of the extent and content of the financial reporting rests with the corporate management, the supervisory board. The section 404 which demands an establishment and retention of an adequate internal control system about the financial reporting has been accepted. In this respect one attestation is demanded by the inspector about the valid -effectiveness of this internal control system.[243] The step was obviously long overdue, even if limited to the enlisted enterprises. In tandem with the functional tasks that was the first time that the issue of the personal liability of a manager in regard to organizational success was addressed.

Literature on similar models is extensive, but they mostly fit in with the character of the private sector.[244] These are the accepted and repeatedly integrated steps for risk management. Most of the commonly used frameworks have different aims, for example reduce the negative implications by not valid annual reports; but the process steps remain the same. All in common is contribution to leadership behaviour based practical elements:

Table 18 Enterprise risk management support for strategic decisions and resource allocation

---

[243] Tarantino, A., *Manager's guide to compliance*, Wiley, Hoboken, p. 22, 2006

[244] Barton, T./ Shenkir, W./ Walker, P., *Making Enterprise Risk Management Pay Off*, Prentice Hall, Upper Saddle River, p. 151,2002; Ehrmann, H., *Risikomanagement*, Kiehl, Ludwigshafen, 2005, p. 37; COSO, in: Schirmbrand, Michael: "Information-Risk-Management als integrativer Bestandteil des Corporate-Risk Management" in: Ertl, P., *Risikomanagement und Jahresabschluss*, Linde, Vienna, 2006, p.127; Schmitz, T. & Wehrheim, M., *Risikomanagement*, Kohlhammer, Stuttgart, 2006, p. 19

Source: by author, based on Province of British Columbia, *Risk Management Guideline for the BC public sector,* Province of British Columbia, 2012, p. 5

Support for management leadership:	
1.	Identifying risks all across the organization
2.	Identifying overlapping areas of risk factors
3.	Determining and communicating organization-wide priorities and strategic goals
4.	Discussion and determination of tolerable and compensable risks
5.	Planning future goals and the way to reach them; determining divergences and measures to cope with

Challenging for practitioners and creators of mathematical programs remain the gain of information. Sensors or personal evaluation of received information, also combinations of several indices or their relationship have to be involved in a processing of data for better understand the holistic picture and more precise forecasts.

4. Tendencies concering risk management practices in public admin

4.1. Comparison of expected effects of risk management in private sector and public administration

Each of the described models and principles emphasizes to protect the interests and the financial engagement of share- and stakeholders of an organization. Structures are similar and focus to an Enterprise Risk Management (ERM). The province to British Columbia summarizes the definition of ERM in the context of public sector as follows:

"ERM describes the integrated and coordinated application of risk management congruently across ministries and public sectors agencies, and through each organization, from cabinet, ministry executive, division, branch, and work unit, right down to the individual employee providing front-line service."[245]

Different hierarchical organizational and procedural structures in different Europeans countries lead to a wide spectrum of operational and strategic risks. The legal objectives are accepted to be the most important guidelines. Those are accompanied by very stringent operational plans and rules for execution. Administrative laws and regulations dominate day-to-day operations. But laws as such do not necessarily promote efficiency in public service. All representatives interviewed complained about the constraints they faced; they wanted transformation of the rigid bureaucratic hierarchy to a more flexible and dynamic organization, as provided for in the NPM model, even while accepting the legal obligations expected of a public administration. Defined procedures enable a public servant to escape the consequences of his activities. Whether a more flexible legal framework can lead to greater efficiency is a question beyond the scope of this work.

For a strategic and political matter the Local Authority Budget Ordinance of the state of North Rhine Westphalia in Germany requested the following, considering risk management: In each annual status report chances and threats of the future development, considering the sustainable allocation of services and products, are to declare; further it is to present the basement and origins of these assumptions (Local Authority Budget Ordinance, § 48). These legal and formal requirements stand for the

---

[245] Province of British Columbia, *Risk Management Guideline for the BC public sector,* Province of British Columbia, 2012, p. 5

M. Bodemann, *Management in Public Administration*,
Sustainable Management, Wertschöpfung und Effizienz,
https://doi.org/10.1007/978-3-658-22687-9_5

brackets of the thoughts in Part II of this work, about risk management, the consequences and outcomes, eventually measured in comparable and competitive units.

A resolution, passed at the Presidium of the German Association of Towns and Municipalities of 1st December 2009, said: "The gap between the collapsing revenues and skyrocketing costs of the municipalities will become wider in the next years." Alternatives, to cope with that prognosis, range from cutting public spending by offering less or limited public services to creative developing new sources or revenues.[246]

Some argue that risk management for private sector has different objectives than for the public sector. Risks, in the meaning of chances and threats for executing public services and providing products, have therefore different linked impacts to the intentions and desired goals of the players as if to think about risks counterbalancing individual or collective distinctive economic interests at the expense of individuals, collectives, or the society as a whole. Considering the fundamental differences the application and direction of risk management and the basement of risk awareness come in focus. Especially when goals of the public administration are in a situation of competition: The Cambridge Dictionary of Philosophy puts it as follows: "achieving one goal may conflict with achieving another, and therefore require that a rational action by one that best achieves one's goal only when these goals are considered forming a system".[247] It is crucial to develop an organization-wide system to identify, analyze and estimate chances and threads. But also to define standards and indicators to measure especially undesired developments in monetary units. Thereby the tension-fields between politics, society and public administration have an own influence.

Literature on similar models is extensive, but they mostly fit in with the character of the private sector.[248]

From a practical view the representatives of the examined municipalities were all convinced that with an appropriate system uncertainties could be eliminated, at least reduced and adverse effects minimized. But all of them argued that paucity of resources should be kept in mind when it comes to working out any risk management strategy – data gathering restricted to a small scale and additional responsibilities imposed on the existing staff kept to a minimum. Such a limited approach leads to a

---

[246] Kalb, A., *Public Sector Efficiency*, Gabler Research, Wiesbaden, p. 1, 2010

[247] Audi, R. (ed.), *The Cambridge dictionary of philosophy*, Cambridge University Press, Cambridge, p. 129, 2009

[248] Barton, T./ Shenkir, W./ Walker, P., *Making Enterprise Risk Management Pay Off*, Prentice Hall, Upper Saddle River, p. 151. 2002; Ehrmann, H., *Risikomanagement*, Kiehl, Ludwigshafen, p. 37, 2005; COSO in Schirmbrand, M., *Information-Risk-Management als integrativer Bestandteil des Corporate-Risk-Management* in Ertl, P. (ed.), *Risikomanagement und Jahresabschluss*, Linde, Vienna, p.127, 2006; Schmitz, T./ Wehrheim, M., *Risikomanagement*, Kohlhammer, Stuttgart, p. 19, 2006

limited effective system. Without allocation of necessary resources no risk management would yield the desired results. The following representative steps are important for any kind of organization and are part of the risk management models mentioned above:

Administration's / Organization's strategic objectives/ goals/ missions
(Depending on internal and external environments)

- legal conditions
- stakeholder/influence of stakeholder
- financial conditions/budgets
- voluntarily duties
- political streams on governmental/state and local level

Risk assessment

a) **Risk identification and classification**
   a. strategic
   b. financial
   c. operational
   d. political/social
   e. market
   f. hazard/natural
   g. residual
   h. reputational
b) **Risk analysis**
   a. probability
   b. potential measurable max. damage/loss
   c. opportunities/chances/saving of resources
   d. qualitative approach
      i. reason/source
      ii. effects
      iii. consequences/results
      iv. monetary/material/financial consequences
   e. thresholds for activities
c) **Risk evaluation**
   a. influence to operations, finance and reputation
   b. normative approach further than technical approach
   c. model of risk cube
d) **Risk aggregation**
   a. using of model
   b. statistical evaluation
   c. computer-based simulations
e) **Risk inventory for CEO/board**
   a. daily/weekly/quarterly status
   b. inter-municipal comparison
   c. grade of compliance

Risk Monitoring

- Control of thresholds / forecasts
- Supervising and communication

Decision

Risk Treatment/Steering

Figure 27: Chronology of risk management[249]
Source: by author

Awareness of long-term objectives helps identifying events or activities that could stand in the way of achieving of established goals. The strategy will be the most important vision, both for the right orientation towards inner and outer relationships,

[249] Derived by author according to literature research; considering current recognized and suggested practices.

and to serve as guidance for all levels which are involved and decision-authorized in the risk identification process. Based on different intentions and grade of accountability four types of risk manager can be identified: While the cowboy is characterized by a high risk appetite and a low level of control effort, the typical entrepreneur is weighting both control effort and possible losses for best performance. Based on the organizational and hierarchical culture and confirmed by researches on accountability risk overexactitude is the predominant behavior.

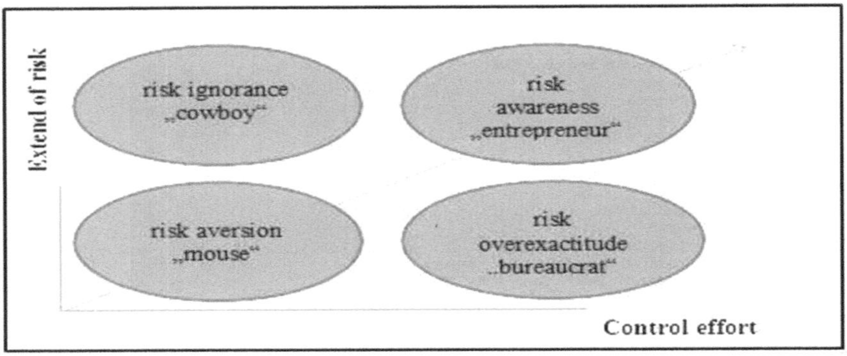

Figure 28: Archetypical taxonomy of risk
Source: Romeike, F. & Hager, Peter, Erfolgsfaktor Risiko-Management 2.0, Gabler, Wiesbaden, 2009

In comparison, while private firms seek to increase their market shares by improving the quality of their products and enhancing the capital structure of the company, the public sector organizations do not take that kind of trouble – after all their duties are laid down and allocations assured. Performing what is assigned to them without getting into trouble is all what most of them aspires to do, as Van der Wal et al.(2008) found out in their survey.[250]

Still the public administration could strive to optimize its products and services to improve the quality of life of the citizens and resolve not to allow cost- or time-overruns and reduce debt levels. Public sector could also follow the directive to avoid new loans and reduce the tax burden for the private sector. Compared with the private sector, the objectives are often not very precise and will be based on some soft and societal factors, which are finally hardly to define. Remarkable in the survey of the public annual reports, except of infrastructure and demographic change, no other strategic goal is cited to depict the correlation between risk and objective awareness.

250 Van der Wal, Z./ de Graaf, G./ Lasthuizen, K., *What's valued most? Similarities and differences between the organizational values of the public and private sector,* Public Administration, Vol. 86, No. 2, 2008

In private sector risk management is determined by different rules and regulations. There are open assessments, but also hidden assessments, for example to evaluate whether a debtor is able to pay back a credit or whether a presented business plan is based on valid historical data and reliable assumption about markets and chances. As mentioned above risk management, though not sufficient specified, is demanded for the all New York Stock Exchange listed companies by the Sarbanes & Oxley Act (SOX). In Germany 1998 forced the German Corporate Sector Supervision and Transparency Act (KonTraG) enterprises and companies to implement and apply a risk management. At least the municipal code in Germany includes a short passage about the reliable presentation of chances and risks for the sustainable operations of local public administration by a risk recognition system.

Both sectors have to cope with the following range of management; the full left or right positions are extreme values, which are unlikely to be reached in a realistic environment:

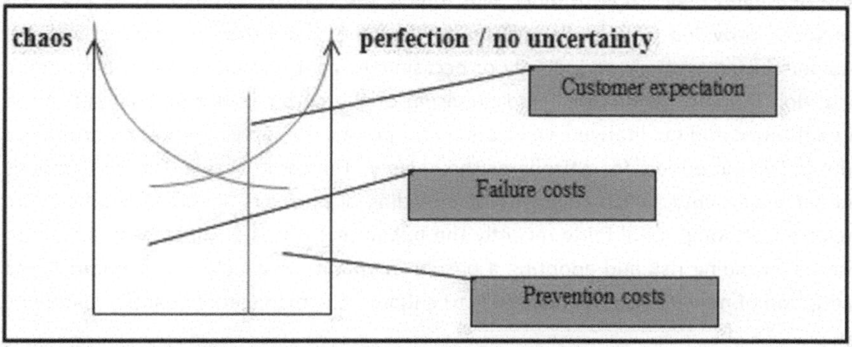

Figure 29: Costs for full chaos and full perfection and the position of customers
Source: by author

In the equilibrium between prevention and failure costs best practice could lie; but a more risk seeking position, moving to the left corner can offer more opportunities and vice versa. Customer expectation of public management behaviour will differ from expectation of a shareholder of private sector management. Extreme positions of risk seeking or risk aversion lead to higher costs than a position around the equilibrium.

Public organizations act in their given legal and physical environment and have a mandated purpose, given by law. These purposes vary, depending on location, size, duty, legal and political importance. They tend to act as Weber demands as exactly as possible as a machine with routine purposes. The system was designed to deal with a wide variety of work in routine. Strict guidelines are set and impersonal rules limit the interpretation of operations and processes. Processes should be freed of personal irrationalism or emotions. They are more perfectly the more depersonalized the organization and processes are oriented. It is expected by the public that the managerial processes are as close as possible to be failed-save and risk free. But that means that the public administration should be excluded of searching for opportunities and chances to reduce certain essential expenses.

This is an initial contradiction what has to been solved politically and legally. The active seeking for chances and intentionally using uncertain decisions is generally prohibited, resulting from the trustee position. But being more effective and efficient and to be market oriented and acting entrepreneur-like need a switch in the legal and political commission of the public administration.

Failure in processes affects regularly more than selective customers, for example the delivery of social security payments on time or the implementation of new software for motor vehicle registration. Affected citizen are in a peculiar situation. On the one hand they are customers, which have the right to demand the offered and regularly provided product or service; on the other hand they are indirectly shareholders based on their periodically or occasionally contribution to the public administration funding. So the expected provision of the citizen is not only aimed to the quantitative and qualitative specification of a product or service; more important are the individual effects for citizens or the society. The same is relevant for decisions under uncertainty, which could threat providing of products, if some conditions are realized, although until fairly recently the public sector was perhaps best characterized as avoiding risk and adopting a bastion mentality that delayed acceptance and adoption of new instruments and tolls to enhance the managerial quantity and quality.

Public sector agencies face different tasks and duties, a variety not complete comparable with the regular private sector organizations. Dixit (2002) speaks about a multiplicity of dimensions of tasks.[251] In comparison with an almost rigid organizational and procedural structure risk awareness could not be easily implemented. This complexity of tasks combined with a stringent separation of execution of tasks leads inevitable to conflicts in the inner and outer environment. In addition to a contrary attitude to risk awareness what is expected. As proven above awareness of risk and determining factors have to be established, knowing the differences considering individual affects and guaranteed existence. Critical are models to slip over the general used model.

---

[251] Dixit, A., *Incentives and Organizations in the Public Sector: An Interpretative Review*, Journal of Human Resources, Vol. 37, No.4, p. 697, 2002

Also the effect of multiple actions is diversified, often not to measure or less interesting for further needs of strategic orientation. But in comparison to private sector organizations the measurement of outcome, measurement in basic or additional utility for citizens or other consumers, are at the beginning stage.

Rainey at al. (2000) identified in their research the following current theoretical and practical challenges for the public administration, which themselves will have direct influence to the integration and application of risk management. They note:

- privatization of public services
- allocation of functions and tasks among sectors
- nature of the sectors themselves
- dimension that define the sectors, including their overlapping and blurring with the third and non-profit sectors
- administrative reference and organization change
- individual motivation and work attitudes[252]

Intrinsic incentives, like individual motivation, have to be placed by the employees of a public administration themselves. The individual worker of each level has to be aware of the results of his activities and the targets, set by politics, rules and laws. If they are convinced by shifts, experiences or statistics, that projects will fail as planned, they will react independent to save the expected result or set active countermeasures to prevent the failure.

In private sector those activities are developed under the label of continuous improvement and change management. Contrary to dynamic ways and hierarchical decision structure in public sector constraints and the absence of delegated responsibility complicate a fast reaction, as discussed above.

The researches of Van der Wal et al. (2008) onto values in the public administration and the results of Kuhlmann et al. (2008) show that the bureaucratic strings often prevent the organization to be proactive in tackling risks.[253] Every step in the process is determined by rules and the communication is transmitted to the next higher level only, and there is no guarantee it would reach the very top. Although Kuhlmann (2006) confirmed, that the initial progress and success with NPM now is

---

[252] Rainey, H. & Bozeman, B., *Comparing public and private organisations: empirical research and the power of the a priori*, Journal of Public Administration Research and Theory, 10 (2), p. 450, 2000

[253] Van der Wal, Z., de Graaf, G., and Lasthuizen, K, *What's valued most? Similarities and differences between the organizational values of the public and private sector*, Public Administration, 86 (2), pp. 465 – 482 / Kuhlmann, S./ Bogumil, J./ Grohs, S., *Evaluation administrating modernization in German local governments: success or failure of the "New Steering Model"?*, Public Administration Review, Sept.-Oct., p. 851, 2008

sobering; more a modern kind in the meaning of restoration of the Weberian kind of bureaucracy is the mid-term result.[254] An entrepreneurial behavior including participation in negative and positive results should be the final stage.

A research of Van der Wal et al (2008) worked out that as most valued characteristic for executing the job in public sector was named accountability, this could be accepted as accountability to the next hierarchical level or to the citizen in front of the counter. Responsibility in the meaning of continuous proving of effectiveness, efficiency and objective orientation is seldom ascertainable. So the leading levels to the top tiers of management complain about the inflexibility of decision and procedural ways to act.

For risk management a fast response and information ways are essential to prevent threats and damages. Just as the providing of collected data and statistics to those functions that are in decisive positions. Assume that an employee worked over a long period of time in an area a project is planned. Milestones are given, a staff to realize is implemented, and expertise is called. The divergence in time and financial frame could be recognized by a worker of operational level. Caused by the stringent hierarchical order suggestions for adjustments will reach, in most cases, the decision level too late to react.

As pointed out above profits or surpluses have never been the focus of the public administration. Civil servants seem to accept that it is not part of their mandate. Especially when they are trustees of the taxpayer's money, they shouldn't spend public funds in uncertain securities, they say. This kind of a mindset only creates a fundamental risk-averse attitude. To cite a glaring instance, municipalities don't seek to go for competitive insurance premiums rates though so much is happening in the insurance market for the last years. A remarkable exception was the solution of the municipality of Weinfelden, Switzerland. They engaged after years of static and defaulted payments an insurance broker to analyze all insurable risks, whether necessary in law or taken up voluntarily. This broker developed a specific and customized computer program to analyze the obligatory risk insurances, the voluntary risk insurances and sought to compare policy payments with compensation payments vis-a-vis the probability of damages and losses. With this program the municipality is able to check and control every year the current risk insurance situation to update the status of polices and to optimize insurance payments.[255] It was also confirmed by a CEO of the department of municipal services in Herzebrock-Clarholz,

---

[254] Kuhlmann, S., *Hat das "Neue Steuerungsmodell" versagt? Lehren aus der "Ökonomisierung" von Politik und Verwaltung*, Verwaltung und Management, No. 3, p. 149-153, 2006

[255] This information was provided by the mayor during an interview, conducted on Oct 13th, 2009.

Germany; where only one policy was cancelled as a result of the situation in the last 14 years. The maximum loss of an adverse development was only three times the amount of the yearly policy. Still as some compensation reserves were built up there was some savings in this case, too.

Theoretical models for improvement of efficiency through development of experts for a small segment, to do only a fragmental part of a coherent process, are contrary to the model of effective influence to processes in the case of an uncertain environment. The intrinsic motivation to react and to point to a divergence, of predicted and realized path, is an essential precondition for effective risk management.

This kind of awareness culture has to be introduced and vivid all over the organization. Propper and Wilson defined risk management and the spread out "as part of an attempt to improve the performance of the overall organization."[256] This by oneself leads again to a further critical point of performance measurement in the private sector.

Contrary to private sector the positive effects of an individual behavior will not be rewarded, at least not with money or additional salary. The behavior to be risk and outcome aware is currently an expectation and trust by the citizenry of the organization of public administration. Overall objective has to be the careful use of public money which is been spent by the residents for fixed objectives and tasks. So the expectation is equal to economic activities, allocation of scarce resources among alternatives, used for the maximization of want satisfaction, as main target.[257] To create a framework and valid estimation of satisfaction is another task, beneath political decision making.

The individual awareness of each employee involved in the organization, integrated in information- and workflows, has to be established in the process of adapting management tools. Internal discussions have to be made to implement bidirectional information flows, avoiding time lags and allowing access by each member of the public administration. The expertise of each individual should contribute to set up appropriate project plans or decisions about investments or other activities. Already in 1995 Hayek pointed out that "ultimate decisions must be left to the people who are familiar with these circumstances, who know directly of the relevant changes and of the resources immediately available to meet them."[258] Among others this delega-

---

[256] Propper, C. & Wilson, D., *Use and Usefulness of Performance Measures in the Public Sector*, 2003, CMPO Working Paper Series, No. 03 (73), May, p. 4, 2003

[257] Williamson, O., *Why Law, Economics, and Organizations*, Annual Review of Law and Social Sciences, No. 1, p. 369 - 396, 2005

[258] Von Hayek, F., *The Use of Knowledge in Society*, American Economic Review, No. 4, September, p. 522, 1945

tion to experienced persons is often interrupted by politics based on the claim to have sufficient information for special decisions.

The possibility of inter-municipal-comparison is currently neglected or intentionally ignored, based on prioritization of local sovereign decisions. Like in the medical sector, using Diagnosis Related Group (DRGs), a standard of cost model for all municipalities and therefore resulting in transparency could be a further step for a country-wide economization based on a virtual competition.[259] Also the reference class models for specific projects or product.

Transferred and derived instruments, now and for future use, are first steps to prepare the public sector for a substantial reform. Knowledge management, as explained in the efficiency-oriented model of F.W. Taylor is a good instrument to be made use of to improve awareness. [260] Such a process could eventually lead to better risk management in public sector.

Threats to attaining goals laid down should be identified early to contain damages, even though the consequences might not be of the same order faced in the private sector. For the private sector threat is an event, as defined by its impact on the company or organization and the probability of its occurrence. Though both sectors have contend with issues, like support of stakeholder groups, human and financial resources, societal changes and customer preference, for the public administration the artificial barriers and challenges by laws and regulations are additional threats; although the consequences could be comparatively less severe as explained above. Considering the challenging task of sustainability of decisions risk management will get a more noticeable management tool.

4.2. Critical factors for public administration reducing effectiveness of risk management

Managing, communicating, re-evaluating and learning from risks have become a crucial task and challenge for any organization. This includes identifying and choosing between different alternatives, each of them combined with a bounded capacity to make a definite forecast with definite consequences.[261] Economists and philosophers see risk as a natural part of business life; the profit for an entrepreneur depends, among others, on the position and the ability to handle risks. Slywotzki and

[259] Article 91d Basic Law Germany is typically directed to that kind of comparison, but few municipals offer and use it.
[260] Taylor, F., *The principles of scientific management*, Cosimo, New York, reprinted 2006; Original by Harper & Brothers, London, 1911
[261] Kaplan, S. & Gerrick, J., *On the quantitative definition of risk*, Risk Analysis, Vol. 1, No. 1, p. 11, 1981

Drzik (2009) complain about the missing acceptance of risk and the opportunities. For them most managers have not yet systematically addressed for example strategic risks, although especially strategic risk causes a lot of value destruction.[262]

Uncertainty as term dominates human live in every stages. Although many computer scientists are working on models to collect information by receptors and process the data immediately, the models remain limited: Either a model represents a fragment, based on all data but with a limited scope or the model is more holistic, but with limited data collected and processed. A certain grade of uncertainty remains. This grade of uncertainty is accepted in business, often it is the reason of sizable income for managers; higher risk and generated success means higher salary and bonus. Thomas Sowell describes that risk is an inseparable part of investment, thereby a part of an investors or business live.[263] Despite the negative emotional context of risk the correlation of these three terms, certainty, risk, and uncertainty, will enlighten the application for risk management and will open the discussion of appropriate operational use of public value in public administration in German local government as indicator of efficiency. Merely the ramifications and outcomes have to be measured in different values.

The following contemplation reflects a combination from scientists, scholar, theorists, and the summarizing of the questionnaires and the empirical analysis of the annual reports.

An assumed convergence in the last two decades leads to the assumption that both sectors adapt processes and structures from each other; both triggered by the necessity to produce goods and services which are compatible with consumer and customer requirements. Risk management and the source of existence have a stigma as all models to virtualized economics: They have to fight the dilemma to produce models which have to be proven in the real world, with more or less assumptions to limit the fully reality virtualization. But some of the assumptions, which allow the model to be functional, will not survive in reality.

The history of the public sector shows an absence of the necessity and consecutive absence of the striving for profitability. But although in an almost certain internal environment the overlapping with the private sector and similar management functions uncertain developments challenge the public sector. Strategic plans come along with uncertainties; forecasts of economic development, timeframes of market reactions, or behaviour of competitors are important information for managing and

---

[262] Slywotzky, A. & Drzik, J., *Countering the biggest risk of all*, in "Harvard Business Review on Managing External Risk", Harvard Business Press, Boston, p. 42, 2009

[263] Sowell, T., *Basic Economics*, Basic Books, New York, p. 295, 2011

steering an organization. Despite of the relatively long lifespan with only marginal modifications and the quasi-monopolistic position for public services and goods, uncertain developments of financial transactions or material engagements remain.

In the case of guaranties demands to react as requested could approach to the given municipality with devastating results, caused by guarantees additional and unplanned expenses strain the budget. Given guaranties are often motivated by politics, not really under control of the administration. In one case a guarantee was given with unlimited term and financial engagement. After recognition of this gap of control the guarantee was taken back and substituted by an appropriate and limited guarantee. But the field survey presents that other external and inevitable impacts could threat the ability to act as ordered for the citizenry. Decreasing business taxes, decreasing transfers from federal and state level could affect the planning and execution. The permanent adjustments of budgets for local public administration are named as negative and relatively uncertain factor; in few cases the new calculation of contribution is considered as a positive factor; but both parties stated their answers with a hint to the volatility. Influence to federal and state level delegation of tasks is limited. For different reasons the centralized management of tasks could be more effectively and efficiently executed on local level. For example a central solution and the proceeding of social aids could lead to less qualitative results. But delegating tasks to local level is usually combined with the threat that calculations of transfers for the execution are not realistic; or will cause not compensated expenses in the future. At least the federal level with the legal authority and competence could influence the forecasts for specific tasks and thus increase the financial and personal burdens.

Simulations are currently too complex and time consuming, e.g. if the majorities in the state parliament changes. Some of these changes confront the municipalities with new or extended tasks; seldom accompanied with a maintained and appropriate compensation.

Like the private sector mathematical formulas will help to develop a critical path to steer and control a process or project. With an appropriate quantitative and qualitative basement and processing of information the selection of the decision to get the desired results is calculated through some algorithms.

Variances outside of a prepared and planned path have to trigger countermeasures to reach back. Statistical data, fast exchange of information, conversion of signals in usable data are numeric basement for a preparation of countermeasures. But the municipalities need instruments and resources for countermeasure; already the insight that the decision has to be done recognizing a combination of uncertain influence factors, is important for further steering and managing. The awareness of uncertainty, the certain insight that a variance from the predicted path can happen, is only one prerequisite for detection and acceptance. To be prepared and able to influence the quality and quantity of ramifications the public sector need personnel, material, financial, and information resources to cope with changed realities.

For private sector management reserves are regularly built up and spent for uncertain developments. But in public sector reserves are prohibited or allowed only for specific purposes; if allowed the reserves have to be kept for a minimum; and always important arguments necessary. A controversy occurs in the estimation whether current consumption leads to a higher grade of utility instead of future consumption. Political interests and social needs will lead to a minimum of reserves; spending public funds for current public needs is higher prioritized than to be prepared for eventualities with negative consequences for the budget. Because of the almost financial safety, reserves were regarded to be superfluous.

Question to be answered is who decides based on which priorities for which project? Political decisions are seldom predictable, as explained, and not focussed to efficiency, a complex structure of reasons to act has to be considered. The notion leads to the following notion:

Political decisions are based, among others, on personnel skills and experiences, public benefit, political benefit, personal involvement, feasibility, relevance, strategic goals on local and regional level, competition and markets, finance. Institutional crises, whether in public or private sector, could be triggered if material and personnel resources are stretched beyond a certain point or if debts accumulate to unmanageable proportions, in the case of uncertainty, if compensation reserves or insurances are insufficient.

Currently for public sector organizations in Germany a governmental parachute is guaranteed and insolvencies could be staved off, even if temporarily; effects of uncertainties about future developments will remain. In Switzerland this fall back situation is not given; several pubic administration had to admit insolvency, for example Leukerbad in the 90ies. The personal debt of each inhabitant of Leukerbad had come to a total up to 200,000 francs. Especially in public sector the situation is relevant for every resident and citizen: They all have to compensate future financial burdens. In a cost-effective oriented business with almost certain budgets as planned, instruments for dynamic and outcome-oriented behavior seems to be superfluous. But risk management is a part of a strategy and will be an integral instrument; the function is identical to the description of Porter, that every organization needs a strategy to deliver superior value to its customers.[264]

---

[264] Porter, M., *On competition*, Harvard Business School Publishing Corporation, Boston, p. xi, 2008

Thus it wasn't remarkable that the public sector in general and public administrations in particular are affected by the crisis of 2008, as seen in a fall in tax incomes, accompanied by cut-backs in budget, not to mention the indirect impact of damages elsewhere in the economy. Clearly changing fortunes of the private sector do adversely affect the public sector.

Three alternatives could lead the way to face the challenges:

- increasing resources via levying new taxes or increasing current taxes
- prioritizing of tasks/ relinquishment
- increasing efficiency and effectiveness

Which of the traditional pillars of the welfare state could whet or stifle the appetite for risks and thus engender a stable risk culture?

To be aware of threats and to see chances to gain advantages are the typical day-to-day operations of an entrepreneur in the private business. The organizational forms are changing, new models are introduced, and management-instruments are proven and applied. Emphases of the current management systems are changing over the time to be competitive with time, information volume, quality and technology. Unfortunately though, the current concept of management in public administration doesn't seem to factor in such issues.[265]

Since 40 years public sector and public administration is triggered by the notion and realization of changes and reforms of objectives, outputs, optimizing, and processes. Risk management became one of several tools for evaluating current and future situation for transferring and converting to public sector. Although there are certain similarities and also differences between both sectors, as discussed above, decisions are made lacking to appropriate and valid information of possible developments and outcomes or ignoring any awareness about the consequences. Missing risk awareness and the traditional process-orientation are attempts to explain and the excuse the yearly deficits and the increase of debt levels all over Europe.

Alison (1980), Rainey and Bozeman (2000), Novell (2009) and Bodemann (2014) have shown that transferring and application have already taken place.[266] Add-

[265] There are some notable articles about behavior of government under uncertainty from an economical point of view. For example: Arrow, K. & Lind, R., *Uncertainty and the Evaluation of Public Investment Decisions*, American Economic Review, Issue 60, pp. 364-378, 1970

[266] Allison, G.T., *Public and private management: are they fundamentally alike in all unimportant respects?* Journal of Public Management, 127 (1), pp. 27- 38, 1980 / Rainey, H. & Bozeman, B., *Comparing public and private organizations: empirical research and the power of the a priori,* Journal of Public Administration Research and Theory, 10 (2), pp. 447 – 469, 2000 / Novell, G., *Public vs. private managers: a new perspective*, Journal of Business Economic Research, 7 (3), pp. 1-6, 2009 / Bodemann, M., *Can corporate management tools be successfully applied in public administration – A German based case study,* Management & Marketing, Vol. 9, No. 2 (34), pp. 227- 238, 2014

ing the constitutional task to take care for increase welfare, depending on survival and ongoing prosperity, risk management is considered since the 90ies as tool for public administration. A risk imposition seems to be acceptable in the case that the total benefits that can be reached by taking risk outweigh the total costs in the case of loss. A numerical comparison, often presented using monetary values, give a better notion of the exposure and the net outcome for the society; both possible sides are to recognize. Gomez and Meynhardt (2009) mentioned that the society has to accept that public managers have to search, initiate and use new methods and processes to restore and improve and administrative and political trust.[267] Output and outcome are measurable quantities which are comparable over time and offers transparency and benchmarking. Comparing the current risk status with data from the past depict the divergence and the grade of awareness to cope with the challenge intentionally taking risk to gain something. Expressed by a measurable value, later is public value used as substitute, and converted into economic units in currency, will be useful for analysis and orientation for public managers and politicians. Risk awareness can be thereby created by inevitable information. "...the manager of risk informs permanently the leaders of the organization and it will brief them on the risks identified and actions seeking approval for the treatment of the risks..." as Hohan, Olaru and Pirmea point it (2011).[268]

a) Decision situation

Decision-makers in both sectors have the freedom to choose between a minimum of two alternatives. But a choice must be made. And hence the outcome for managers of both the sectors is equally determined by probabilities and expected gains and losses. In business decisions are made between locations, between products or markets. The freedom of choice is directly linked with chances and threat.

Different is the situation in the public sector, where everything should be determined after the traditional Weberian Model, by laws, regulations and guidelines, following a political program. Bogumil (2008) described those constraints as the reason for the lack of dynamism.[269] When responsibilities of a civil servant are laid down by law and by various guidelines, dynamic action or flexibility is unlikely. Without the

---

[267] Gomez, P. & Meynhardt, T., *Public Value: Gesellschaftliche Wertschöpfung im Fokus der Führung*, in Seiler, S. (ed.), „Führung neu denken – Im Spannungsfeld zwischen Erfolg, Moral und Komplexität", Orell Fuessli, Zurich, 2009

[268] Hohan, A./ Olaru, M./ Pirnea, C., *Case study regarding the implementation of an integrated risk management system in local public administration*, Supplement of Quality-access to success, II (125), pp. 246-251, 2011

[269] Kuhlmann, S./ Bogumil, J./ Grohs, S., *Evaluation administrating modernization in German local governments: success or failure of the "New Steering Model"?*, Public Administration Review, Sept.-Oct., p. 851, 2008

authorization for fast and autonomous separated decision, the classical functions of a public manager remain: To execute and follow regulations while implementing political and legal programs. Strategic initiatives, for example building a new bridge or a sports field, are generally left to the political executive, and officials themselves have little say in such issues and hence discussions at the operational level are very rare. The main focus in the public sector is therefore to reach the planned objectives, independent of the financial or personal status.

b) Active or passive behavior

Business is always determined by the choice made by entrepreneurs – irrespective of whether the decision means to act or simply not do something that could prove damaging to the enterprise. A good example could be the case of waiting to see what other actors on the market will do. To wait for new technologies, to wait for new products, maybe to copy them, are only a alternatives. Options for local administrations are relatively limited; they face responsibilities and time-critical decision-situation. It is expected that preventive measures are prepared for almost every eventuality.

When there was only a minor progress in technological advancement, the authorities could content themselves with some protective measures. Protection by dams became a possible bulwark and everyone involved; both politicians and administrations, has to go for it, despite the costs involved. Perhaps some of them could weigh up data and choose not take any proactive measures arguing floods are unlikely. But doing so carries a lot of threatening factors, they may have to face the ire of the citizens in case of sudden floods, apart from the fact they themselves might be affected by the floods.

For the private sector, it is important to act instead of waiting and watching what the competitors will do or what happens in general out there. The board of directors has to develop a clear and realistic strategy including prescribed and defined actions in order to secure the existence of the company.

Current market trends or changes in consumer interests must be keenly monitored. Whether it is energy-saving products, like cars or fridges, or natural products in the bio-market, they are all affected by various developments, including demographic changes. For instance, consequent on a rapidly ageing population, changes in housing architecture might be necessitated, say smaller flats or special designs to cater to the needs of those suffering from disabilities. Especially these aspects are content of reporting systems, developed in Australia and United Kingdom. [270]

---

[270] HM Treasury, *Public sector annual reports: sustainability reporting guidance 2014-2015*, Crown, London,

While such changes will affect both the private and the public sectors equally, the latter is hamstrung by a plethora of legal constraints. And so the local authorities are, more often than not, forced to adopt a passive stance without freedom to act, as delineated by the Weberian model. Every step, more or less detailed, is determined. If only the managers look ahead, factor in the risks on the anvil and take necessary pre-emptive measures everyone will stand to benefit. The rules and regulations governing their actions should be such as to lend them enough flexibility and dynamism in larger interests.

c) Rational behavior

Markowitz, 1959, implicitly introduces a model of preferences. He combined the model while developing the main-variance portfolio allocation framework. This became later part of financial and economic heritage.[271] Markowitz assumed an investor who places positive value on the expected return and negative value on the variance of return. For his rationality the trade-off between the set of different outcomes depends only on the mean and the technical variance. Gough in 1988 replenish this view by the expected social-utility a decision maker or an investor is intended to consider during his action.[272] She distinguished the following preferences:

- value preferences
- time preferences
- risk preferences.

The detection of these superficial but important preferences seems simple; more important and later considered in the developing of a model, to measure preferences and expected influence to public value, are the following three categories of preferences:

- revealed preferences
- expressed preferences
- implied preferences

In the application of risk analysis another factor plays an important role: Public administration works in a legal framework, but preferences are brought in by political programs, political majorities and indirectly by lobbyists. In the questionnaire, the political influence is considered as important factor; so political determination is in-

2015 / Farneti, F. & Guthrie, J., Sustainability reporting by Australian public sector organizations: Why they report, Accounting Forum, September, 2008

[271] Coleman, T., *A practical guide to risk management*, CFA Institute, Amazon distribution, Leipzig, p. 13, 2011

[272] Gough, J., *Risk and uncertainty*, in "Information Paper No. 10", Centre for Resource Management, University of Canterbury and Lincoln College, p. 39, 1988

volved in the process of risk estimation and risk management. Trigger for a preference in general or in particular will be an overall program or a personal perception, both individual and collective, in the meaning of positive or negative consequences. In this context the Royal Society pointed out, that most favoured ways of analysing risk involve the use of revealed preferences, cost effectiveness in the meaning of risk reduction and risk balancing.[273]

In the case of public risk management the decision makers, public manager or politician, are legally demanded to decide with the overall goal of ensuring and developing societal wellbeing. The tools to reach this goal and the individual perception of consequences to the individual or a group depend often on politics. This political influence will be increasingly delegated from the local, to regional, national and European levels.

From a technical view risk is represented by the product of maximum expected or calculated damage and probability. This numerical value only focuses to negative consequences consist of two opposite outcomes, if simplified: First the chance, a positive development in the desired way, and threat, in the meaning of variances in an undesired way.[274] Therefore a variety of future developments is possible. Forecasts with only two possible alternative final stages are seldom; in most cases multiple outcomes at different times are likely.

It is the duty of the controller to check the developments in the realm of finance and to report to the board when differences occur. But as pointed out above, not all risks are can be monetized and hence thresholds other than in financial values have to be developed.

To survive in private sector the decision-maker has to keep in mind the set and declared goals; those have to be reached with the help of the given instruments, material and personnel. Goals like growth, competitiveness, the loyalty of the customers, improvements of quality or innovation have also to be kept in mind.[275]

In addition the decision-maker is to be provided with most complete information. Even if he is not, he still has to make a decision, though fully aware of bounded rationality. Using irrationality in the sense of individuals: Not to follow own interests and goals.

The bureaucratic model dominates the municipal administration. Most of the procedures are governed by a set of laws and regulations and hence the freedom for individual initiatives is limited. Even the mayor, the town councillors and the CFO are

---

[273] Cited in Gough, J., *Risk and uncertainty*, in "Information Paper No. 10", Centre for Resource Management, University of Canterbury and Lincoln College, p. 40, 1988

[274] Romeike, F. & Hager, P., *Erfolgsfaktor Risiko-Management 2.0*, Gabler, Wiesbaden, p. 81, 2009

[275] Ehrmann, H., *Risikomanagement*, Kiehl, Ludwigshafen, p. 39, 2005

not in a fully independent position to plan or to choose. They are subject to the political settings or strategic planning and regulations. All representatives of the examined municipalities affirmed that they frequently wanted to be free from constraints. The freedom of action has its limit in the position and function of a trustee; as long as nobody is personal involved in results in mismanagement, the objective limits act as guideline and criterion for examination.

As a result rational behaviour is limited by legal constraints. The municipal administration rarely seeks to emulate partially the best business practices of the private sector in this regard. In such setup economic use of resources means to choose the cheapest available, mostly concentrated only on the cheapest bidder, not on the expected quality of execution.[276]

Rational behaviour in municipal administration is reduced to a mere fulfilment of complex regulations. But such an attitude could prove self-defeating.

d) Subjective and objective intentions

In the different approaches to the three-component-model researchers brought up the question of an absolute definition and an absolute value of all three, considering probability, expected maximum or minimum gain or loss or a proposition to be true or false. In all cases a further distinction is used to complete the notion: Subjective and objective interpretations. Insider transactions at the stock market all over the world are a good example to illustrate the different approaches to stocks in the case of asymmetric information and thus a different awareness of the current status and future expectations. While using the objective interpretation probabilities are taken to be real, in the case of subjective interpretation probabilities remain human beliefs. According to Knight, probability depends on the observer's lack of information; a decision is then made based on factual ignorance. Keynes extended the model by suggesting that in some situations of uncertainty objective probability cannot be assigned. This distinction will be used by the approach to heal subjective ignorance or probability. Adopting the legal demanded transparency by Basel II and III, a similar data provision and processing could be applied in the public sector, too. Using that basement of data, consistent of gain or losses and the fitting probabilities in classes or clusters will contribute to decrease the grade of subjectivity and increase the grade of objectivity according to risk and uncertainty.

e) Future-oriented

Thoughts about positive and negative impacts are future-oriented. The actor, private or public, has the duty to manage the circumstances in an attempt to get at

---

[276] A research on choosing the provider purely on cost considerations could prove interesting.

some desired result or other. If the chance to influence is gone, the probability of contrary results is almost a hundred percent. If the municipality lacks to instruments to create a flooding area or an appropriate dam structure to secure suburbs from the ongoing flood, but seeks a position to mitigate the damage, say by evacuation or by providing relief to affected citizens, the risk becomes a threat with almost known effects.

Therefore risks in a narrower view are factors with negative impacts which are difficult to handle. Reaction with no or ineffective influence are considered not to be future oriented.

f) Information structure

Councillors and agents try to gather relevant and essential information to develop a comprehensive and pertinent information basement for strategic decisions. Statistics from other companies in similar situations, experiences of other developments in the past and estimates of experts contribute to make precise forecasts and offer probabilities of results. In some cases known statistics of probabilities or derived values are not consistent; the information basement is very poor. In both sectors the information basement has the same effect on the decision-maker.

In the last decade the focus of the public administration was to fulfil its service requirements as laid down by the law, but well within budgetary constraints. Comparing the planned and finally realized public projects, Flyvberg showed that managers were determined to complete the projects irrespective of cost considerations, invariably overshooting the budget. The results of the questionnaire confirmed that assumption; costs of 50% of building projects, also 32% of the infrastructure projects are more than 10% underestimated.

These results of mismanagement, in monetary terms, have to be externalized. Flyvberg offered two possible explanations for the situation - either the setting of the projects lacked realistic or precise parameters, making additional measures necessary or, simply, the budget calculations were based on incorrect assumptions. Either way, the information quantity and quality were insufficient and so additional outlay became necessary.[277] Decision in an incomplete information environment determines the role of an entrepreneur. His pioneering decisions leads to new products and development of new markets, weighing up future benefits and utility with the continuation of the current status.

---

[277] Flyvbjerg, B./ Holm, M./ Buhl, S., *Underestimating costs in public works projects*, Journal of the American Planning Association, Journal, Summer, Vol. 68, No. 3, p. 279, 2002

g) Orientation to objectives and goals

Planned strategies or goals and objectives are the basement of all projects and programmes. Still pursuit of some objectives might be bedevilled more not to foresee influence factors than others. For instance, trying to achieve growth, by entering new and unknown markets, could pose a lot of threats, but simultaneously chances for any business. To be in a decision-situation demands to know what the direction of an organization and what are the strategic goals.

Objectives could be determined by a number of factors – including

- the size and the status of the business
- the power of shareholders
- ownership and leadership
- long- and short-term objectives
- external and internal pressure
- corporate and business culture
- financial status[278]

The provision of services and products alone will not guarantee the survival of a company. Objectives are important and relevant for employers to have a guideline or a better measuring instrument for temporal comparison to prove efficiency and effectiveness. Another aspect is the grade of fulfilment which is important for share- and stakeholders; for example performance of the stock price as indicator.

Important for the evaluation of potential losses: With a set of precise goals and measurable objectives deviation or divergence can be identified and qualified; especially in monetary terms. Even minor deviations could cumulatively lead to a disaster at some point of time if left unattended to when they occur. Well considered decisions, taken with a view to attaining some objective or another, are what makes a company prosper. Development of market shares are among the objectives that can be laid down clearly and properly evaluated.

Though, historically the main objective of public sector business has been provision of public services to enhance public welfare; since the 90ies, public sector organisations tried to act business-oriented.[279] Pollitt and Bouckaert (2004) offer the following aim: "...public management reform consists of deliberate changes of the structure and processes of public sector organizations with the objective of getting them to run better..."[280] Governmental organisations should operate like private sector companies, including in such areas as measurable objectives and output- and out-

[278] Hall, D. et al. (eds.), *Business Studies*, Causeway Press Ltd. Harlow, p. 32, 2007

[279] Schedler, K.& Proeller, I., *New Public Management*, Haupt, Berne, 2006

[280] Pollitt, C./ Bouckaert, G., *Public Management Reform*, 2nd edition, Oxford University Press, Oxford, p. 8, 2004

come-orientation. The government at federal and state level expect them to operate efficiently and offer cost-effective and quality services.[281]

The role of the political executives is dicey. On the one hand they have to give the leadership, study challenges on such fronts as demographic or hydrological aspects, and come out with action plans in consultation with experts. Unfortunately their initiatives can also be circumscribed by election constraints, like what would win them and what would not. Bureaucrats have no option but to fall in line.

What considerations will sway the voter is another complicating factor. If, for example, a promise to rebuild the town hall, could win more votes than, say, improving the drainage system; then obviously the politicians will go for the former option. Anyway laying down objectives and factoring in risks that could thwart the attainment of the objectives are keys to successful running of a public administration toward increasing welfare.

h) Measurable objectives

Clearly laid out objectives are essential to execute controlling and supervising functions. The board of directors or the analogous management bodies must be provided with necessary information on variance from the objectives and also on developments on the periphery.

When a company is looking for payment surpluses,[282] the board should be informed in time of the uncertainties resulting from inner and outer environments. Management instruments try to recognize very early variances from the given objectives, so that the board or the governing body could take necessary pre-emptive measures.

In the private sector, as pointed out above, precise and sustainable objectives and goals are set to define the overall strategy of the company. In public administration there are four power streams which may determine the objectives. In such circumstances, it might be difficult to lay down clear, precise and measurable objectives. The forces are

- legal framework, rules and regulation
- public meaning (parliament and district council)
- public administration as an executive function
- interests of citizens and inhabitants

---

[281] Hall, D. et al. (eds.), *Business Studies*, Causeway Press Ltd., Harlow, p. 32, 2007. In Germany the latest legal highlight was the introduction of the double entry accounting, which was introduced Switzerland in 80ies of the last century and is introduced for Austria since 2014.

[282] Gebhardt, G. in *Enzyklopädie der Betriebswirtschaftslehre*, Schaeffer-Poeschel, Stuttgart, p. 1714, 2002

All of them have a role in evolving objectives and the plan to reach them. Even while granting that the aspirations of the citizens expressed legitimately through the political executive have to be fully accommodated, questions will remain: How clear and measurable are the objectives defined? Reflect the articulated targets the majority and how to satisfy the minority in the pursuit of objectives? Are there measurable effects or results which will be useful to identify uncertainty or potential negative effects to the public administration itself? Are there qualitative and quantitative values to compare? Business principles, like EVA (Economic Value Added), have in focus the difference of net operating profit, the cost of capital and the operating assets. The equation could be applicable in the public administration, too, especially after introducing the double-entry-bookkeeping. But on the other hand adjustments in assets and a fixing of an objective market value are often hardly to determine.

It can be argued that simple measurable determinants are fixed in the regulations, for example in the municipal code or the yearly budget guidelines. Such regulations mandate the administration to spend the available resources in an economical way. But when money is saved by some enterprising manager, he could end up drawing flak for not using up the money allocated. Hence no manager bothers to save. As far as the subject of concrete services and products are concerned, qualitative and quantitative guidelines are published by European, federal and state level. In the position of executor of political programs the local public administration is dependent; this dependency limits the effectiveness of management.

In addition nowhere is fixed that a building planning is to finish within a limited time. Time is obvious a dimensionless value: The private owner has to wait until the process is done and the certificate is handed out for that building. But service improvements are part of the NPM: For example in one city in Germany the duration of a planning permission was reduced from 40 days (2001) to 10 days (2003).[283] For active use in public administration time is regarded as unlimited factor; the capital-airport in Berlin is delayed several times, based on several routine challenges; the opening is scheduled now for 2017, but there are further risk factors which could delay this fixed date. The objective was to present and to provide a modern airport in the south of Berlin as an appropriate successor for the current used airport in the north. In the aftermath of this project compensations have to be paid; another form of threat for available public funds although the project cost and the determined objectives are measurable.

[283] Kuhlmann, S., *Hat das "Neue Steuerungsmodell" versagt? Lehren aus der "Ökonomisierung" von Politik und Verwaltung*, Verwaltung und Management, No. 3, p. 150, 2006

i) A chance to gain something as a desirable result

Considering the origin and fundamental statutory tasks and combined functions of the public administration, e.g. to contribute to a steady increase of welfare state, gains and losses could have different meanings for the participants. One example from Australia enlightens the spectrum of assumptions for political and rational reasons: The Public Accounts Committee predicted in 1994 that a reduction of investments in highways as one of the spinal column of business with the mainland, will save a lot of money, but on the long run a reduction of the GDP (Gross Domestic Product) by 3.5% and an increase of unemployment by 2.2 % were expected. Both consequences are measurable. In addition the effects of a decision will not harm the organization itself. Public managers or employees are affected not in their function as contractor to the public administration, but as citizen, as part of the society. In private sector an entrepreneur is forced to make rational and future-oriented decisions. The alternatives with the highest probability, and, in comparison, with proportionately less potential loss, will be chosen. Rational business is focussed on a target-oriented system. Results are market shares, revenues to develop new products, followed by new technologies to attract new and more customers.

The negative result of investing in uncertain finance businesses was an additional burden, which had to be compensated: Mussari stated in 1996 that local governments remain in believe to find the reason for their existence within themselves and their method to execute the given tasks.[284] Further he argued that ramifications of decisions will not affect the organization, a department or a municipal administration, neither the functional leaders nor the politicians will held directly accountable for the results. Keeping that personal safety desired and not desired effects will be considered in the political and administrative discourse,

- by more loans/ supplementary budget
- by a changed taxation policy and
- by delayed or given up projects.

More important, all the additional cost consequent on the blunders of the local authorities fall on the tax payers. On the other side the managers and employees do not participate at the results. Their salary will remain constant, also when gains are realized. Incentives, comparable with private sector, are not part of the private sector. Rainey (2009) is of the opinion that this static orientation is a hallmark of public administration, to focus on stable and clearly defined structures and processes.

---

[284] Mussari, R., *Autonomy, responsibility and new public management*, Conference on New Public Management in International Perspective, St. Gallen, 1996

Organization-wide goals are always clear. For public managers is left to design and steer the organization in the most efficient, repetitive, machinelike procedures to maximize attainment of political and financial determined organization's goals.[285] Currently, sustainability of activities is in focus, deviation from the current state of term public value as proxy for gains and losses, can support a more focused and measurable managing.

j) Threat of the loss of something as undesired result

Personal, material, financial or reputational effects could be observed in both sectors. But the consequences are different. Financial losses or other losses are possible in both sectors. But it affects the managers differently and the collateral impact is different. For instance if the reputation decreases he will start losing customers and market-shares immediately.

But in the case of a public administration, even if losing reputation, say following unhappiness over the procedures in place for granting planning permission, the authority will keep its patronage – for the simple reason the customer has no option or alternative; he has to go back to the same local public administration for his needs. The administration has a real monopoly in certain areas and there is little market competition. Only under some specified conditions such services are devolved on private providers. It can be argued that in monetary and reputation values the public administration acts almost in an isolated environment, with all the collateral impacts to follow, whereas its market shares and customer patronage are virtually fixed.

Looking at annual reports of municipalities, one can receive the impression that managers seek to escape the consequences of their decisions, leaving citizens at large to bear the consequences. In Germany a few municipal administrations invested a lot of money in derivatives or in cross-border-swaps. Most lost their money, at least a considerable part of it. This topic was discussed in the media, especially the question of personal accountability and responsibility.[286]

The following figure illustrates the exemplary spectrum in which the results of a decision will affect different groups; some of the members are multiple members, often with contrary interests.

---

[285] Rainey, H., *Understanding and managing public organization*, John Wiley & Sons, San Francisco, 2009

[286] For example: Kirbach, R., *Die Rathauszocker*, http://www.zeit.de/2009/30/DOS-Swap,retrieved 17.07.2009; Shinde, S., *AIG-Deals kommen Kommunen teuer zu stehen*, in: http://www.handelsblatt.com/unternehmen/_b=2195969,_p=,t=ftprint,doc_page=0;retrieved ,1709.2009

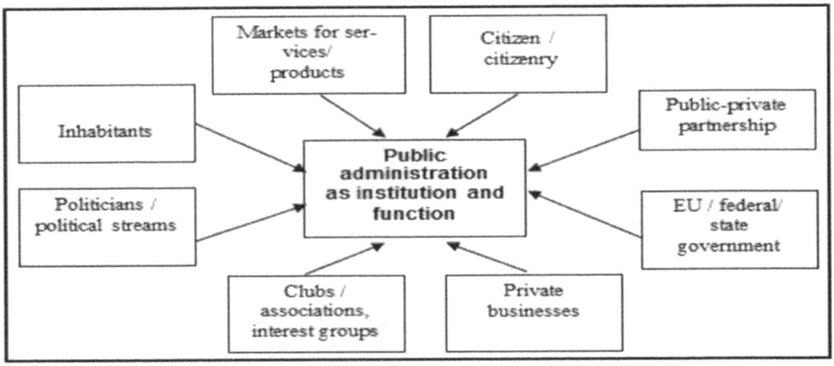

Figure 30: Influence and pressure groups for public administration
Source: Developed by the author

k) Mutual relationship between loss and reward

As pointed out by Wolke (2007)[287] the handling of risks is comparable to the two sides of a coin. Both sides are conclusively linked. An investment at the stock exchange could bring in lucrative returns, but you can also stand to lose it all. Maybe with some reliable information, one can hope to minimize the losses, but uncertainty remains.

General objectives of any business organisation are already pointed out - staying in the market, increasing the market share, to secure and optimize the production lines and to gain an appropriate surplus for new investments. But such risks are part of the game, as it were, if an enterprise is to break fresh grounds. Girotra/ Netessine (2011) go further; they argue that companies get a competitive advantage by being better in managing their risks.[288]

It is difficult to apply the term of risk and reward in the public sector. Profit maximization or paying dividends to the stakeholders that are in the figurative sense the citizens, is not part of the mandate for the public managers. As later discussed, the grade of fulfilling objectives could be related to public value. Risk requires both exposure and uncertainty, but in the public sector an exposure often is indirect, also for the managers. Positive exposure, still increased revenue, could mean increased financial freedom; but this doesn't seem to be realized by anyone as a research by Flyvberg (2002) reveals.[289] Realized threats could result in the straining of limited

[287] Wolke, T., *Risikomanagement*, Oldenbourg, Munich, p. 1, 2007
[288] Girotra, K./ Netessine, S., *How to build risk into your business model*, Harvard Business Review, May, p. 6, 2011
[289] Flyvberg, B./ Holm, M./ Buhl, S., *How (in)accurate Are Demand Forecasts in Public Works Projects*, Journal

budgets. John Maynard Keynes might have proposed spending one's way out of a crisis with his "General theory," but there are limits to such a strategy.[290]

That's why representatives of politics and administration go for borrowing to tide over crisis situations, but they should bear in mind warnings of David Hume, made as early as the 18th century, against such an approach. Kuhlmann (2006) added that especially politicians have less interest to transparency and verifiability; interests in power and re-election are the dominating factors.[291] From an idealistic view administration has a stance between both, public and political will of transparency, efficiency and effectiveness.

If the municipal administration acts as a trustee and works with the money received from the taxpayers, one should carefully weigh the options and decide whether the potential gain is higher than the anticipated loss, hence the decision to invest in uncertain financial transactions should be well discussed and politically secured.

From a practical point of view the mutual link between risk, reward, and loss is visible when making investment choices: Stocks are generally riskier, so the investment could be a total loss, but they also promise to generate higher returns over long term contemplation.

But then when it comes to such categories like pension plans, one can't be too careful in both sectors - safe investments are necessary. Some bigger municipalities have indeed done highly speculative investments in swap-business in the last years. The results are devastating. The officials blame the financial sector by incomplete advices; the financial sector argues that uncertain investments could fail, also if done by the public administration. Losses raised up to € 50 Mio € and have to be compensated.

Risk taking, as accepted potential event, plays an important role in spurring innovation. The desire and the practical need to develop better and more sustainable products and market them have always been a major influence in the further development of companies. Innovations are invariably the triggered by the need to beat competition to stay on and flourish, an element that is certainly missing in the public sector.

---

of the American Planning Association, Vol. 71, No. 2, Spring, pp. 131-146, 2005/ Flyvbjerg, B./ Holm, M./ Buhl, S., *Underestimating costs in public works projects*, Journal of the American Planning Association, Journal, Summer, Vol. 68, No. 3, p. 279, 2002

[290] Willke, G., *John Maynard Keynes*, Campus, Frankfurt/ New York, p. 44, 2002.

[291] Kuhlmann, S., *Hat das "Neue Steuerungsmodell" versagt? Lehren aus der "Ökonomisierung" von Politik und Verwaltung*, Verwaltung und Management, No. 3, p. 150, 2006

l) Personal involvement

In the traditional bureaucratic model, a lifetime employment is guaranteed with prospects of promotion, depending on one's qualifications and career, though. In Germany the employment contracts are subject to wage agreements which are re-negotiated every two years. Any financial crisis will not affect the scheme of things for they are all governed by the relevant regulations.

Additionally in Germany federal laws don't allow municipal administrations to go bankrupt.[292] Thus the existence of the administration is constitutionally guaranteed as also by the voters who choose their representatives, a mayor or head of administrative district. The assumption is that the administration carries out some key public tasks and hence those in charge have to have a comparative job security. Anyway they are all governed by a complex set of regulations to ensure they do their job well.

Similar changes could be observed elsewhere in the world. When the state of California, USA, was hit hard by the financial crisis, it could not pay thousands of civil servants, from town councillors to policemen, even if only for a short period. In the review that followed, as many as 20% of the civil servants were dismissed.[293]

It can be argued that from a theoretical point of view personal involvement is one of the most important determining factors for risk: As Gough (1988) pointed out, threat and chance follows a subjective estimation of potential risk perception of the degree of personal involvement. She argues from a medical point of view, but this can be transferred analogue by monetary terms.[294] Without any personal consequences the term risk as combination of chances and threats could not be applied. To be more critical for determining risk for public administration: Absence of consequences of personal involvement excludes the existence of risk. For an integrated risk management personal involvement has immense influence of behaviour and personal awareness. Also accountability is connected with personal involvement.

m) Accountability

Accountability is laid down by the law of course, but there is also a subjective element to it in that how much a civil servant believes he is accountable for what he or she is doing. In case of damage or loss, in certain circumstances individual bureaucrats can be prosecuted and punished. That apart the corporate culture one works in also determines how much one feels responsible for his or her actions. Coming from

---

[292] § 12 German Insolvency Order; the same in other countries: Chapter 9 of the United States Bankruptcy Code.

[293] Financial Times Germany: 18.02.2009, http://www.ftd.de, retrieved 20.04.2009

[294] Gough, J., *Risk and uncertainty*, in "Information Paper No. 10", Centre for Resource Management, University of Canterbury and Lincoln College, p. 18, 1988

the German language roots, accountability is seen when somebody will stand up for his actions as also for the consequences thereof. In English accountability and responsibility are used to describe these two states.

Dictionaries describes as human taking responsibility for all possible consequences of an activity.[295] The judicial dictionary defines accountability as a human response to a situation and the level of accountability will decide the quantum of punishment too in case of a negative consequence.[296]

Personal accountability in the private sector is linked with the position and the freedom to choose or to act. Consequences of failure could also mean negative impact for the person concerned.

But in public sector the interpretation of accountability deviates from the judicial definition. For Van der Wal et al. accountability arises in the context of organizational values, when one is willing to act and justify one's actions to relevant and important stakeholders.[297] Accountability and responsibility have to be separated; meaning on the one hand the willingness to realize the needs and demands of citizens, on the other hand to be personal involved in processes and their results.

Consequently personal damage on the negative fallout of a decision is avoided by citing rules; real loss of resources is later than externalized to the society; whether by missing convenience, by time-consuming activities and at least by tax collection.

Personal involvement and desire to achieve greater effectiveness and efficiency is constrained by the necessity to follow as exactly as possible laws and regulations in order to avoid damage to one's career in case of negative consequences. There is minor room for flexibility or dynamism in such an environment. More important is the functional dimension of accountability. Public sector administration is a guided activity, first by an unambiguous, manageable acting program; secondly by a well mapped-out steering instrument, whose effects are known and comprehensible; third it doesn't allow one to follow individual goals or objectives and interests, but defer to the goals already laid down. The administration could also be said to be virtually independent of the external environment while executing its duties and hence considered closed.[298]

Promotions might not come one's way if found violating rules or acting against political interests of whoever is in power. But sanctions, like trials against, are rare. Of course some do lose their jobs in case of public major disasters. The British minister

---

[295] Bünting, H., *Deutsches Wörterbuch*, Isis-Verlag, Chur, p. 1245, 1996

[296] Köbler, G., *Juristisches Wörterbuch*, Vahlen, München, p. 486, 2003

[297] Van der Wal, Z./ de Graaf, G./ Lasthuizen, K., *What's valued most? Similarities and differences between the organizational values of the public and private sector*, Public Administration, Vol. 86, No. 2, p. 465, 2008

[298] Kegelmann, J., *New Public Management*, Verlag für Sozialwissenschaften, Wiesbaden, p. 63, 2007

of social department resigned from his position, as he lost his mobile data-disk with unencrypted and unsecured data during a train journey; the disk contained social security data of millions of British citizens.

4.3. Considerations of current financial situation and consequences for decisions under not-certainty in public admin

Continental Europe is seldom regarded as a first comer in terms of introduction and application of tools from the New Public Management (NPM) – toolbox for public administration. In this context the public sector is defined in the meaning of parts of an economy owned by government: This includes state-owned enterprises like public transport or railways.[299]

With the application and the adoption of some of the elementary columns of NPM the public municipalities and counties in Germany tend to transform themselves towards a service- and output-oriented provider. The sector has to focus all efforts to enhance welfare as constitutional task, but also to follow political strategies and local constraints. Main distinction between both sectors lays in the strategic objective: Private sector organizations have in focus profit maximization; public administrations tend to improve welfare, among various efforts to reach this goal cost-efficient. So the organizational and procedural environment should be used in a very dynamic way to cope with the requirements of resources by the different parties. Already Woodrow Wilson (1887) had pointed to these permanently changing demands.[300] However, obviously the local public administrations are already over-challenged for many years. Causes could be the internal structures, but also the imbalance between resources and expected outcomes. The gap between the provided resources and the demands by politics and society appears very clearly in the indebtedness degree of the public sector.

4. 3. 1. Financial situation in public administration in EU

Increasing social welfare commitments means more responsibilities for managers in the public administration. But more than half of the chief financial officers of the public administrations interviewed, feared that financial and personnel resources

[299] See also: Lagassé, P. (ed.), *The Columbia Encyclopedia*, Columbia University Press, p. 895, 2000

[300] Wilson, W., *The study of administration*, Political Science Quarterly, Vol. 2, No. 2, pp. 197 – 222, 1887

at their command might not be commensurate with their increased responsibilities.[301]

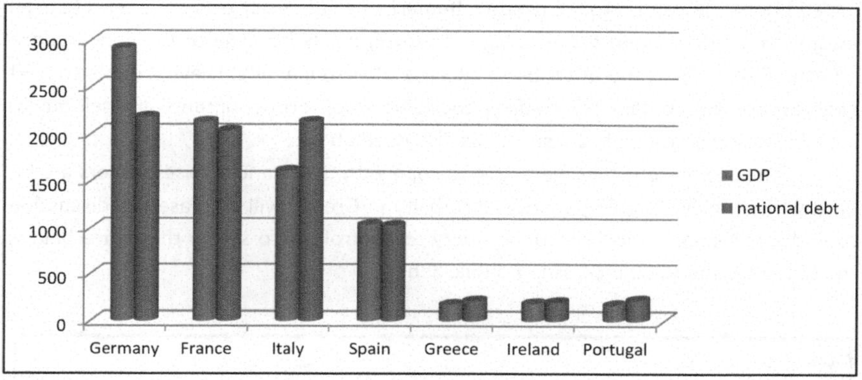

Figure 31: Shares of national debt 2014 over GDP in Mio. €
Source:http://de.statista.com/statistik/daten/studie/198957/umfrage/hoehe-der-wirtschaftsleistung-und-staatsverschuldung-im-laendervergleich, retrieved 28.10.2015

Forecasts draw a different picture of the financial developments for the next three years. While measurements in Greece are expected to pay off, in the Euro-zone the debt level will proportional increase in comparison to the GDP.

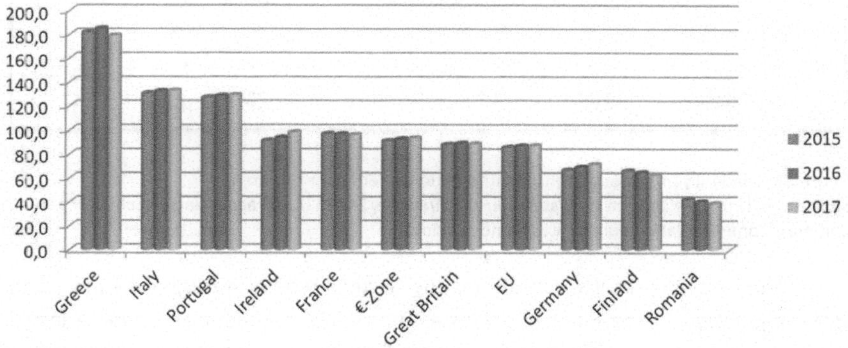

Figure 32: Forecast of shares of national debts from 2015-2017 over GDP in %
Source:http://de.statista.com/statistik/daten/studie/207261/umfrage/prognose-der-staatsverschuldung-von-ausgewaehlten-europaeischen-laendern, retrieved 23.03.2016

[301] Result from the field research conducted. The research results are augmented by a survey of Kienbaum in 2009 in: Innovative Verwaltung, 1-2/2010, p. 21: The research covered 45 big cities in Germany. More than half of them confirmed that the trade tax incomes decreased in 2009, t between 15- 25 %. In addition the social aids costs increased by 79% of the examined cities.

Under those financial circumstances, every deviation of a planned path, causing additional debts, has to be avoided. Remarkable various efforts on federal to local level were made to stop the running debt level, partly because of the convergence criteria of the EU, on the other hand because of sustainability. Leaving debts to next generations will contain their ability to steer. Long-term programs are seldom to identify, based on the political strings as discussed above.

While some countries were able to cope with the financial crises, others are hit hard with a delay. Ongoing political instability in Greece will increase the discussion over the European Union and their ability to control. As to see in the figure below, the tendency shows an increase of public debts.

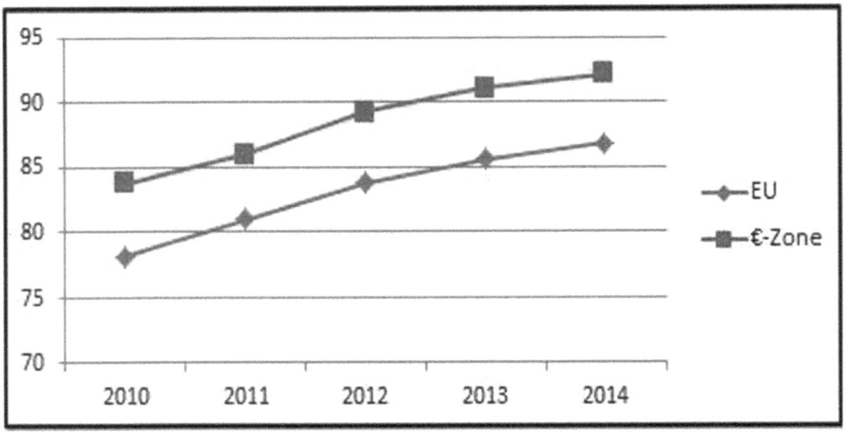

Figure 33: Tendency of shares of consolidated national debt over GDP in %
Source: http://de.statista.com/statistik/daten/studie/247033/umfrage/staatsverschuldung-in-eu-und-euro-zone-in-relation-zum-bruttoinlandsprodukt)

The following results, considering the German federal states, give a more concrete impression of the financial status as entire look. Without appropriate instruments to control costs and identify undesired expenses, at least those under direct influence of politicians and administration, this level will expectedly rise for the next years.

Table 19 Debts of German municipalities, counties and associations in Mio. € excluding Berlin, Bremen, and Hamburg 31.12.2014
Source: Statistisches Bundesamt, Wiesbaden; https://www.destatis.de/DE/ZahlenFakten/GesellschaftStaat/OeffentlicheFinanzenSteuern/OeffentlicheFinanzen/Schulden/Tabellen/SchuldenGemeinden_311214.html , retrieved 24.05.2016

German Federal States	Sum total in Mio €	Bond debts in Mio €	Short-term debts in Mio €	Loans
Baden-	7,152	-	199	6,953
Bavaria	14,14	122	290	13,727
Brandenburg	2,088	-	770	1,318
Hessian	18,81	-	6,335	12,483
Mecklenburg-	1,979	-	690	1,289
Lower Saxony	12,48	180	3,248	9,055
North Rhine-	52,05	700	26,160	24,198
Rhineland-	12,48	275	6,080	6,130
Saarland	3,627	-	1,988	1,638
Saxony	4,323	20	100	4,203
Saxony-Anhalt	3,148	-	1,204	1,944
Schleswig-	4,163	-	766	3,396
Thuringia	2,972	-	200	2,772
Sum total of all federal states	139,436	1,297	48,031	90,108

The presented monetary values give cursorily an impression of the perception of the financial challenges to cope with in short future. But the values symbolize premises of future tasks for public administration as executive level of political programs; the debts are symbols for further restrictions and barriers to break, in pursue to improve public welfare as contribution to the economic cycle and as mandatory task. Especially the local individual developments to battle the demographic change or encourage settlement of new enterprises are limited or completely at a full stop. Identified factors for positive and negative developments are presented later for the state of North Rhine-Westphalia. Moreover the sum of all public debts in Germany rose in 2009 over 2.0 trillion € and remained high.[302] The question is whether the public support and legitimacy is behind this development, considering that no forecast copes with forcing back.

[302] www.destatis.de/DE/ZahlenFakten/GesellschaftStaat/OeffentlicheFinanzenSteuern.de;retrieved 15.02.2016

Currently the resignation of the municipalities, especially in Germany takes places. The liabilities for municipalities for example in North-Rhine-Westphalia, increased. In the period from 2000 – 2008 the regularly debt level, based on mid-term/long term loans was more or less constant and surprisingly decreasing in the last three years.[303] The reasons were diffuse: On the one hand the interest rates were very low; a chance for redistribute loans was acceptable to gain monetary advantages. Otherwise an instrument, known from the "Cameralistics", was used more in these years: The so called "Kassenkredite" (Cash loans), short-term loans, which are not part of the regularly debt level, are used to compensate financial bottlenecks and to remain operational. From 2000 with € 2.4 Bn. € to 2008 with € 14.6 Bn., the volume increases nearly six times more than ten years ago. This is a signal that the financing of the annual budget is based on loans and has to be compensated on the long run by the taxpayers, inclusive interest rates, which are significant higher, because of the short-term conditions. 2005, in addition, have 198 of 427 municipalities in North-Rhine-Westphalia declared that they are unable to present a balanced budget, so they are forced to take additional loans. The expectations are similar today.

With this divergence of additional delegated tasks, more complex duties, which require more complex equipment to handle, less financial compensation and an increasing demand by the public for support through the public administration, the decision-makers face the futility trap: Not only directed to the budgetary constraints, but especially directed to the application of integrated risk management. If the decision-maker and the local parliament are not able to fulfill the tasks within the financial resources, the development will be contrary: Regularly or new tasks are financed by loans, the debt level will be raised and the costs for interest rates will increase the yearly expenses, too. As result the scope to act or to compensate surprising activities or duties is decreasing. The cost of the attending current duties and tasks will be prolonged to future budgets and generations.

But the situation of state bankruptcies is recognizable over centuries. Austria/ Hungary or Spain has declared nine resp. eight times insolvency since the year 1800.[304]

---

303 2000: 25.347 Mio. €
2004: 24.576 Mio. €
2008: 23.583 Mio. €
Source: Minister for the Interior of the State North-Rhine-Westphalia, *Report of the status of finance of the municipalities*, September 2009 (Kommunalfinanzbericht 09/2009)

304 FocusMoney, *Trauma Teuerung*, Nr. 26/2011, p. 45, 2011

In other European countries the situation looks similarly menacing and challenging as Figure 31 shows. One important and continuous effort remains: To bridge the gap between the given budget and the costs for increasing duties and surprising expenses; for example by cutting the budget, being prepared by collected reserves, or by avoiding surprising and undesired expenses by an appropriate organizational, informational, and functional system; for better results the process view has to be chosen to act more efficient.

To frame the later discussion about uncertain future the following conditions determine the current challenges of public administration:

- decreasing financial budgets
- uncertainty about fiscal income
- use of financial title often criticised
- critical interests of citizens and interest groups
- transparency through new accounting standard
- increasing number of tasks to execute without appropriate financial support or compensation, by federal or state law[305]
- raising competition with private sector
- sharing or pooling of sovereignty with Brussels and the institutions of the European Community; agreeing to trans-national regulations to provide border-free competition or freedom for personnel and material resources[306]
- expectation to adapt instruments from business sector[307]

4. 3. 2. Challenges for dynamic response to environment in public administration

At the end of the 19th century Woodrow Wilson already stated that public managers have to track the legal and formal aspects and requirements; they also

[305] As one result of the field research 83.3 % of the examined municipalities expect additional duties without compensation through the next higher administrative level.

[306] Duggett, M., *What can we say about the Westminster Model today?*, PSA Conference Manchester 2009, p.2, published also in PMPA Review, January, 2009

[307] Critical to this intention by: Thieme, W., *Kaufmännische Buchführung in der öffentlichen Verwaltung*, Die öffentliche Verwaltung, No. 11, June, p. 433, 2008: Among others he criticizes the unconditional transfer of instruments used in business companies to public administration; the political and not business function is only insufficient considered.

should have to be aware of minor and major changes and adjustments in inner and outer environment.[308]

It became obvious, demonstrated by the actual desolate financial and operational situation of several public administrations in Germany, that a reform of traditional kinds of decision-making and bureaucracy is needed; first, to gain initiative, second, to cope with the more and more complex duties, third, to comply with the increase interest in the society considering the execution of political and legal orders.[309] In some cases the execution of mandatory tasks is endangered, investment backlogs delay a further development in infrastructure. More it is elusive that the execution of constitutional tasks will be reduced or back-delegated to state or federal level. And the pressure will be increased, including the hosting, managing and integrating refugees from the Arabian States since the civil wars around the Westside of the Mediterranean Sea.

As discussed above NPM or the German adopted version of NSM opened the public sector for an increasing number of applied private sector management methods and tools. The differences between both remain; financing, competition, or provision of public goods, only a few to name. But Simon points out that one result of actual researches is the increasing blurring of both sectors on management level and on operational level.[310] More transparency and comparability are only two effects that will follow after the reform established and the tools maintained. Within the trend a more future-oriented management, with a focus to uncertain events, will follow. Beneath the interest of the public in public administration, branches and companies use increasing pressure to take over parts of the provision of public goods and services. The financial sector is waiting also for more precise information of the current situation and the expectation for further development of management of public administration. The rules of Basel II and Basel III demand certain measures and reliable premises and estimations of current and future states for provision of credits. They have to check debtors by their credibility, liquidity and the expected short- and middle term development of finances. The former privileged position of public sector is no longer a safe haven. Denhardt and Denhardt see in this presentation further an increase in accountability while estimating the consequences of decisions.[311]

---

[308] Wilson, W., *The study of administration*, Political Science Quarterly, Vol. 2, No. 2, pp. 197 – 222, 1887

[309] Bodemann, M./ Olaru, M/ Pirnea, C., *Risk awareness as competitive factor for public administration - a German case study*, in "Proceedings of the IE 2015 International Conference", p. 499, 2015

[310] Simon, H., *Why public administration*, Journal of Public Administration - Research and Theory, Vol. 8, No. 1, pp. 1-11, 1998

[311] Denhardt R. & Denhardt, J., *Public administration: An action orientation*, Thomson Wadworth, Belmont, 2009

As seen above the term risk is often used in a variety of meanings. In the legal requirements the term chances and risks is explicit chosen, but both terms are not defined. Without a clear and common understanding of risks as causes, effects or outcomes, risk management will less contribute than expected, argues Bodemann.[312]

Public managers could therefore choose the wide variety of cause and effect relations leaving the intended transparency and comparativeness. Concrete numbers are addressed only a few times. The term public value will be discussed to complement the link between chances and risks and the expected and desired outcomes for the citizens. It is further used as efficiency indicator. It becomes evident by analysing the public annual status reports that the public managers had left with a wide variety of causes and effects, desired and undesired consequences. While some define clear the conjunctions between causes, effects and the consequences for the execution of tasks, others use the status report as a forum for general, often political, complains of the current situation or as political statement. Some of the reports content neither any combination of chances or risks nor a forecast of expected developments or possible events or a mutual relation of damage and probability.

Shifting the budget from one project to another was under "Cameralistic Accounting Guidelines" impossible. Under special conditions a shift between different budget items was possible. Using the double-entry-accounting makes the steering and prioritizing of project in the public administration easier. The results after ten years of initial application of NPM and the first years with double entry accounting are ambivalent.[313] For the private sector dynamic reactions to market, customer interests, and technology changes were essential to survive. In the public sector the strict separation of different departments was strong; effectiveness and efficiency of an administration was slowed down by the individual interests, ignorance, and the distinctions between the departments. Management and steering of such an organization, based on selective awareness of necessities, are difficult.

Interviews with the representatives confirmed the silo mentality and the direction of the heads of department to stay in their budget as most important challenge (input-orientation), partly regardless of the outcomes. Combined activities, recognizing the main objective to serve the citizens and to provide services as governmental representative for the welfare state, are only at the starting line. Tasks, duties and dimension of the governmental structure were controversial discussed. It depends on the political level, how much share of authority from government and state are

---

[312] Bodemann, M. / Maier, D. / Sandru, M./ Weber, G., *Risk awareness after the adoption of New Steering Mod el in German public administrations – a case study*, Procedia Economics and Finance, No. 23, p. 1052, 2015

[313] Sartoris, J., *Doppik zeigt nur die halbe Wahrheit*, Der Neue Kämmerer, Issue 5, Dec 2008

enough to manage, to steer and to develop. On the individual level it depends on the range of services, duties and transfers, expected by the citizens. The participation differs, but has influence in the consideration about risk and risk management in the public administration.

Analogue to the analysis of consequences of supplemental budget opportunities and threats, resulting from uncertain conditions, the consequences will affect the citizenry. Important projects, i.e. modernization of the communication infrastructure will be delayed, planned announced and then delayed; connections to highways or railroads will affect the settled and potential businesses.

Local public administrations have a further instrument to steer their revenues: Taxes, at least property taxes and trade taxes, are instruments to manage and are used as source of income. All of them are directed to finance the public budget, partly to participate in the success: From the collective and societal view to involve the business in the external effects and as compensation by businesses in the position as beneficiary of infrastructure, land and other supporting installations. Tax is also a steering instrument, for example the "polluter-pays-principle". Provided infrastructure which is used frequently by the business, pollution of air, land and water are compensated, at least partly, by revenues of this tax; although the revenues are not used for precautionary or cleaning measures.

Entrepreneurs trust the planned and published tax policy on local level. Their budget plans are strongly combined and up with the governmental tax policy. As confirmed by the questionnaires, not only private business recognizes policy changes for taxes; adjustments create a relevant field of uncertainty. Changes could endanger projects, new investments and the development of a whole organization; effects of a changed tax policy have relevant influence to businesses and their further expectations. Effects are strengthen and itself a reason for uncertainty if the tax policy is changed belatedly. A change in trusted indexes make the planning unsure, the perspective has to be adjusted by expected results. The instrument of tax changes could affect every resident, but could also lead to selected affected persons and organizations.

An externalization of internal unpreparedness or ignorance will happen, the tax payer have to bear the additional burden. Risk, as an essential part of entrepreneurial life, affects the owner and the people who are working for that management as function. Customers will not be affected by wrong strategic decisions, by false production planning. Only stakeholder and shareholders are affected in the case of vital interests and the threat of existence of the organization. An implicit motivation by the employees on every level is created; personal effects are obvious and transparent for every worker. In contrast to the public administration where on physical level only minor motivation and incentives are created by the system. The live-long-career is therefore regarded as one break shoe for a modernized and lean administration. It is intentionally organized to handle all equal; but the reverse effect is that without incentives and rewarding an absence of awareness for necessary and appropriate improvements is present.

From a business perspective, to remain on the market, following peculiar conditions have to be met for durability:

- Liquidity
- Profitability
- Growth

The municipality exists to support the welfare state and to render certain services and hence characteristics of a firm as set down by Erich Gutenberg are invariably not met; there is no effort to make profits. Where there is no principle of private property, there is no inducement to make profits anyway. For a direct comparison between public and private sector a definition of growth has to be determined. The same will apply to estimation of profitability, too. What means profitability for the public sector? The relationship between the invested capital to the profits does not fit in with the conception of a public administration which is supposed to have to come into being to render certain services to the people – hence making profits is not part of its managers at all. Flynn (2007) summarizes as follows: "Whole purpose of public service is not to make money but to collectively provide protection, help, restraint, education, recreation and ease outside market relationships."[314] This functional description leads to the assumption that applied principles have to be replaced by other management principles.

Another relevant difference is the threat for existence. As discussed above a public sector organization is per law not able to declare bankruptcy. While such a threat is always existent for any private firm, their institutional survival is constitutionally guaranteed.[315] The municipality, the state government or, in the last instance, the country stands as a guarantor behind the public sector. This is one of the most important differences between public organizations and private companies. If a private entrepreneur is unable to pay the invoices, maybe he gets some loans from the banks. But beyond a point, say if the business is not seen as flourishing, he has little option but to shut down.

---

[314] Flynn, N., *Public sector management*, Sage, London, p. 5, 2007

[315] Wollmann, H., *German local government under the impact of NPM modernization and new direct democratic citizen rights"*, Proceedings of „International Conference on Reforming local government", Stuttgart, Sept. 26th, p. 4, 2002

Municipalities have a wide span of duties to fulfill, constitutionally laid down apart from some taken up voluntarily[316] – water, power, and infrastructure and, in most cases, education and health system, too. In view of such key responsibilities devolved on them, their fund flow is guaranteed by law. In the changing circumstances though the municipalities do tend to raise loans for various projects, at which time their performance is rigorously analyzed and they are loan-rated, hence the need risk-focused management. In Switzerland already the municipalities are being ranked;[317] indeed it could be argued that Germany attempted to introduce ranking and benchmarking from another direction, by switching to double entry and accrual accounting. There have been other measures to improve efficiency in the public administration. Interviews by the author show that an official ranking is not yet made, but internal rankings do take place, leading to a range of reactions, from reduced loan limits to higher interest rates.

So then in adherence to the NPM principles: The public sector organizations have to try and avoid incurring fresh debts, but, instead, offer their services within the planned budget. They also have to professionalize the internal structures and processes. Optimization and standardization of processes are in focus. With an appropriate risk management system, the local administration could indeed deliver the results expected by the citizens and within the legal and budgetary requirements.

But persistent deficit financing, resorting to loans, could only a huge burden for future generations. In some European countries discussions are on to scale down debts and develop a sustainable use of available resources. This is discussed under the label an inter-generation-fairness. In addition the convergence-criteria impose a ceiling on government debts. As early as the 17th century, David Hume warned against the danger of transferring debts to the next generation. Keynes argued that in the case of a recession, the market forces have to be supported by investments in the public sector to stimulate the markets by anti-cyclic demands by the public sector, recently applied in Germany to cope the impact of the financial crises using a stimulus project over two years to support local businesses. Weak spot of the model is that the actors involved have to build up resources before. If, on the other hand, debts keep piling up, with no long-term plan to reduce them, what is one to do? How to spend the allocations in a given period? In addition, politicians often use a current

[316] Hoppe, W. & Uechtritz, M. (eds.), *Handbuch kommunale Unternehmen*, 2.edition, Dr. Otto Schmidt, Cologne, 2007

[317] Rehfeld, D., *Rating von Kommunen*, in Stephan, G. & Meurer, E.(eds.), „Rechnungswesen und Controlling", Haufe, Stuttgart, 2005

necessity to justify expenditures beyond the planned budget.[318] This amplifies deficits by overstretching the legal framework.

4. 3. 3. Strategic approaches of risk management practices in public administration

The term in the Local Authority Budget Ordinance to describe chances and risks contents a bandwidth of vagueness and freedom to interpret. Most of the examined public administration used this legal demand for a political statement, predominantly the downside, not desired events and consequences are described. Only in a few cases expected positive effects are presented. For a more precise description and therefore a better analysis of the current status of chances and risks, the terms have to be better defined; especially the distinction of causes, events, consequences and the conversion to monetary values will enhance the meaningfulness of this part of the reports, in best practice in direct correlation with the financial statement. Exogenous impacts or events could be influenced only superficially; the framework of adjusting screws lay often outside of reach of the local government. Exogenous impacts are to handle like pure risks, they could be absorbed politically or monetary prepared and combined by laws and political will. By comparing the reports of a certain period of time a correlation of risks, deviations from a planned budget, will be recognizable; using the identified chances and avoiding risks contributes to cope sustainability with the mandatory task to improve welfare.

Among others, current articles from scientists and practitioners provide the following spectrum of named causes for uncertain future developments:

Social challenges	**areas of social responsibility**	social inclusion / integration of disabled persons in schools and society, according to legal requirements
		accommodation and assistance of immigrants and applicants for asylum
	state/ public schools in the responsibility and supervision of public administration	infrastructure / Investments
		school program development

[318] The indexes presented by a local double entry bookkeeping will create more transparency and a greater awareness of the situation by the citizens and of the needs of the citizens by the politicians.

		inclusion / integration
	youth welfare services	support of young families
		youth welfare services in general
		extension of kindergarten services
	demographic change	change in maintenance of infrastructure
		services to the society
		total population
	public order / protection	fire prevention measures
		containing robbery and violence
Provision	**Infrastructure**	streets / bridges
		buildings / protection/ precautionary measures
		street lightening
	Legal and political framework	pending lawsuit
		delegated services without appropriate financial support
		legislation on federal and European level
Revenue relevant objectives	**commercial interests**	shareholding
		given guarantees
		letter of responsibility
		resettlement of armed forces
		commercial spaces
		real property
	revenues	income tax
		business tax revenue
		development of fees and charges
	dependence of single enterprises/ organizations	financial operations
		interest payments
		financial liquidity
		requirements of BASEL II / III
		transfers payments (in / out)
Ecological purposes	**Environment**	environmental protection
		wildlife

		climate protection
		energy-serving measures
	Infrastructure/ supply	water/ waste water
		energy
		gas
		waste disposal

This not finalised spectrum shows the wide area of possible disruptive factors for public administration. In the case of autonomous decisions processes could be prepared, to react in an appropriate matter, in consistency with given objectives by weighing up. Involving the political directives will stretch the process and under given circumstances opportunities are missed. Risk management, including political objectives and societal estimations and preferences could enforce decisions in the meaning of optimizing public welfare.

The current financial situation of public sector in Europe shows two trends: One trend represent all states which try to cope with the legislative framework and to increase efficiency and effectiveness to stay within the given budgets; the other trend represent all states which increase asymptotical the debts levels without any strategy to pay back or to initiate deep reforms to correct past mistakes in financing the private sector or to drew back privileges for few in the favour of the society.

Developments in the past and expected developments of the national debt levels are indicators that a change to more economizing, structural change, process optimizing and application of other management tools is inevitable.[319] Øvretveit (2005) argues that public sector is less competitive in comparison to private sector. But culture and objectives for public sector are partly different, so the used instruments and results are recognizable different. Embedded in a variety of different political systems, interactions and integration of political programmes, the priority of political majorities and the grade of dependency or independency from central government have direct influence to local public managers and efficiency for executing tasks.

Scientific articles with different results about similarities and differences between both private and public sector organizations essential reasons and objectives for adjustments are defined, for example Allisson, (1980), Rainey and Bozeman (2000), Van der Wal et al. (2008), and Novell (2009). Gaining something of making some profit, i.e. to save a part from the given yearly budget, is not in the sense of

[319] Øvretveit, J., *Public service quality improvement*, in Ferlie, E., Lynn, L.E. jr., Pollitt, C., (eds.), "The Ox ford Handbook of public management", Oxford University Press, Oxford, p. 537, 2005

public administration; also building up some reserves for uncertain developments is limited. Main effort remains to cope with the execution of mandatory tasks.

The privatization of departments, for example public transport during the era of Prime Minister Thatcher in Great Britain, transferred public services to private organizations. In Germany some former governmental departments, for example the German Railway (Deutsche Bahn) or the Postal Service (Deutsche Post) are privatized by gradual transfer to private legal capacity, in the majority public limited companies. Individual or collective interests are of less concern in the pursuit of profit. The results of privatization are for the most part regarded negative for citizenry and society: According to Forrer et al. (2010) that kind of massive privatization is led by the presumption that private vendors can provide some public services more cheaply than governmental agencies.[320] But the range of services is in most cases channelled to the most profitable products and services; meeting the requirements by all fragments of the society leads to a shrinking of the range of services and products. Figure No. 3 shows the overlapping areas public administration has to cope with. Thus these areas represent divergent interests, but are legally, functionally and personally inevitably connected and have to be considered while reengineering public administration.[321]

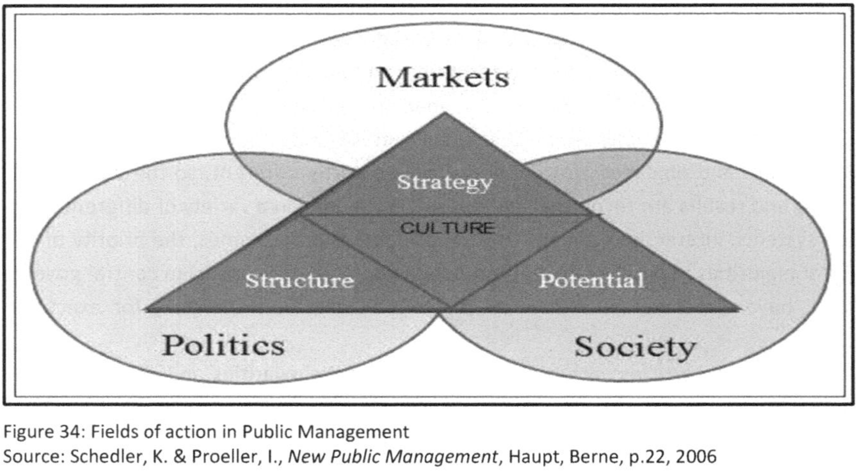

Figure 34: Fields of action in Public Management
Source: Schedler, K. & Proeller, I., *New Public Management*, Haupt, Berne, p.22, 2006

[320] Forrer, J. et al., *Public – private partnerships and the public accountability question*, Public Administration Review, May-June, pp. 475-484, 2010

[321] Hilgers, D./ Schauer, R./ Thom, N., (eds.), *Public Management im Paradigmenwechsel*, Trauner Verlag, Linz, 2012

Beneath others in Europe the German federal system traditionally is based on a three-tier-mode: First a governmental/federal level and second on state level, in which the states are so called "Länder", and on local level municipalities and counties. In a long-standing practice the German states delegate the most of policy and political program implementation and the basic administrative tasks to local administrations.[322] In this applied separation of duties and implementation of objectives, on local level very concrete measures and activities, pointed direct to the citizen, should contribute to the welfare state. The measurement of deviations of the status of welfare state and the individual consumption of public goods will be later introduced as substitute to the conventional numbers for the processing in risk management and measuring efficiency. Local authorities are held responsible for almost every social assistance scheme, providing the poor and needy, not covered by the general social security scheme. In addition for the whole community one important and legally codified task is the provision for the every-day-existence; this term covers i.e. water supply, sewage water disposal, public transport, supply of electricity, and gas as well as the operation of municipal or – county-owned saving banks. Further the basement of health services and education. Idea behind is that the local authorities know best what to provide in an appropriate quality and quantity in the identified interest of the individuals or groups of individuals.

Summarizing the given examples, which could differ, depending on the geographical, economical and socio-economically situation, there is a wide scope of responsibilities of local governments focused to public services and public utility. Premises for strategic planning have to be developed by references and forecast.

A general model is presented in Figure 34: From a starting point rational decisions and activities are started, influenced by events and risk factors, and intended to change one or more of the three subsystems. Risk management works during that transformation stage and support public managers by analysing and evaluating risk factors and events and their potential ramification for the initial decisions and the target system. By measuring the expected change in the subsystem compared with the expected changes in start stage provides an indicator of efficiency.

[322] Wollmann, H., *German local government under the impact of NPM modernization and new direct democratic citizen rights*, Proceedings of „International Conference on Reforming local government", Stuttgart, Sept. 26th, p. 4, 2002

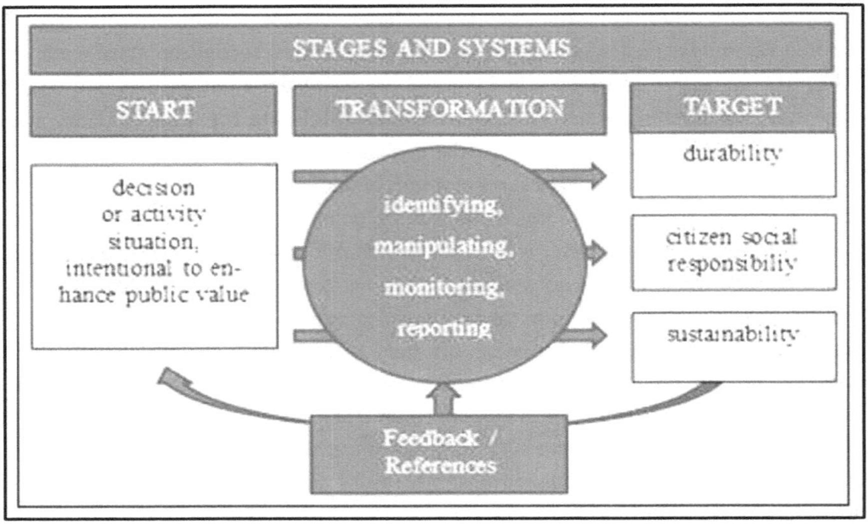

Figure 35: Stage model for outcomes of public administration activities
Source: by author

This broad spectrum makes it on the one side very important to develop and maintain a forecast system to identify uncertainty and influence factors for sustainable provision of mandatory and voluntarily tasks. On the other side, this spectrum is a complex system, influenced from the in- and the outside and founded on the ever changing and volatile notion of public welfare. For strategic risk management especially targets have to be established and indicators for measurement identified.

5. Study on the opinions of enterprises regarding the evolution of

5.1. General context of the research

For private sector risk management is legally demanded; it strenthgens the position of share- and stakeholder by implementing a system to identify, evaluate and manage decisions and potential outcomes under the conditions of no certainty. This is the typical environment a entrepreneur is acting in. Analogue public sector recognized the necessity to rethink processes and tools to manage their routine work and to develop systems which are able to support the decision-maker. The intended objectives are to cope dynamically with the increase complexity and number to legally tasks and to avoid, at least mitigate, undesired consequences from decisions or processes. Appropriate systems should alert the management in the case of deviations from a predicted plan, can process several data to present consequences and offers tactics to regain the management ability. Risk management systems for public sector have been early adopted in Australia and New Zealand, later in Canada and United Kingdom. In Switzerland, Germany and Austria risk management systems are legally not demanded, although obviously risks for sustainable operations are to manage.

5.2. Objectives and research methodology

To get a general overview of the current states of risks, uncertainty, efficiency, and potential consequences by changes in the inner and outer environment, a field research was conducted in Germany, Switzerland and Austria. The research based on two parts: First part was a questionnaire, based on 45 questions. The questionnaire was followed by a structured interview, based on 22 questions, with mayors and/or Chief Financial Officers of local public administrations. The interviews were conducted in the public administrations and offered several occasions to complete the view to a public administration. Several public administrations denied their support or refered to already existent statistics; others pointed out the confidential treatment of the information.

M. Bodemann, *Management in Public Administration*,
Sustainable Management, Wertschöpfung und Effizienz,
https://doi.org/10.1007/978-3-658-22687-9_6

5.3. Research results

5. 3. 1. Research results in evaluation of efficient project management in public administration

Comparative studies of real and estimated costs in public transportation or infrastructure development, for instance, are rare.[323] Pickrell in 1990 concludes that cost-estimates are highly inaccurate, with actual cost being typically much higher than estimated cost. But Nijkamp and Ubelles came 1999 to the conclusion that cost estimates could indeed be correct.[324] In general it all depends on projects and the assigned project-manager.

Incidentally Flyvberg also pointed out that comparisons with private sector organizations didn't exist; nobody knows whether private projects perform better or worse than public ones regarding cost underestimation. Interesting example is the maiden flight of the military transport Airbus A 400 M at the 11.12.2009. The planning schedule was two years behind the estimated time, the costs turned out to be 30% higher than what was first planned.

Still there is a vital difference: When there is a cost overrun in the owner could decide to pull the plug, whereas public sector projects are guided by political compulsions and hence the project is persisted with whatever the cost.

Flyvberg also observed that forecasts of costs, demands by citizens and other aspects of planned projects have remained constantly and remarkably inaccurate for decades.[325] For the analysed 70-year period accuracy in cost forecast remained significantly at a poor level.[326]

The results of the research draw a similar unsatisfying picture of handling projects in local public administrations. While the cost of IT are in 30% higher than expected, for building more than a half of the project are finally more expensive.

---

[323] Bruzelis, N./ Flyvberg, B./ Rothengatter, W., *Big decisions, big risks: Improving accountability in mega projects*, International Review of Administration Science; Vol. 64 No. 3, pp. 423 – 440, 1998; Pickrell, D.H.: *Urban rail transit projects: Forecasts versus actual ridership and cost*, U.S. Department of Transportation, Washington, DC 1990

[324] Nijkamp, P. & Ubbels, B., *How reliable are estimates of infrastructure costs? A comparative analysis*, in "International Journal of Transport Economics", Vol. 26, No.1 pp. 23 – 53, 1999

[325] Flyvberg, B., *From Nobel prize to project management: Getting risks right*, Project Management Journal, August, p. 5, 2006

[326] For transportation infrastructure projects the inaccuracy in cost forecasts on constant prices is on average 44,7% for rail 33,8% for bridges and tunnels 33,8% and for roads 20,4%. Values from: Flyvberg, B., *From Nobel prize to project management: Getting risks right*, Project Management Journal, Vol. 37, No.3, August, p. 6, 2006

Table 20 Variances in budget in projects
Source: by author: Questionnaire 2009 – 2012

	more than 10% more expensive	up to 10% more expensive	as planned	less expensive	more than 10% less expensive
Buildings		52.6 %	42.1 %		
Infrastructure	15.0%	30.0 %	50.0 %	5.0 %	
IT		28.6 %	71.4 %		

Similar in the case of a given timeframe: In no case the final stage is reached faster than planned, IT projects are fastest; almost half of the infrastructure projects are delayed. Reasons given are the unexpected hindrances, for example public resistance to cut down trees or exploration of ruined buildings

Table 21 Variances from planned time frame
Source: by author: Questionnaire 2009 - 2012

	slower than 10%	less than 10%	as planned	faster than planned	faster than 10%
Buildings		29.4 %	70.6 %		
Infrastructure		45.0 %	55.0 %		
IT		21.1 %	789 %		

A deviation from estimated costs leads to reduction in the allocation to other projects or have to be financed by new loans; both of them have negative impacts on public value.

5. 3. 2. Results on intentional risks - given guarantees in public administration

Although David Hume warned the public sector against accumulating debts as early as in 1752 developments in Europe demonstrate show no one has bothered to heed the call.[327] The debts levels are ballooning, with no sign of declining in the near future. Investment opportunities, promising higher returns, could look attractive, but

[327] Hume, D., *Essay IX: Of Public Loan,* in *Green*, T. & Grose, T. (eds), *David Hume – The Philosophical Works*, Aalen, 1992

there is always a flipside. And the flipside has come to haunt the local bodies now. In some cases whatever was invested is gone, severely affecting the finances. Public administration acts as a trustee of the tax-payers' money, and so while dipping into it, the managers have to be extremely cautious. But apparently they plunged headlong without a proper risk evaluation. Berlin's mass transit company BVG took a massive risk financing new trams and subway cars, at the time it sounded attractive. Many followed suits. Between 150 and 200 cities and towns across Germany used such deals to finance everything from public transportation to sewage systems and garbage incinerators.

Traditional sectors/areas of the services and products are:

- Finance, to develop strategies and procedures to raise necessary resources to fulfill legal obligations
- Revenues, steering of tax adjustments to maximize the revenues
- Education, providing an appropriate education, from pre-kindergarten to high school, in the local area, partly competing with private providers
- Social services, to provide income support and other welfare activities
- Industry and commerce: to develop a modern and adequate infrastructure for necessary for enterprises
- Demography: keeping track of population growth and planning for necessary civic amenities
- Also to cater to the sports, cultural and social networking needs of the community

Any situation has two potentials, positive (desired) and negative (undesired). Categorization helps narrow down to specific issues and work out appropriate strategies to head off the possible negative fallout.

Examples are given guaranties to third parties; in this case public administration act as guarantors for obligations of others, like public hospitals. This sector is, in the case of publicly owned, not run to gain profit, but provides medical healthcare as a constitutional task, notwithstanding the costs involved. In the circumstances private investors or creditors look for governmental or public guarantee for their investments and loans as provider of medical care. Currently some of the public owned hospitals are not able to survive without such guaranties. So also in infrastructure, like transport or cultural establishments, like sporting clubs and museums, the municipal administration steps in even if the providers are privately run or they are taken over by private organizations from the government.

In some such cases guaranties were neither time-bound nor was there any financial ceiling. Any kind of financially unlimited guarantee is a risky proposition; still such courses of action are common in many places. One results of the research brought a diffuse figure of identified uncertain threats. As to see in the following table municipalities have given guaranties to public owned or private owned organizations. In one case a guarantee for pensions was given for a local but public owned and managed hospital. In the case of denied guarantees the hospital has been closed in a short period of time. Political reason for the guarantee was to preserve services in the medical sector and to attract more interested patients in the area. But if realized at one time the financial burden for the budget of the district administration would be over 1/7 of the yearly budget (on average of the last 4 years): A significant part of the budget that could not have been saved by reducing or delaying other projects. The table illustrates the financial dimensions by given guarantees in comparison to yearly budgets:

Table 22 Sum of given guarantees in comparison to yearly budget
Source: by author: Questionnaire 2009 – 2012

No.	Given guarantees (alphabetic order of respondents)	Shares of guarantees over yearly budget
1	25,100,000 €	55.78 %
2	99500,000 €	130.92 %
3	7,262,839 €	2.08 %
4	23,422,000 €	11.71 %
5	4,500,000 €	22.50 %
6	1,900,000 €	7.90 %
7	15,000,000 €	7.35 %
8	2,400,000 €	2.77 %
9	50,000 €	1.25 %
10	22,825,471 €	61.69 %
11	10,316 €	0.02 %
12	574,000 €	1.64 %

Remarkable is the proportion between annual budget and given guarantees. In the case, that all given guarantees are realized in one certain time, the results will be disastrous. Liquidity will immediately washed away, additional loans will be necessary, no compensation by own resources would be possible, in one case more than a full yearly budget is bounded. A lack of responsibility is recognizable using this disproportion as indicator. The threat remains to spend the money for an unplanned and undesired project if the external planned activities will fail or not pay off. In contrast, in Switzerland guaranties by public administration are legally prohibited.

In more than two-thirds of the deals, German cities insured their assets, for example with AIG or Lehman Brothers. After those two pillars of U.S. finance crumbled, German cities suddenly faced the risk of having to make huge payments — as much as € 30 billion, according to some estimates — to their American investors.[328]

In more than one research Flyvberg showed that in most cases both the time line and the financial planning as well as the expected benefits for the public were missed. After all the cost overruns and interminable delays in execution, it was found that public patronage was much less than what had been hoped for. Particularly so with bigger projects, like building, bridges or complex IT ventures. More than two thirds of the examined administrations acknowledged that such was indeed the case. The public administration in general faces jammed investments in public buildings and infrastructure, although few stated a good balance for investment in the surveyed annual reports. Poor planning and the inter-departmental cooperation were considered the most important contributory factors. As one result it remains an awareness of the need for better project-management, particularly holding the contractors to their promises on the time-frame and quality of products. For the IT-sector the so called SLA (Service Level Agreements) are basement which enables a precise assessment of deviations, for which the contractor can be penalized. From the Flyvberg research, it becomes clear then that realistic assumptions are more effective than politically-driven time-lines; but it remains the privilege of political interpreted premises and bandwidth of decisions.

In Germany the increasing investments and the fixed assets expenditure requirements are obvious. They are partly caused by intentionally saving money for other projects, partly caused by the expectation to sell the assets to private investors. But in case of delays in attending to maintenance issues, the expenses for the administration will go up as any way at some point of time they have to be sorted out. In a worst case scenario personal injuries could result as if roofs of public buildings are

---

[328] "Now German towns and cities are appealing to the German government to bail them out." from: http://www.time.com/time/business/article/0,8599,1890418,00.html#ixzz0vFhui2jV; retrieved 31.07.2010

not properly maintained or repaired. In the private sector particularly the costs of such renovations are heavy: Hence to avoid nasty shocks at a later date, long-term planning is needed.

5. 3. 3. Results identifying and ranking external and internal influences

The results from the questionnaire proved that there are uncertain circumstances for administrative decisions. All of them have their own probability and are often political driven, therefore often outside of any rational and predictable development. Chosen from a variety of fifteen different sources, the following ranking was the result of the questionnaires:

Table 23 Ranking of threats for executing routine duties, ranking by average value
Source: by author: Questionnaire 2009 – 2012

1.	Declining tax income	2.42
2.	More duties without adequate compensation	4.17
3.	State politics	6.54
4.	Delayed necessary investments	7.00
5.	Limited freedom to act	7.08
6.	Attraction of location	7.35
7.	Federal politics	7.46
8.	Demographic change	7.58
9.	Deficits by shares	8.17
10.	European politics	8.42
11.	Addition political expectation	8.67
12.	Less qualified employees	9.04
13.	Increasing demand by society	9.38
14.	Climatic change	10.87
15.	Negative development of transactions	12.95

For example declining transfers from the federal or state level have impact on all sectors of municipalities: Delegation of duties without appropriate financing will be confirmed by the analysis of the annual risk report.

Table 24: Development of transfers from state or federal level
Source: by author: Questionnaire 2009 – 2012

Significant increase	0.00 %
Increase	18.18 %
Constant	27.27 %
Drop	54.56 %

More than half of all addressed and examined public administrations complain a drop in transfers from state and / or governmental level. Without appropriate resources execution of political programmes will lead relentless to increase of debt levels.

Following changes in the expense structure were given by the surveyed municipalities:

Table 25 Increase of expenses over the last 5 years in %
Source: by author: Questionnaire 2009 – 2012

material costs	significantly increased	7.7 %
	increased	88.5 %
	constant	3.9 %
personnel costs	significantly increased	3.9 %
	increased	76.9 %
	constant	15.4 %
	decreased	3.8 %
social aids	significantly increased	41.7 %
	increased	29.2 %
	constant	16.7 %
	decreased	12.5 %
interest rates	increased	12.0 %
	constant	44.0 %
	decreased	44.0 %

These costs have different meaning for operations and for strategic planning; while material costs are a factor which can be influence by using electronic workflows instead of paper-based cases, the social costs raised over-proportional over the last 10 years with a tendency rising further. That depends on several factors, including demographic changes. In the annual reports this risk factor is named by almost all of the examined public administrations. The costs for the refugees fleeing from the Arabic states will increase these costs additionally.

It remains the question whether pensions or social aids can be categorized as risk; there are certain indicators for forecasts, for example life expectancy. Influence to public value could be on macroeconomic level several changes in pension policies or the steady discussion about working life time.

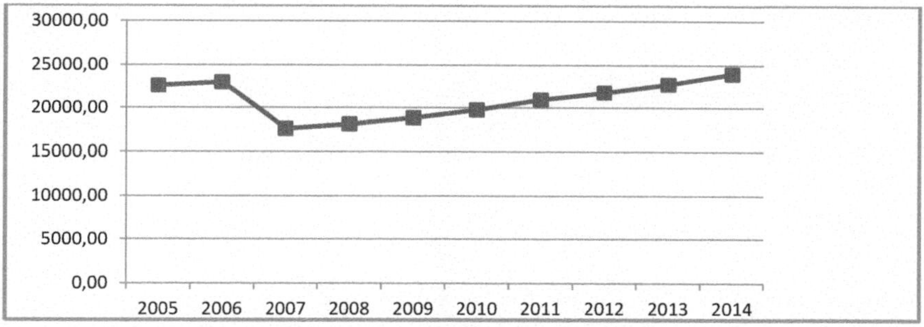

Figure 36: Development of social aids in Germany over the last decade in Mio. €
Source: Statistisches Bundesamt, www. Statista.de, retrieved 22.04.2016

The decreasing interest rates are no signal of good management or better use of resources; the interest rates decreased and so the expenses for interests also.

Combining the current status, the development of resources and duties and the identification lead to an existing risk awareness; nevertheless the interviewed persons declared that they are imprisoned in a kind of futility trap: Opportunities identified and used will lead on state level to an expected solidarity; savings will not be spared to reduce debts, but the political will prefers immediate consumption rather than sustainable measures.

6. Study on the identification of risk management practices and risk factors in German public administration

6.1. General context of the research

During 500 years of so called Cameralistics, based on a cash-accounting system, the political and administrative responsibility was focussed from fiscal year to fiscal year and election to election. Long-lasting investments were suppressed by change in political majorities, higher authorities, like the federal government, the legal branch or the European Union. Especially the real estate and other fixed assets are ignored in this kind of accounting. The new kind, similar to the double-entry-accounting, was introduced in NRW in 2005 – 2009. The adoption of principles and standards of the German Commercial Code (Handelsgesetzbuch, HGB) is a first step for transparency in the inner and outer sphere, replaces the Cameralistics, and adds the fixed asset accounting. By applying the double-entry-accounting, the analysis of current state of financials and liquidity is possible, developments over more than a year and appropriate countermeasures are possible and legally demanded. Converting the accounting system lasts planned from 2005 – 2009; other German states changed simultaneously, others follows, but without a binding schedule or content.

„Risk management function has become a central feature of the operation of debt offices in many jurisdictions", so the OECD in 2005.[329] The OECD focussed in this paper to cope with debt as strategic objective. But risk management is recognized as one tool to improve efficiency, impartial from debt management, and to contribute appropriate and valid data for strategic decisions in both private and public sector. In the public sector reforms are in progress and are accelerated by internal and external pressure, demanding more efficiency and effectiveness. While in private sector risk management is legally demanded and has direct influence in the intersection with the external environment in public sector the current situation is diffuse. Several states work on concrete and compulsory standards; others delegate the responsibility of strategic and operational steering to the local authorities. In Germany tools from NPM are introduced, but only selective. That creates the notion that public sector can be compared to similar private sector organizations. Because of the subsidiarity principle the progress is different and the elaboration lies at the state level. Since 2005 the state of North Rhine Westphalia uses tools of NPM. Standards for risk management, similar to Australia or UK are not defined; the municipality code demands hints

[329] OECD, Overview of advances in risk management of government debt, 2005

M. Bodemann, *Management in Public Administration*,
Sustainable Management, Wertschöpfung und Effizienz,
https://doi.org/10.1007/978-3-658-22687-9_7

about chances and threats in the annual status report, but lacks on links to risk management standards to be used or measurable objectives to be reached. The following research enlightens the current practices to cope with the notices about chances and threats in local administration in North Rhine Westphalia, the range of given risk factors, the origins, based on internal and external environment and categorizes the given risk factors. Later the characteristics are analysed for use to create a standardized risk catalogue, roots and causes and how to deal with them. The risk factors can also serve as reference classes for further categorization and benchmarks.

6.2. Objectives and research methodology

The results of this part of the survey are based on the annual report of local public administrations in the state of North Rhine-Westphalia. Germany itself consists of independent sixteen states, the size ranges from the areal of Bavaria of 70,550 km^2 to the areal of Bremen of 419 km^2, the population ranges from 17.571.860 for North Rhine Westphalia to 657.390 for Bremen. With an area of 34,110 km^2 the federal state of NRW is ranked 4th, but has the highest debt level of all federal states (2013: 208.26 B€). [330]

The selected state is located in the western middle of Germany. The area reaches from the formal city-region of the city of Aachen in the West, and the smaller county of Höxter in the East. North Rhine-Westphalia has the greatest population in Germany and represents the whole spectrum of branches: From the domination of farming in the East and North-West to industry and production for all purposes and branches in the so called Rhineland and Ruhr-area in the West.

The macrocosm of the research contents 397 local public administrations and 30 counties. Counties are governed by a county council (Kreistag) and a district administrator; the municipalities are ruled by the municipal council and the mayor. For the results of the research the annual status reports of 72 local public administrations (18.2 %) and 12 county administrations (40%) are evaluated and the results interpreted in the following systematic approach:

Similar to private sector, municipalities in North Rhine-Westphalia have to prepare and to publish an annual financial statement, including a compulsory status report, according to the communal budget ordinance, § 46 GemHVO. Beneath other information, e.g. precise defined standard reports to present the current financial

[330] Source: http://de.statista.com/themen/1098/bundeslaender-im-vergleich/ retrieved on 15.10.2015

status and the developments in the past, the board has to present chances and threats, both affecting the sustainable mandatory tasks.[331] Similar to the private sector determination for the execution of this systematic approach, only a few hints describe the framework to articulate the risks for a public administration. There are no binding questions to be answered, no form to be filled out. As consequence the implementation and the maintaining of risk management is delegated in terms of content to each individual public administration.

The research is directed to analyse, process and collect the identified uncertainty factors of public administration in the state of North Rhine-Westphalia to evaluate their outcomes in terms of efficiency and contribution to public value.

By using the origin and the possibility to influence the factors by themselves different singular risk factors can be distributed in endogenous and exogenous risks; in the meaning that the factors are administration-inherent or given by the outside-environment; for example economic developments, societal development or politics from state to federal level.

Table 26 Range of risk factors of public administration
Source: by author

Desired outcomes of chances and threats of factors		Not desired outcomes of chances and threats of factors	
Endogenous	Exogenous	Endogenous	Exogenous

Identification and depiction as content for the chance and threat summarization is on the one hand an indicator that the public administration is aware of not-certain, but possible developments; on the other hand developments in the out- and inside sphere are detected as influences for the result to public value.

The factors of uncertainty, sources and results, can be used as reference of the individual risk awareness status of each public administration and show the trend of risk awareness; further a distinction in endogenous and exogenous chances and threats is made to show factors to be influence and outside-given factors, depending on the economic development, rules and regulations, and the societal development, only to describe the most important factors for further expectations. Kind and number, frequency and severity of factors will influence the operational level of public administration. The given results reflect the general awareness of uncertainty and the

331 Loevenich, B., *Der Umgang mit operationellen Risiken in Kreditinstituten – Vorbild für öffentliche Verwaltungen?* in Niedostadek, A., Riedl, R., Stember, J., „Risiken im öffentlichen Bereich", Lit Verlag, Berlin, 2011

ability to identify sources of desired and not-desired factors. For operational and analytic purposes using a risk map, quantifying the own risk, can enlighten reason and source for influence, including:

- cash flow at risk/ liquidity factors
- earnings/ revenues at risk
- economical capital at risk or
- market value / public trust at risk

By using the identified factors, a measurement of ramification and consequences is possible.

6.3. Research results

6. 3. 1. Risk categories by annual status reports

Loevenich (2011) reviews risks in the following approach: Operational risks are based on organizational-operational facts and therefore so not-economic risks which could cause damage to the organization.[332] Loevenich distincts between operational risks, economic risks, business risks and strategic risks, while economic risks are described by loss of debtors, market price risk or liquidity risks. For a better estimation and notion of the risks, we have to distinct the origin and possibilities to show the effectiveness and efficiency of countermeasures. At least, all of them will have a direct impact to the liquidity and the available finance resources, for mandatory and voluntarily tasks. Compressing the often described, partly hidden hints to factors, following categorisation is done by the examined public administrations:

Results from the research are an aggregation of local city and county administration. In cases both kinds of administration are surveyed different, it is declared by the description.

Table 27: Categorization of exogenous risk factors
Source: By author, annual status reports of public administrations in North Rhine-Westphalia, Germany

	1.1. Negative factors:	**1.2. Positive factors**
Social development:	integration of disabled people	Demographic development

[332] Loevenich, B., *Der Umgang mit operationellen Risiken in Kreditinstituten – Vorbild für öffentliche Verwal tungen?* in Niedostadek, A., Riedl, R., Stember, J., „Risiken im öffentlichen Bereich“, Lit Verlag, Berlin, p. 260, 2011

	youth welfare	
	kindergarten	
	education	
	social benefits	
	demographic change	
General:	connectivity principle	geographic status
Finances:	transfers	transfers
	Basel II / III	
	interest payment	
	financial operations	
	taxes	taxes / revenues

Similar to the assumed exogenous factors, endogenous factors could be categorized. Separation between positive and negative factors contents a blurring area; interdependences between categories are possible, each local public administration has an own peculiar estimation.

Table 28: Categorization of endogenous risk factors
Source: By author, annual status reports of public administrations in North Rhine-Westphalia, Germany

	2.1.Negative factors:	**2.2.Positive factors**
Social development:	public safety and order	commercial factors
General:	reconstruction	reconstruction
		own equity
Finances:	guarantees	holdings / shares
		interest payments
		taxes
Provision of services of general interest:	waste disposal	street maintenance
	energy, water	
Operations:	personnel costs	energetic measures
	law suits	economic stimulus
		city development
		organizational improvement
		internal control systems

		public works
		co-operations

All in common is the feature that they are regarded by the public administration as uncertain factors referring to probability and consequences, in monetary or other terms. The categories used in the table result from the given spectrum of questions about identified chances and threats in the context of the annual report. The categories reflect all given answers presented in the partial report for risk management: The generic terms are used to collect similar factors in one category: For example "Finances": In the category finances reasons for chances and threats are combined which are direct linked with finances. The added asset accounting after "Kameralistics" allows proving the increase and decrease of fixed assets and uncovers former shifts by liquidity stability. By the analysis and benchmarking of banks the credit conditions will be adjusted in the case of a significant decrease or bad ranking. Transfers to get or to pay have as well direct influence of the liquidity and potential short-time credits. By analysing and synthesising the essential parameters all given risk factors and their consequences will be measured with models like Value-at-Risk.

The next figure presents the given exogenous risk factors by the examined municipalities; the spectrum of different negative factors (12) is significant wider than the subcategories of positive risk factors (4). That leads to the assumption that uncertainty in terms of negative consequences is linked with the outside. Different are the results of the subcategories of the endogenous risk factors as to see in Table 27 and Figure 25: The proportion is in reverse; subcategories in negative expected results (9) are outclassed by 14 assumed positive risk factors. One quantitative feature in this analysis remains to support a trend in risk identification and estimation in public sector: The sum of all named negative factors is 238, in comparison: Positive risk factors are only named 95 times.

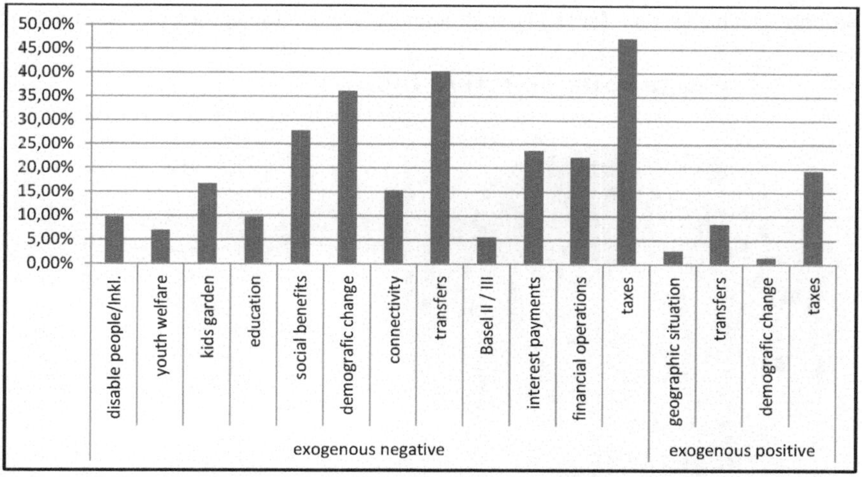

Figure 37: Desired and not desired exogenous influence factors, named by public administration in %
Source: By author, annual status reports of public administrations in North Rhine-Westphalia, Germany

Selecting all exogenous factors five main components of the whole spectrum are named most: The demographic change with all consequences including aging society, different needs for older people, or less experienced workers. Especially the rural regions in the north and in the east of North Rhine-Westphalia indicated the demographic change as challenge for the future: Professionals will move to the bigger cities, without a qualitative and quantitative workforce new settlements of organizations will be unlikely. Taxes as important income factor follow cyclic movements; in the crisis of 2008, the German government started an initiative to stimulate the economy, especially local medium-sized companies. By using the instrument of stimulation of anti-cyclical demands by public sector these companies are supported, but to the threat of increasing debts on the long run. On the other hand, some of the public administrations expect further positive developments in the available public funds and a more appropriate distribution, as one of the expected external positive factors.

The following charts show how many public administrations named exogenous negative factors; in focus are especially the development of taxes, the dependent transfers from state and federal level and the demographic change. Interesting is the geological position of a city or county: The isolation can be compensated by a good infrastructure, the efforts to attract businesses and people are estimated over-proportional higher than for local public administration in the vicinity of metropolitan areas.

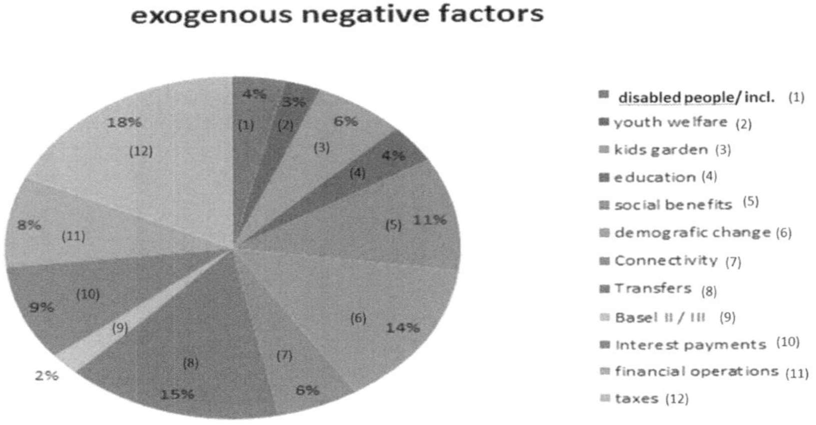

Figure 38: Expected exogenous factors for undesired developments
Source: By author, annual status reports of public administrations in North Rhine-Westphalia, Germany

The range of external positive factors is significant smaller, only for risk factors are named. Main concerns are the taxes and transfers, an indicator of remaining input orientation in the public administration. As seen in Figure 36 the number of indications is also significantly lower.

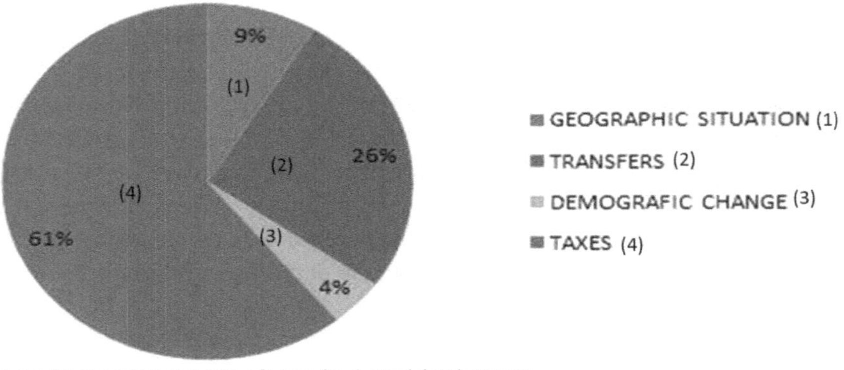

Figure 39: Expected exogenous factors for desired developments
Source: By author, annual status reports of public administrations in North Rhine-Westphalia, Germany

Beneath external origins of risk factors, each organization has to cope internal uncertainty factors which can directly or indirectly influence the grade of compliance with of legal or internal objectives. Originated from sources inside the responsibility of the local administration; decisions under no certainty are made by decision makers by political, strategic and/or rational choice. Set up of origin is located in decision by the local administration/ local political parliament.

Examples: guarantees, delays in maintaining buildings, size of staff. In this case, although current status is a result of past decisions, only few risk factors from the inside management are given.

Almost a third of all examined public administrations declared an investment jam considering reconstruction. That will lead to immediate investments, partly out of planning. As seen in Table 23, given guarantees are wide spread as tool to substitute public duties and general public interest to societies or associations. If properly used and selected, guarantees enable the public sector to delegate origin public duties to third parties, by offering them support and in worst case scenario the creditors safety for repayments. Guarantees have to be monitored, premises for decisions determined, and possible extensions considered, because the probability of loss will change during the term of provision.

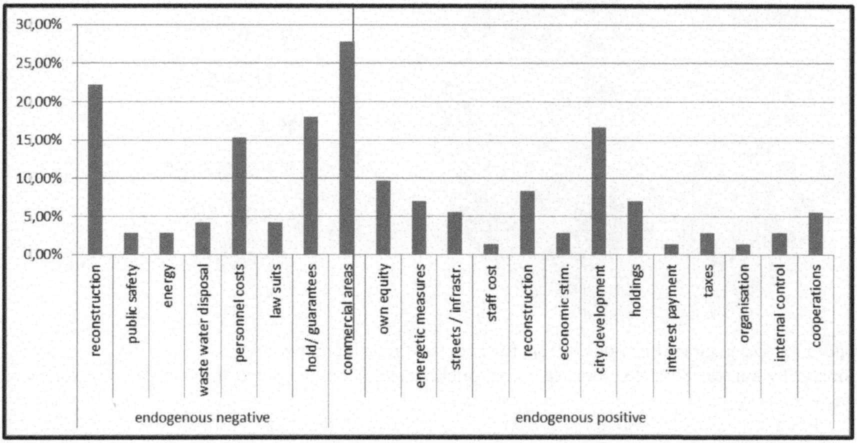

Figure 40: Expected endogenous factors
Source: By author, annual status reports of public administrations in North Rhine-Westphalia, Germany

One third of the examined public administration announced that the current state of reconstruction and infrastructure have to be reconsidered and appropriate measures executed; not only to maintain but also to restore the use or as compliance to public safety. Beneath material factors, the personnel costs are identified as possible negative factors for the future. Collective wage agreements have direct influence to all departments and organisations in the public sector; but also the former explained demographic change will play a role: Public sector is bound in the wage agreement for most of the public clerks. By decreasing population the competition for qualified employees will increase, but the public sector is not compatible to attract these qualified persons in time and number to substitute the retiring employees. In addition the increasing aging of the population increases the monthly payments to civil servants, one of two forms of employment contracts. Civil servants will be paid by the public administration as debtor, with an increasing number of retired civil servants and a higher life expectancy the annual financial burden will increase. The uncertainty factor is in this case a systemic factor. Increasing payments for retired employees could be moderated by savings during their active time. Some public administration try to avoid live long career public managers, they prefer to offer the regular employment contracts with constant payment for pensions by the employee and the public employer during working time.

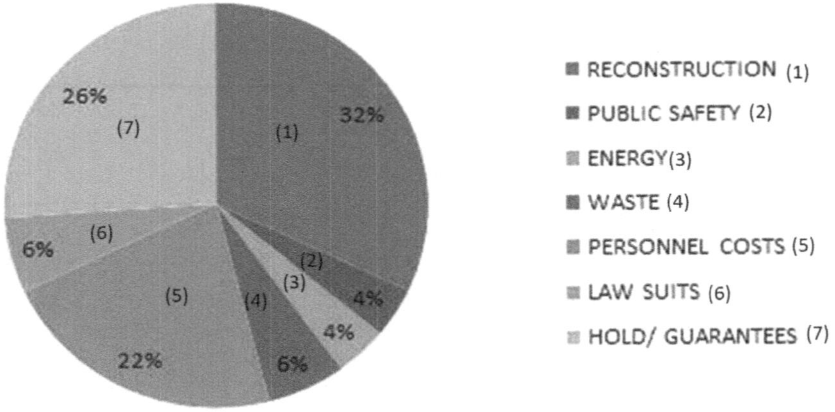

Figure 41: Expected endogenous factors for undesired developments
Source: By author, annual status reports of public administrations in North Rhine-Westphalia, Germany

Contrary to publications at the end of the last century high uncertain financial transaction play no significant role in the annual status reports. Some of the risky transactions, using complex financial instruments, for example interest swaps, had to be partly or completely written off with enormous consequences for the annual budget of the responsible municipality.

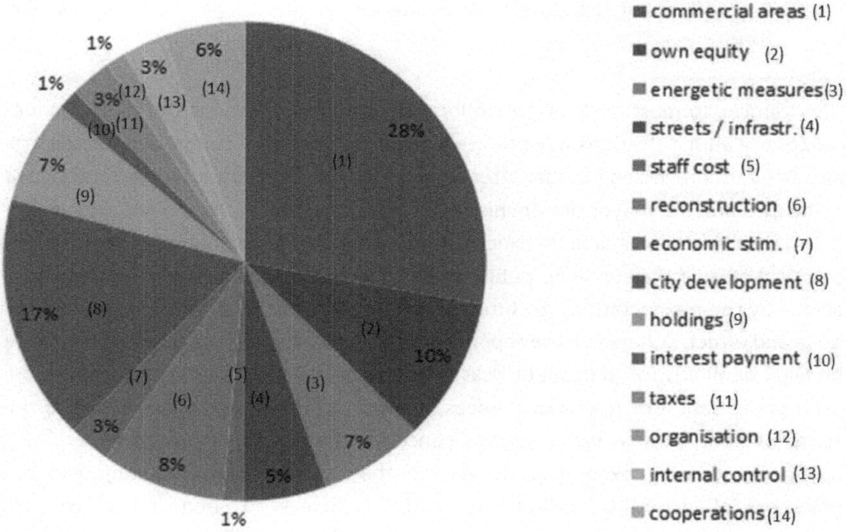

Figure 42: Expected endogenous factors for desired developments
Source: By author, annual status reports of public administrations in North Rhine-Westphalia, Germany

The results of the annual reports draw a clear statement: Uncertainty is in 2/3 cases combined with negative expected results, chances coming with uncertain developments are less in focus of the public administration. Similar is the view onto factors from outside and inside. The variety and the grade of affection are significant. Endogenous risk factors could be steered and manipulated by the public administration and are measurable in monetary units. Developments of commercial areas as trigger for encouraging settlements of companies, followed by families of the employees, reflect the positive expectations. Combined with a general city development for increase of attraction is almost 20% named by the examined administration.

Concerning risk management, local public administration is able to act within a limited freedom to choose; for examples to give guarantees, to plan and order personal developments, or choose different kinds for financing mandatory or voluntarily tasks and projects. That leads to a different approach analyzing the presented risks. As to see in Fig.45, the spectrum of named risks is wide, almost 44% complained, out of an input oriented view, the forecasts of fiscal income.

6. 3. 2. Research results on correlation to size and annual budget regarding risk factors

Similar to most of the German local public administrations the municipalities and county administrations have to prepare and to publish a compulsory statues report. Beneath processed number after a given scheme, the report, written and signed by the CFO and the mayor or administrative head of a county, has to describe chances and risks for the sustainable execution and provision of mandatory and voluntary tasks.[333] Some of the surveyed public administrations describe very clear and in detailed way their expectations for future developments and give a clear estimation of cause and effect. Others use the report for a general political discussion; a few ignore the legal demands for part about risks and chances. While some expect a more detailed presentation of risks and chances in the fast decreasing of own equity or increase of debt level to prove serious concerns, the results are more widespread. Maybe the missing experience to handle the double-entry-accounting and the awareness of increasing transparency and the chance to conduct best practice benchmarks keep some public managers from better results.

Remarkable is the proportion of the given influence factors: The given internal influence factors, factors which can be actively steered by the public administration, are in total 21 categories. These categories are created by the author to compress the findings in the research. On the exogenous side 14 categories are given, also divided in negative and positive factors.

The given 21 given influence factors which will decrease the quantity and the quality of the provision equals almost the given positive factors, while positive factors are mainly seen in the endogenous framework.

One indicator for a higher awareness of risk factors can be the correlation between the current debt level and the number of identified risk factors. As to see in the Figure 43 the correlation is wide spread; the most numbers of risk factors are given by municipalities around a debt level of 30%. In this graph positive and negative and in- and outside risk factors are displayed. As one result high debt level are not necessarily combined with a higher awareness of uncertain influence factors.

[333] Loevenich, B., *Der Umgang mit operationellen Risiken in Kreditinstituten – Vorbild für öffentliche Verwaltungen?* In Niedostadek, A., Riedl, R., Stember, J., „Risiken im öffentlichen Bereich", Lit Verlag, Berlin, ß. 257, 2011

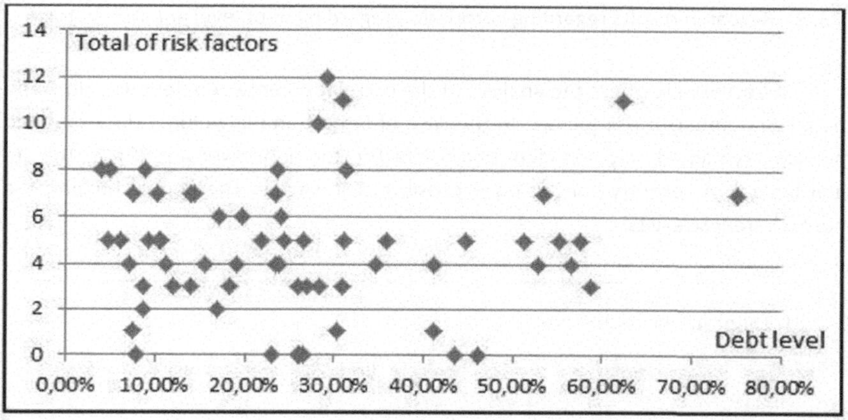

Figure 43: Correlation between debt level in % of annual budget and number of given risk factors for municipalities
Source: By author, annual status reports of public administrations in North Rhine-Westphalia, Germany

The absolute numbers of given risk factors is significant smaller in county administration than in municipalities. This is one effect of the financing of the annual county budget: It is demanded from the municipalities which are part of the county. The financing is therefore guaranteed; incentive for acting cooperatively is the political harmony. As to be seen in the next figure, the debt level is significant lower than for municipalities; a clear function between debt level and named risk factors is not recognizable.

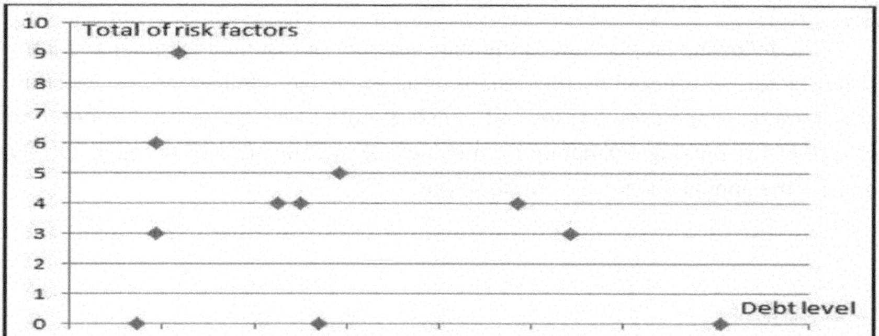

Figure 44: Correlation between debt level in % of annual budget and number of given risk factors for counties
Source: By author, annual status reports of public administrations in North Rhine-Westphalia, Germany

6. 3. 3. Research results regarding correlation regarding debt level and risk factors

A better view offers the analysis of the correlation between debt level in € and the given number of risk factors. In the case of largest annual volume the examined municipality named only one identified risk factor, the debt level was 30% of the annual budget. A contrary conclusion is possible: The smaller the annual budget, the more awareness exists.

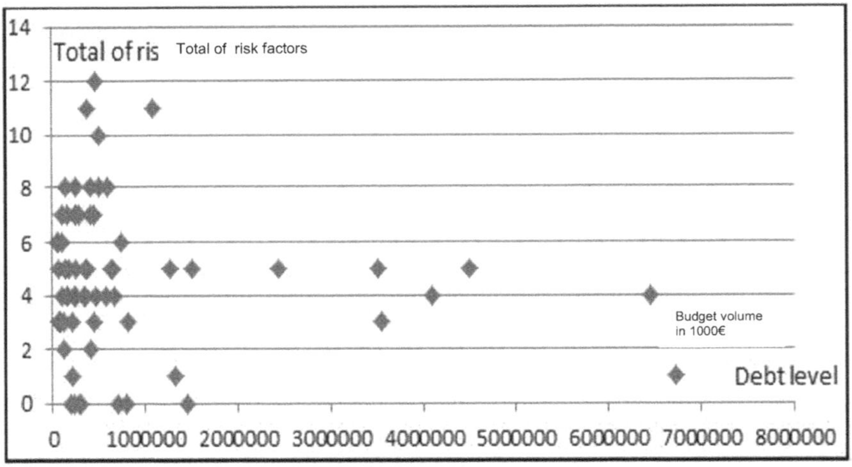

Figure 45: Correlation between annual budget in 1000 € and numbers of given risk factors
Source: By author, annual status reports of public administrations in North Rhine-Westphalia, Germany

The following graph showed the full spectrum of assumed external and internal risk factors, presented by their share of all examined administrations. Most important are developments in taxes and transfers, both based on an input orientation. Because of the missing estimation in monetary terms, the consequences in correlation with the annual budget are not displayed.

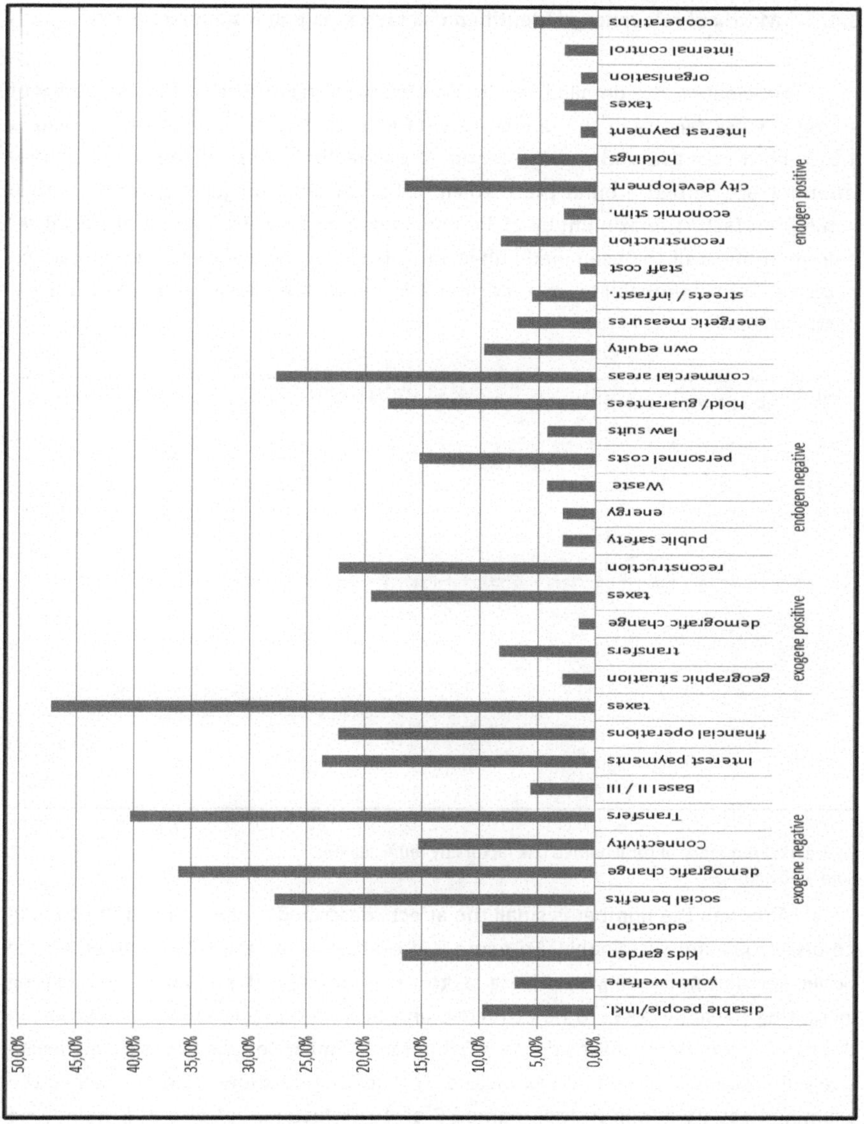

Figure 46: Categories of risk factors and their shares overall
(Source: By author, annual status reports of public administrations in North Rhine-Westphalia, Germany)

6.4. Matrix of relevance of identified risk factors in public administration

Anticipating the detailed results, the following figure shows the frequency of addressed risk factors in the annual reports of municipalities, while the median is 4.625, both negative and positive assumed risk factors. Most of the public administrations are settled around the median, a half of all is ranged between 4 and 6 named risk factors, maximum by 15 by one, minimum 0 by six; without any legal requirement most of the examined public administrations renounce to mention an expected severity, probability, or time frame in which the causes and effect are expected to realize.

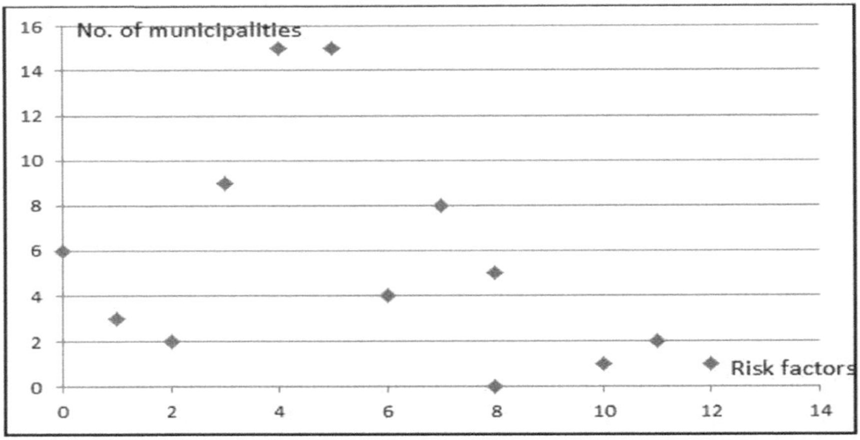

Figure 47: Frequency of total named risk factors by municipalities
Source: by author

Although the number is small the affects described in the annual report could be disastrous and sustainable. To name is the situation on the labor market, where public sector competes with private sector. Few describe the situation anticipating increasing personal costs to be attractive and to fill the gap in human resources. In the case of county administrations the situation is similar sobering considering exclusively the quantity of named risk factors. The next figure shows that the half of the examined county administration named 3 or 4 risk factors, but also 25% named no specific risk factor.

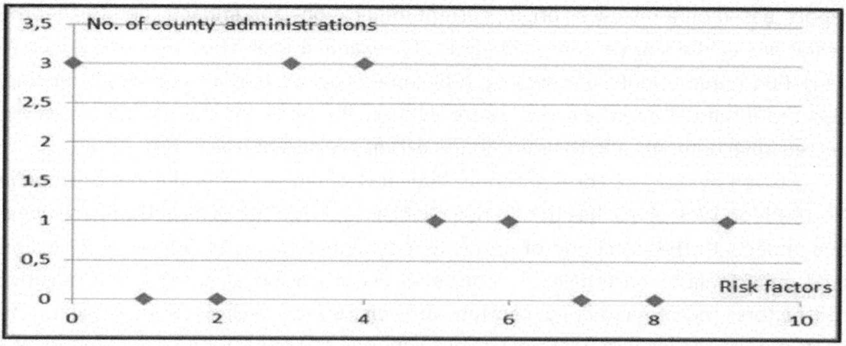

Figure 48: Frequency of total named risk factors by county administrations
Source: by author

There could be two assumptions for explaining the significant difference between the results:

a) County administrations declared themselves that they are not exposed to risk factors, at least in a lower grade and /or lower affects for their duties
b) Public managers, responsible for declaring the risk status in the annual reports, are not aware of risk factors

Because of the different funding situation county administrations are allowed to finance their routine duties and projects by shares of municipalities. By demanding appropriate funding they could be more output-oriented than focusing to input. Both types of public administration started during the period between 2005 and 2009, the experiences with risk and risk factors, their roots and causes are similar.

The complacency in the public sector managers is slowly fading under the impact of reforms most countries across the world are opting for. One has to work hard to justify one's salary and they are all being motivated to be more efficient and raise revenues. Dominating factor for individual and collective risk awareness should be the orientation to the outcome of the products or services.

6.5. Analysis of the risk awareness based on the identified risk factors

6. 5. 1. Reflection of risk awareness as result of the survey

The annual status report is only one fragment and provided results of a vivid risk management system. Legally demanded, the report focused to a description of a status at the end of the year. Only few of the examined status reports give a situation report, based on a review of origin, current implications and impacts, and further expectations of the source. Metric analyses, for example evaluation of monetary compensation requirements, are missing. It becomes obvious that a risk policy is missing, also the intended or grown risk aware culture. Premises for the estimation of expected developments and their maximum extent are absent, too.

Given by the § 48 Local Authority Budget Ordinance, the local administration in North-Rhine-Westphalia has to describe chances and risks. Risks have therefore negative impacts to the execution of duties to local administrations. 50 out of 72 examined municipalities have given a comprehensive overview of positive and negative risk factors; the remaining concentrate in their reports exclusively to negative impacts or miss the legal required risk status. Options and opportunities are limited by a high threshold; sometimes timely and in terms of content: The opposite side, chances, therefore desired events and consequences have to be declared also. But the quality is very diffuse. Few described in a very detailed way the origin of the current financial status; others complain in general the finances and the expectations. Because of the short definition of risk and chances in the ordinance, origins, consequences, outputs, and outcomes for the provision of public services are used in a wide spread way. Some stated the results without a timeframe, others described clear the genesis of the current circumstances and expectations. Remarkably, no one of the examined municipalities tried to convert the risks and chances into monetary values or in consequences for their operations. Doing so can be used as argument to save publicly-owned money. Compelling consequences are described only in a vague way. Periodical audits, reports or benchmarks, that can describe the current risk states, are never presented or mentioned. Compliance with the lean requirements at the end of a fiscal year is focus.

The following model of a financial statement shows the private sector standards, measuring objectives and gives examples for calculated numeric statement, for better comparison, with data from the past or with similar organizations:

Table 29 Strategic objective metrics relating to the statement of financial position
Source: Monahan, G., Enterprise Risk Management, John Wiley & Sons, Inc., Hoboken, p. 2, 2008

Objective:	**Metric:**
Increase assets	Total assets
Reduce liabilities	Total liabilities
Return on assets	Profit/assets
Return on equity	Profit / equity
Asset turnover	Sales/asset
Financial leverage	Assets/equity

Debt to assets ratio	Liabilities/assets
Debt to equity ration	Liabilities/ equity
Current ratio	Current assets/ current liabilities

Obvious, objectives following, services, and products provided by public and private sector are not similar. Measurement of success is different because of the reasons pointed out above, but in general the government's job is to protect the public from undesired events and outcomes after all.[334] So it is remarkable that the reports neglect pure risks, like change in severe weather or weather phenomena like dry outs, heavy rains, or thunderstorms. There are no final empirical findings that a climate change is ongoing in Europe, but the intensity is increasing, the intervals decreasing. Preventive measures by rules and regulations, to ensure the public safety, based on models of the last century; but to enhance and to act as an guarantor of public safety, as one segment of public welfare, those consequences have to be kept in forecasts for measures and costs. Beneath the direct effects to the public, indirect threats are also ignored: No one of the examined public administrations has argued that the growing dependence to IT-based services and the internet creates a holistic threat: IT-Systems could be hijacked or disturbed. As one result the basic provision of fresh water, electricity and energy could be stopped sharply. In February 2016 a hospital in the near of capital of North Rhine Westphalia, Düsseldorf, had to stop all surgeries for few days, because the computer system was infected, radiographs or patient charts were not available.

Bodemann (2012) argues that one key for efficiency lays in the combination of technology, processes and security. Leaving the focus to maximize the utility of information-technology public administration will be decoupled from progress.[335] The consequences are not scientific examined, rather than a plan for establishing of minimizing the consequences established. Results of the internal analyses of past developments, current and anticipated events, and the consequences are predominant from a financial standpoint. Missing are holistic notions, analyzing public risk administration in legal, social, contractual, and financial environment. Applied risk management systems or methods for evaluation of risk factors are only sporadically appointed,[336] partly because of lack of resources: The smaller the public administration,

[334] Moss, D., *When all else fails – Government as the ultimate risk manager*, Harvard University Press, Cambridge, 2002

[335] Bodemann, M., *Technologie und Vernetzung – Integration von Verfahren in kommunale good-practice IT-Strukturen* in: Hilger, D./ Schauer, R. / Thom, N., "Public Management im Paradigmenwechsel", Trauner, Linz, 2012, pp. 785-802

[336] Previously such tasks were the responsibility of the CFOs/treasurers in consultation with the board of directors in the private sector or heads of department, councilors and mayor in the public sector.

the lower the level of risk awareness and integration into organizational structure. The change from the traditional model of input-orientation to an outcome-governance supports the integration of risk management. It is to be expected that if executives of individual departments are more and more accountable for their output and, derivatively, for the outcome too, efficiency in public services will increase.

Risk management has to keep in mind that factors like liquidity risks, market risks or operational risks that can affect the annual budget - positively when some uncertain revenues are realized, negatively in case of additional cost, for example through compensation payments or higher insurances rates. It can be argued that combination of risk management with the other known principles or to calculate them by the expected return and comparison with certain returns[337] will work; at least all of them try to implement instruments to monitor, control and to intervene in the case of an undesired development. For the managers at operational level, the model of NPM includes decentralized accountability of resources. The risk-bearer or risk-owner will have to be guided by objectives as laid down by the political executive. He is responsible for the risk management, organizational and technical, including the sector-uncertainties, linked with chances and threats for execution of duties. Also formal activities in the case of foreseeable variances from the given path have to be determined and monitored. Such actions at departmental levels can help the management at board level to cope with risk factors for the company/ organization as a whole. When drawing up a risk inventory, the correlation of uncertainties ahead, and possible consequences have to be worked out. Directly linked uncertainty factors as collateral uncertainties are to be identified and to be discussed with other departmental executives to get a larger view.

The following graphic should illustrate the relationship between the cause, the realized negative effect, and the other uncertainties, which are further linked to other events:[338]

[337] Arrow, K. & Lind, R., *Uncertainty and the Evaluation of Public Investment Decisions*, American Economic Review, June 1970 (60), p. 367

[338] Result of analysis of political work; author was member of the county parliament of the district of Höxter from 1999 – 2009; also: Rudzio, W., *Das politische System der Bundesrepublik Deutschland*, Leske+Budrich, Opladen, 1996

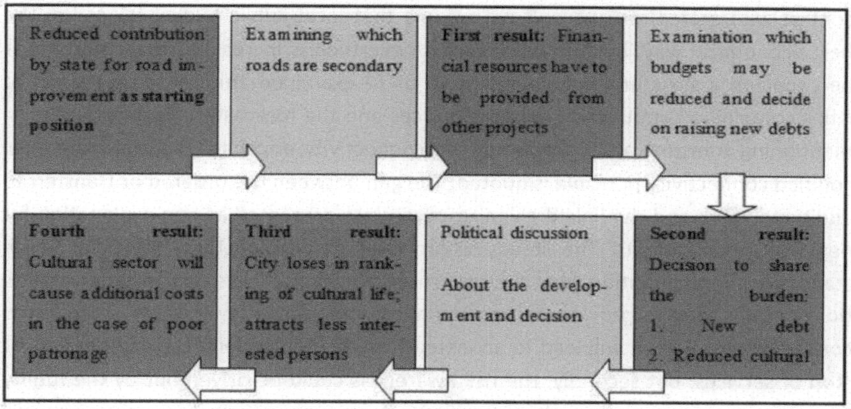

Figure 49: Chain of negative reaction in the case of undesired results
Source: by author

Knowledge of the degree of uncertainties as their possible impact on the functioning of the organization is a vital part of risk management. More than the possible positive effects in focus are potential negative values of impact and the flexibility to act as a public organization, considering precisely defined hierarchical information and activity ways as another prerequisite to success.

6. 5. 2. Integration of risk factors in status reports in public administration

For a successful application with effective outputs providing services to enhance welfare risk awareness has to be established all over the organization. Some will argue that the application of the Weberian Bureaucratic Model prevents the organization on the one hand to act as an entrepreneur; on the other hand personal involvement in results is intentionally excluded. The elements of absence of personal responsibility in the case of correct execution of rules and regulations, hierarchical structures and workflows, and no direct participation to success and failure are presented as reasons for the peculiar organization and processes in the public sector.[339]

Recognizing these important cultural and organizational distinctions leads to another important perspective: The public administration in Germany was established as an executive organ for governmental programs at the different levels. Local politics, given by the local and decentralized parliament and governmental policies, given by the federal and state government, are in conflict with local demands and in

339 Weber, M., *Wirtschaft und Gesellschaft*, Zweitausendeins, Frankfurt, org. 1922, reprint 2008

conflict with scarce resources. If we assume that local public budget is used in the best economical way, but the debt level is nevertheless increasing, than there must be expected a structural imbalance. In 40 of 72 examined annual status reports of cities complained about the limited resources and the forecast of financial budgets, mentioning transfers and violation of the connectivity principle. Especially the legal codified connectivity principle is quoted: The gap between the ordered or transferred additional tasks and the linked given resources are presented as one explanation for negative developments. The steady violation of that connectivity principle, which stands for the assumption, that the governmental level, that is responsible for additional duties, has to provide an appropriate compensation, will lead to undesired consequences. First, it will lead to an increase of the debt level, delays of projects or stop of services; but secondly, the risk awareness could be driven out by the futility trap. That means that it doesn't matter how effective and efficient any institution will execute her duties, the negative development is determined because of the imbalance of additional costs and additional compensation. The trap based on the estimation that, although using every measure to stay in budget and increase efficiency, additional duties and increasing costs, the public administration has to cope with additional debts. Beneath the NPM wave the focus is directed to change: Reforming the organizations from governmental level to local administration as one instrument to ensure the sustainable provision of public services and products. For Fernandez and Rainey (2006) most important is to communicate the need for change, analogue managerial leaders have to convince the individuals of the need for risk awareness and a compelling model. If one follows the results from Kers de Vries and Balazs (1999) that it is most successful, if argued by the expectation of relief from stress or discomfort.[340] But Fernandez and Rainey put forward another factor for successful organizational change: They see the top-management support and commitments as critical cornerstones for a change.[341]

Summarizing the results of the questionnaire and the researches considering developments for and in public administration leads to the conclusion that an adoption of private sector practices can lead to an increase and future-oriented management. Cultural roots of the organizations and the privilege of politics have to be integrated to fulfill legal requirements and democratic fundamentals.

---

[340] Kers de Vries, M. & Balasz, K., *Transforming the mind-set of organization*, Administration & Society, Vol.30 No. 6, pp. 640 – 675, 1999, cited by Fernandez, S. & Rainey, H., *Managing Successful Organizational Change in The Public Sector*, Public Administration Review, March April, p. 169, 2006

[341] Fernandez, S. & Rainey, H., *Managing successful organizational change in the public sector*, Public Administration Review, March April 2006, pp. 168 – 176, 2006

7. Proposed framework for risk management practices in public sector to increase public value in Germany

7.1. General context of the research

Measurements for saving money will find their limit: Cost-benefit-analysis could lead to another direction, but without changes in the legal environment and in the duty to provide essential duties for people and for enterprises cost-effectiveness is not to realize. Arrow and Lind (1970) suggest that governmental agencies should ignore uncertainty and behave as if they act or react indifferent to threats or chances.[342] They argue that the government is able to pool and compensate risks. The reachable extend is thereby greater than private investors are able to offer.

Other researchers recognize in public risk management an effective tool for better steering on operational level and as support strategic decisions. Beneath the political strings from the local to federal level, aggregation of identified and estimated risks, their origins and expected consequences. In the international comparison Germany lacks clear and present requirements of integrating, maintaining and using of risk management systems. Based on the subsidiary system, selection of tools to be used is delegated to local level; the legal framework is lean and not specifying.

The following thoughts explain the general framework for decisions with variable output and outcome. Risk management acts thereby as catalyst in optimizing the processes and contributing to sustainable decisions and almost determined effective use of resources.

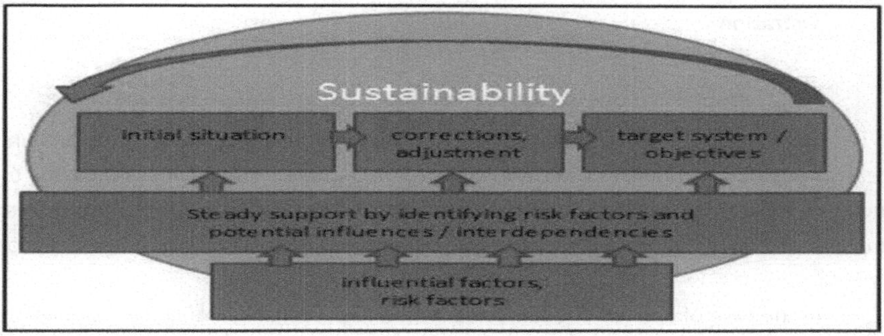

Figure 50: Principle of operations of risk management in context of sustainability
Source: by author

---

342 Arrow, K. & Lind, R., *Uncertainty and the Evaluation of Public Investment Decisions*, American Economic Review, June 1970 (60), pp. 364 - 378

M. Bodemann, *Management in Public Administration*,
Sustainable Management, Wertschöpfung und Effizienz,
https://doi.org/10.1007/978-3-658-22687-9_8

7.2. Objectives and research methodology

Limited guidelines for risk management are available for each risk management concept or system, but also the scope of handling is different: From a holistic view, the spectrum ranges from influence internal and external factors to reduce the threat to present not valid data in yearly reports Considering the aim of public administration to increase public value, risk management has to process other data than business oriented risk management, focussing on monetary values. Assumed as key indicator for success of public administration operations is public value. But public value is an abstract term and can be interpreted and defined in different ways. Combining the results and recognizing the approaches to public value, deviations from a certain status can support to measure influence and outcomes of decisions. Further it indicates the overall performance of a local administration. The following thoughts combine the results and experiences from private sector and the ongoing discussion on public value as substitute to shareholder value. Therefore is risk defined by an almost objective correlation of uncertainty based on historical data and the aggregation of subjective estimations of deviation of the current state of the public value. In other branches, this kind of analysis for strategic and operational meaning are common and legal demanded since years due to the demand by legal frameworks and pressure by the market.

7.3. Development of a model of integrated risk management for public administration

7.3.1. Proposed model as support for public administration decision-maker

For an objective provisioning of all facts all possible actions have to be known, descripted and identified. Further they have to be feasible; rational in the meaning of increase welfare in best legal and economic application under given circumstances, and the probability of possible alternative developments have to be known for processing.

In the case of applied direct involvement and participation of citizen, at least at the beginning stages of the decision-process, following conditions have to be considered and prepared about the information-gap and the outputs and outcomes to be estimated by each citizen for himself.

- information have reached the citizen
- information have to be paid attention to by the citizen
- information have to be understood by the citizen

- information have to be trusted by the citizen
- information have to be complete and valid
- information have to be equal to all citizen
- information contain transfers costs and opportunity costs as alternatives
- information have to show variables of decisions
- estimations have to reach the collecting public administration
- estimations have to be processed in an equal and neutral way
- processed estimations have to be prepared for further discussion and decision
- it must be proven and steadily confirmed that collecting the estimation has influence to the political and administration decision-process

Further the individual estimation of measures and the combined opportunity costs, the overlapping areas, considering the outcomes, of different, but linked measures and personal preferences. At least, how a person will value consumption or the ability to consume in one state compared to a different one, depends on the known or estimated probability, that the expected state will occur. For a numeric value the individual utility from an objective point of view and the grade of affection of this utility has to be combined, similar to the notion of calculating risk. Challenging for mathematical processing will be to get all valid personal estimation in a certain time and with comparable scales. That leads to a snapshot of one person, for a snapshot a benchmark to a former state, all values have to be aggregated.

For better support in a decision-situation numeral indicators can be applied to show a net result estimating an actual situation by expectation values. Individuals are affected by decisions in a different way and grade as pointed out above. Public value calculation thought can be implemented in data-based model for processing and proposing trends and estimations. The scalable values and a representative selection of citizens are most challenging and hence be based on additional sociological researches.

The following steps show a possible calculation considering alternatives and different grade of utility and opportunity costs.

(1) U_t = utility of realized target status

(2) O_c = combined utility of all not realized matters in the favor of U_t

(3) P = preferences for each measure

(4) G_p = grade of passive affection

(5) G_a = grade of active affection

(6) p = probability of realization of U_t

(7) T = Time of realisation / time of use of provided services or products

(8) $\wedge$ U(T) = f($U_t(T)$, p(T), (1-p)$O_c(T)$, P(T), $G_p(T)$, $G_a(T)$)[343]

This formula describes the assumed change of utility as substitute for welfare at the certain time T for one decision to make. As results positive or negative values and deviations are possible. In the case of no change, a decision leaves this citizen equal to the current state. All of the variables are subject to change during the observed or forecast period. To evaluate the expected change of utility for one affected person the following formula could be used:

$$(9) \quad f(U(n)) = \sum_{n=1}^{N} (\mathrm{U(n)}x\, p(n), Ga(n), Gp(n), ((Ocn)(1 - p(n)))$$

Here N are all possible decisions to be made or states to become realised.

Using time as reference the following formula can be used for calculating the changing risk status for all individual at the situation or time t:

$$(10) \quad U_{t\,(all)} = \sum (U_{t(n)})$$

The result means the summary of all subjective utilities under consideration of dependencies of each other. Depiction of strings and dependencies of utilities and risk factors remains a challenging task, some computer programs anticipate such utility functions by simulations.

Adding changing preferences, grades of affection and a decrease of increase of utility of alternatives the processing of all data leads to a notion of development of welfare. In the case of increased utility it can be assumed that while realising the expected status in the future the individual and subjective welfare increases and vice versa. For a notion of the status under consideration of all affected members of the community, all individual estimations have to be processed to get a holistic view.

$$(11) \quad \wedge\, Ut\,(all) = \sum (Ut1, Ut2, \ldots, Ut(N))$$

N in this case stands for all directly or indirectly affected and addressed persons / citizens.

Summarizing all personal estimations will produce a notion of the state of welfare on an objective basement, however processing subjective meanings of expected results under realization of status triggered by current decisions to be made. While

[343] Adapted and extended formula from: Damodaran, A., *Strategic risk taking*, Wharton School Publishing, UpperSaddle River, p. 19, 2008

preferences and grades of affections typically remain individual values, the accuracy of probability could be increased by applying the reference class model, mentioned above.

The given formula substitutes the expected processing of public interest by politicians and demonstrates the high complexity and the steady change in the variables, but also in the results, expressed by increase or decrease of assumed utility.

Premise for processing the data to get useful results the outcome of a decision, is that U has to be determined by several key indicators; these standardised indicators and composite variable have to be used in the same way with the same scale and range to compute the data. Outcomes to an individual and to a group to individuals have to be measured by the same benchmark for the initial status. Especially absorption and derived utility could have a wide spectrum.

Further researches are necessary to determine the scale, giving benchmarks, the measuring points, selection of subjects and the processing of data. For the first approach the value of public value has to be assumed as zero to show the deviation in desired or undesired direction over time. Individual expressed expectations, processed by algorithms and the results as change in the status of public value have to be validated over time and the model enhanced. In addition, more objective sensors for perception and historic data lead to more neutral input than personal estimations.

7.3.2. Combination of public value and probability over time

Collecting and processing of all advertised data can be the first step. Creating a current status of public value supports mediation of different and often concurrent interests, based on the researches to be spent. Limited by thresholds of strategic risks awareness, objectives and resources for realization show possible developments

Risk assessment by the model given above contributes by analysing and presenting trends at a certain time. The selected persons estimate their expected benefits from the decision to be made, weighing up opportunity costs and present their estimation in the case of realization. Using additional information, i.e. probabilities of overstretching time frame or planned finances, will replenish the model and create a more ambitious model. Currently pluralistic decisions, based on referendums or politically mediated public interests, complicate distinction and selection of public priorities.

Individual and collectively interests and strategic targets in combination with estimation of utility of public products and services lead to a wide spectrum of estimated future status and grade of exploitable utility.[344]

The following figure shows the topology of one risk, combining the aggregated estimation of deviation from current state of public value and a probability of the realization. Both sides around the starting conditions are possible. By using the third dimension time, public decision makers get a notion of the volatile development of the estimated situation concerning public value. This topology will change during the running time of observation, based on time frame of a project or timeframe for political discussion. Also in this model risk awareness and publicly discussed risks-thresholds have to be included and respected. Financial and reputational outcomes, based on a long term analyses, are further aspects using this model.

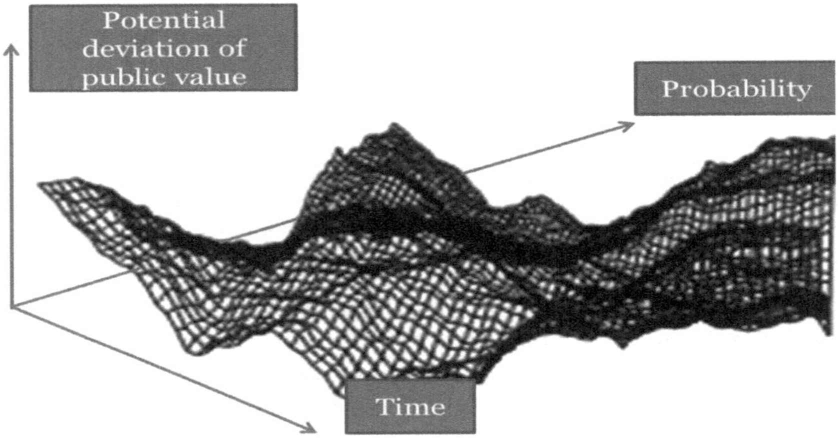

Figure 51: Risk topology for an isolated view to an identified risk, combining gains and threats for public value
Source: by author

As discussed above efficiency in the meaning as relationship between monetary input and monetary output is not the direct focus of this model. Using public value will bring a gradual shift from public administration as closed and processed oriented organization to a more customer oriented organization rather than to generate monetary effects in short time. Customer or citizens interests and choice will shift over time, the graph will change also. Processes and objectives, behind a decision to

[344] Blumenthal, cited in: Denhardt, R. & Denhardt, J., *Public administration: An action orientation*, Thomson Wadworth, Belmont, p. 6, 2009

be made, have to be monitored and adjusted over the planned implementation timeframe. Each delay or increase of costs will have direct influence to the estimation of expected public value. As to see it enlightens possible developments and shows the possible gaps between maximum loss and prepared compensations within the limits of public law.

For the banking sector such models exist to compare the current status and the expected developments for the framework an organization is working in and working with. By collecting and processing more data, for example from stock exchanges or from information traffic, the model will present more valid data. As next steps author will contact and established a contact to other researches in this specific field for exchange of thoughts and to discuss the possibility to adopt the model for the banking sector for public administration under consideration to substitute economic value by public value.

For compensation or be better prepared knowledge about the developments are necessary, especially in a situation without certainty and combined with an uncharted area of action and responsibility. Precautionary measures and building up reserves are also necessary to fulfill the aim of risk management. The next step has to be to re-convert Public Value at Risk in monetary values to establish a system of compensation, for example for sustainable ecologic compensation.

7.3.3. Framework for decisions and influence to public value

In the German constitution and the local municipal codes of each German state increase of welfare and economic and efficient spending of public funds are fundamental tasks. As to see in Figure 52 provisioning of sustainability, ecology and efficiency are codified in the constitution and the local municipality codes in Germany. Management and tools for management aim to these fields of action, executing mandatory tasks without any maneuvering room or voluntarily projects based on a local initiative to attract businesses or increase public value to residents. Other priorities can the set by politics and public administration. Combining them and to analyse the relationship between all areas need a parametrization. For better understanding an Enterprise Risk management (ERM) replenishes the narrowly focussed risk management considering only single programs, processes or projects. Figure 52 shows broadly and abstract fields of action across and through the organization.

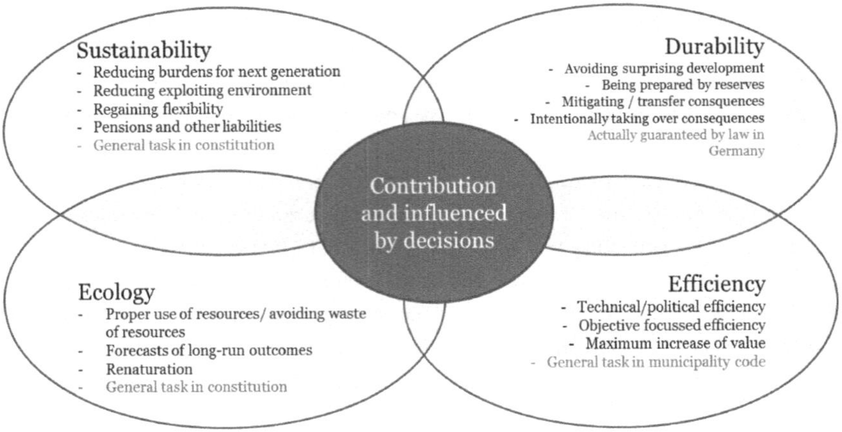

Figure 52: Fields of responsibility of organizations embedded in legal framework for public administration
Source: by author

Main objective to increase value by using risk management has to consider this framework; in other developed countries similar codified targets of execution of politics by public administration can be found. By establishing the fundamental premises for risk, personal involvement is named. The durability of a private sector organization is for the stakeholder one rational objective, for public administration it is guaranteed by constitution. Efficiency can be measured in public value invested and gained, sustainability can be measured in public value gained and, in the not desired way, lost by decisions under not given certainty; ecology can be measured in public value by threatening ecologic reservoirs or variety in species. Especially developing countries ignore consequences for wildlife and especially the provision of drinking water. Public value has to consider these aspects on the long run to, reference class model can support the validity and transparency of the consequences, without restricting the privilege of politics.

7.3.4. Organizational framework for application of integrated risk management in public administration

Embedding of risk management in processes and structure is basement for effective use of risk management. Second part is the application of a management tool, what is able to emulate the internal structure and processes, historic of statistical data and current references for analysis and identification of opportunities, threats and potential gains. The structured process as advocated by ISO 31000 is similar to all risk management system, each with an individual scope of management and objectives, but all in common the aim to anticipate and evaluate potential developments to be prepared for or to use countermeasures.

Combining the general hierarchical structure of municipalities with the organizational adoptions from the already applied risk management systems in the private sector leads to following graphical structure:

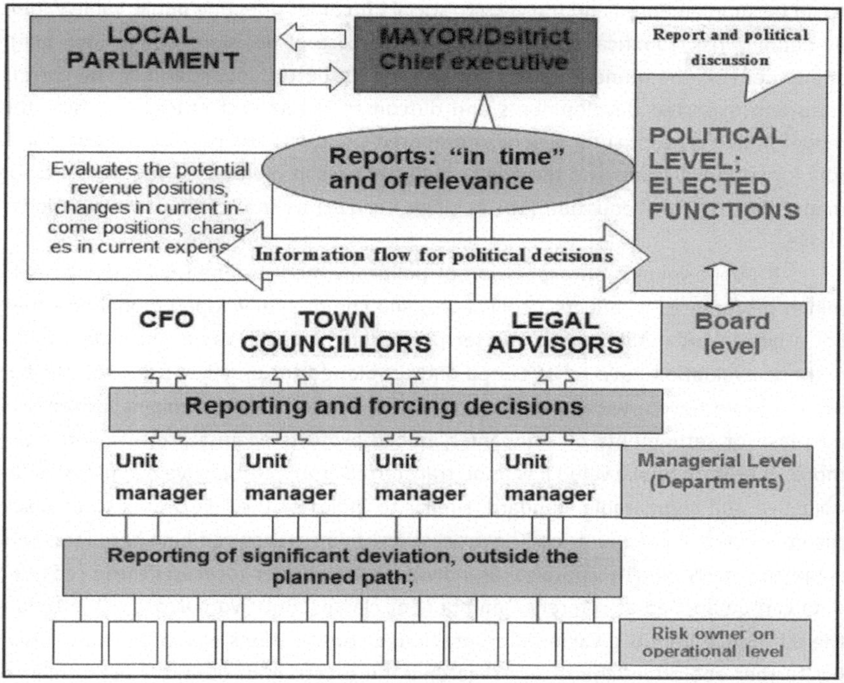

Figure 53: Model for organization structure for small - and mid-sized municipalities (model without added risk manager)

Source: by author

The very diffuse use and content of the legally demanded risk reports lead to the necessity for standardized information to identify, to describe and evaluate risk factors.

Adam Smith characterized the economic value as the expressed utility of a particular object and combined with the power to purchasing other goods with the possession of the object. In result economic value is the exchange value of goods and services, usually based on society sanctioned indices; in most societies this is monetary value, other currencies are possible. For the private sector this statement is proven to be valid. Public value is to be handled different. Public goods and services are different; they wouldn't be produced by all consumers. The production is done almost under the state of a monopoly. Citizens or inhabitants wouldn't be willing to pay taxes and fees in the current volume as their personal dues.

Developing a quasi-mathematical formula converts different variables in net values which could be used as a decision evaluation indicator. Economic evaluation could be supplemented and the view to social outcomes affecting public value widen. By defining risk, ramification and results in the case of decisions under uncertainty and under risk, the numeric values can be used for better understanding the current state and expected developments and outcomes in terms of efficiency. Using this model should prevent surprising or unprepared situations and provide a set of indicators for initial decisions and the need of adjustments in the case of decisions already made, shown in the equation (10) as single- or (11) as sum-estimations mentioned above.

If public value is an expression of politically mediated and collectively determined preferences it reflects a collectively and common developed model of values. For a better understanding and better processing of public value, the model and a numeric evaluation have to be tested and developed for practical use. Indicators to be processed have a wide spectrum, for example number of complains, increase or decrease of settlements of companies, public protests against projects and many more. Therefore public value has to be transferred from a subjective estimation to an objective and comparable standard, similar to indicator the OECD uses to compare the developments of countries. The processing of data has to combine hard facts with subjective made quality appraisal of individuals. For better forecasts these recorded data can be applied as reference numbers or classes. But two persons will estimate the difference in public value different, cloned constellations would be coincidence. For further operations the results regarding the spectrum of potential risks, their influence to the citizens and a numeric value for comparative studies have to be combined in an operational basement for producing, collecting and processing the estimations of public value. The more decisions and the later estimated change in public value processed, the more precise the guidelines and forecasts. With a wide-spread data base for decisions under non-certainty will increase efficiency and effectiveness of local public administrations.

For a concrete application indicators for utility, including grade of affection, duration of affection and conversion the withdrawn utility of alternatives have to be created and tested to validate the applicability of the formula.

Summarizing the presented hindrances to apply private sectors tools unchanged in public sector and the remaining differences between both and the empirical results leads to the necessity to create a own risk management system; especially the aim and objectives of public sector, at least to enhance welfare to the people, distinct both sectors.

To establish this system privilege of politics and the democratic structures have to be integrated. Automatically generated processes and activities have to be decided by the politicians as bundles; short time for decisions, opportunities and flexible response to developments can be realized. That confirms the necessity of comprehensive models of future states, indicators and selections of alternatives which are binding in a certain state.

By using an enterprise- or organization-wide risk management with the minimum requirements supports benchmarks and compliance checks. To measure efficiency in general and in risk management the objective of enhancing public value has to be applied. Expectations and grade of desired and not desired deviations will contribute to best practice evaluation of alternative and the anticipation of final states. Steady maintaining, for example by adopting reference models, and balance between political mediated targets and representative public interests can help to increase efficiency of use to resources to gain freedom to act on local level to fulfill the constitutional task: To improve welfare.

Conclusion

In the current economic context the effectiveness and efficiency in public sector is often regarded as not competitive to private sector organizations. Looking at the debt level in European countries of the public sector, from governmental to local level, it can be argued that most of them have lost their ability to improve and maintain value to the people, the citizens, at their own accountability. In addition, projects in public sector appear not to be steered and often multi-times more expensive than expected with less effects to the people than predicted. The difference lies in the different objectives of both sectors and the way these objectives are reached and which influential factors play a role. Since 40 years scientists and practioners develop tools, reform the public sector, and reach a higher level of the relation between increased level of value and used resources. On the other side kind, complexity, and bandwidth of provided services and products have been increased, based on societal and political notions of public sector organizations; borrowings and adoptions from the private sector can be helpful and successful to increase competitiveness, efficiency, and effectiveness. Debt level of public sector all around the globe increases urgency and necessity, deviations from predicted and desired path will contain the legal functions and the constitutional task to increase welfare. Increase is therefore not only measured in direct outcomes to a citizen but more the present and future outcome to the society, based on durability of the services and products and sustainability of decisions.

Best practices from private sector are adopted, some pay off. The objective to increase public value by increase welfare to the people, but also make sustainable decisions to stabilize the economic and ecologic situations and a robust development, is common and mandatory task of politicians and administration in developed countries. Forecasts of future states and the outcomes to the public can be supported by risk management; culture towards risk is one of the biggest drivers of success or failure. In Australia, New Zealand, Canada and UK, risk management is in focus, concrete legal demands established.

Triggered by the current situation of public sector and focussed to German local public administration following results are presented to step forward to an appropriate use of private sector tools to increase welfare to the people. They will answer the question can risk management be applied effective in public sector organizations and what are the hindrances for conversion the private sector model. As result these key scientific research areas are addressed in the thesis paper

M. Bodemann, *Management in Public Administration*,
Sustainable Management, Wertschöpfung und Effizienz,
https://doi.org/10.1007/978-3-658-22687-9_9

- Definition and meaning of efficiency and effectiveness in the context of local public administration and the applicability in public sector
- Enclosing of purposes of private sector and public sector organizations and enterprises
- Adoption of management tools for public administration and the boundaries for application
- Analysing and interpretation of current studies regarding the introduction of New Public Management tools in general, and the New Steering Model in Germany in particular
- Measurement of success for public administration, considering public and individual welfare
- Risk awareness and risk culture in public administration, based on empirical study of annual status reports
- Avoiding of and/or preparing undesired developments and their effects to public value as substitute to economic value in private sector

In part I, the current state of knowledge is analysed and the basement elaborated; the research will confirm and improve the basement.

Chapter 1 gives an overview of definitions public sector is based on and the combined range of objectives public sector is responsible for. The bandwidth of public duties varies, depending on the current state of reforms, for example the grade of privatization or the intended contracting of the state of institution. The OECD named four branches the public sector in general is working in: health care, justice, education and taxes. In comparison, private sector seeks to provide attractive products to customers who value the use or the consumption of the goods or services. One difference between both sectors, elaborated by different researches and manifested in the legal framework, is the main objective: for private sector, working market-oriented, profitability is the basement for survival and growth; for budget-oriented public sector, from governmental to local level, the focus is on implementation of objectives and the realization by services to the citizenry.

Several approaches describe differences and similarities between both sectors. Based on a combination of bureaucracy, process-orientation and separation, the execution of political programs left minor space to act. Especially influential politics play an important role in notion of welfare and the provisioning of appropriate services. Stake- and shareholders can be considered as very similar, although internal and external frameworks differ in nuances: Public interest and scrutiny are more intense in public sector than in private sector and increased in the last years; partly because of citizens self-consciousness, resources-pressure and the public discussion, what duties are constitutional and have to be executed by public sector; further based on the ambivalent function of the citizen as person: He is on the one hand sponsor of the public administration, but also customer and consumer of public goods.

Another important difference between both sectors is the input- or budget-orientation: The provisioning of products and services was based on the estimated input from revenues. By application of tools of the NPM this attitude will be changed to a more output- and outcome-orientation, similar to the private sector that focus to satisfy needs and demands. Likewise, measurement of efficiency and effectiveness is discussed, several models and ideas developed and arguments placed, that both sectors remain different and need a special kind of treatment. Key performance indicators are hard to install; based on the culture of public sector. Crucial points are the provision of public goods and organizational and procedural structure. Products and services are discussed on political level, politicians are regarded as representatives for public interests; public administration acts therefore as executive for political programs which are increasingly not supported by appropriate financing. One additional effect is an increasing debt level. Performance measurement as indicator for efficiency and effectiveness is currently rediscovered: Without comparable and transparent indicators improvements are hard to testify and incentives ineffective. Delegation of responsibility, for example by the Government Performance and Results Act in the US, lean organization and results from surveys show the trend to reform the processes and to demand more taken responsibility by public managers. Responsible and supervising actors can contribute to a more effective use of provided resources in public sector. Another break shoe is the often monopolistic conditions under which the public organizations operate. Without pressure by competition, at least published benchmarks on common standards, but also by participation in success, improvements are difficult to realize. Without competition and incentives managers in both sectors become unmotivated.

Success can be measured by indicators, which has to be declared. The degree of fulfillment of objectives has to be under steady surveillance. Interdependencies of pursuit objectives, inputs, the grade of efficiency and the consequences for the socio-economic situation will lead to renewed needs and derived political objectives. In private sector already leading function, corporate social responsibility offers a new benchmark and orientation for public sector: Welfare as abstract target of all public sector effort can serve as aiming point. Social responsibility is therefore an overarching principle for public sector without any specific need to be defined. It remains the question of functional or personal responsibility and the binding consequences. Guaranteed incomes, highly secured careers and political influential spheres minimize the grade and acceptance of responsibility, but left the legal social alignment. Benchmarks, regarded catalyst for improving operations, compare performance

measures of one's own public organization to others or to agreed standards. Standards for comparison are also hard to find.
The utility of public sector operations is in addition often in doubt, because of the diffuse absorption of an individual. Public value is regarded and discussed as a more concrete and appropriate measurement point to describe and proof advances and regresses. Beneath monetary values, public value as abstract number can be applied as result a product of the collective use of capital, employees, know-how and other provided resources. The different absorption of public goods and services, temporary interests, and only fragmented utility, complicates the forecasts and later measurement of outcomes to the citizen. The final collecting and processing of the different estimations of potential developments is the most challenging step toward a peculiar risk identification and estimation in an adopted risk management system for public administration. The later empirical part shows that qualitative descriptions of risks are currently common, quantitative values are on negligible level.

Chapter 2 presents the current status of suggested application of private sector tools in public management, predominately triggered by publishing the New Public Management tool box. It further introduces thoughts and ideas from different views from scholars and theorists to prove the current situation of public administration concerning efficiency and economic use of resources. The reforms are characterised by introduction of several management practices, including market analysis and budgeting techniques. Much depends on the expectations of the various parties concerned; the effects to the people can be very different. All in common is the customer orientation, executed either on political but also on administrative level. Based on premises, including the acceptance that state and public administrations are necessary, competition lead to more efficiency and effectiveness, and that politics and administration are capable or learning. Western democracies selected different tools and manifestations of introduction a new kind of public administration. Initial points for considerations are the financial problems and the increase of public pressure to rethink organization and processes, and focus of public administration. Main objectives of NPM are slowing down or better reversing government growth in favor to private sector, but stabilizing public welfare, automation, especially in the IT, and the distribution of public goods and services. NPM stressed the rejection of input orientation to an output orientation and further an outcome orientation in the pursuit of efficient use of resources. Delegation of authority combined with accountability is one organizational adjustment to support the efforts.

But the results are evaluated different: Scholars and researchers complain that the intended goals are missed, in some areas, like delegation of authority and accountability, reverse tendencies occurred. Critical results from Australia and New

Zealand see in NPM a retreat of the traditional welfare state, based in the increase of privatization and the effects for citizens, analogue to the UK experiences in the late 80ies of the last century. Measurement of implemented NPM elements in Germany 2008, after five years of active application are also sobering: Adjustments in the department structures are realized in almost the half of the examined public administrations, but decentralization used only one out of ten. It is argued that the results of the reforms depend on the legal and political constraints which slow down the discussion and the processes. Life-longs careers, only limited use of incentives are counterproductive in the sense of performance gains. Others argue that intrinsic motivation is undermined by applying an incentive system and therefore not intended by the historical and cultural background. On the other hand, proponents of the tools of NPM state that the role and influence of citizens is strengthened. Summarizing the distinctions made by different researches, some arguments remain, including strategic goals, financial goals and budget priorities. On an abstract point of view both sectors serve the goal of customer satisfaction, but each in his peculiar environment. Using a circuit to describe the interdependencies the socio-economic situations is the starting point. Derived from the situation needs are addressed to politicians or the administrations, needs are converted in concrete objectives and resources are provided.

Despite the inhomogeneous setting of public administration, benchmarks within the organizational framework and with similar administrations are regarded as useful tool to determine the current status and to evaluate the progress for further adjustments. One result is in common all of the researches: They regarded the quantification and comparison of public sector within and with the private sector as very difficult. The ratio between input and output tends to be insufficient; outcomes to the citizens are the objectives. While in private sector the productivity can be measured in each routine process, the value of a product or service can be expressed by monetary values. Expected personal utility, based on the specification of the product, is another aspect of presenting a product. In public sector services are provided partly without a direct pricing or payment, interest and individual utility are hard to set in relation to a price to pay. Willingness to pay is an approach to set price for services and products.

The findings show that efficiency could be measured in the conversion process, starting with the output and leading to outcome; the outcome itself is hard to measure because of the individual grade of affection and utility; a complex system of perception points to assess the individual and collective outcomes is necessary to get a valid value, currently it is substituted by representatives in the political opinion-forming process. This process is complicated by ever changing political and social environment and diffuse interests.

Measurement of public sector performance is regarded as instrument to cope with the increased public pressure, to justify applied resources and withdraw of personal consumption and utilization of taxes. The dominant objective of increasing welfare is already in focus. It remains the discussion about indicators of welfare; several terms and definitions are used, the OECD has published numerous indicators. Usually measurement can be done on a macroeconomic level, for example results of the education researches in the EU, measured as ration between dollars spent for education and PISA scores, economic stability, or the development of national average income. On microeconomic level various benchmarks are identified: Severity of floods and the affected estates or persons, number of schools, average time to place of action by an ambulance. Other researchers suggest a data collection to build up references as orientation for public administration projects to reduce the area of potential outputs and outcomes to the people. All in common is the basic result that both sectors are in a blurring process, but peculiarities remain. Cultural hindrances remain to develop and emplace a multidimensional system to measure and evaluate public organizations performance, for transparency and comparability, at least to justify spending public funds for.

Chapter 3 shows the development and different application of risk management, and the several components. Risk management for the private sector is not a novel idea. Actually it is embedded into several international and national laws and regulations. But the comprehensive experience of the last half decade shows that integrated instruments, by themselves, are inadequate to meet future challenges and need to be improved, to prevent further crises and not steerable impacts to the national, European and global economy.

Over mathematical consideration several hundred years ago risk management is now integral part of management tools in private sector. Basement for calculation and combined conclusions about development and various final states are the two components of expected gain or loss and a probability of future states; based on calculations, on references or on instinctive forecasts. Treatises to risk elaborate several aspects about the term risk and the processing and managing of data. By analysis of the main concepts of the model of risk I worked out that three stages determine the initial situation for risk management: Certainty, as proxy for well-known developments with one initial stage and only one final stage; risk, as proxy for one initial stage combined with at least two or more expected end stages and the corresponding gains or losses, and probability; at least uncertainty, either with known future alternatives, or probability and ignorance of a link of both. Missing probability or expected gains or losses lead automatically to a status of uncertainty. The conversion of consequences from quantitative to qualitative statements challenges the modellers; numerous influence factors, each combined with a probability, stand for a wide spectrum of possible outcomes in the case of a decision made under not-certainty. Although public sector is regarded as determined organization, internal and external influence factors play an important role. Public administrations act thereby as catalyst.

Next step was to create a notion of risk, from the identification to desired or not desired results. To cope with uncertain developments, of the internal and external framework, is based on a model of risk, which consistent of a funnel of expected ways of development. Further the results and consequence risk factors, which can influence the development by events in a desired or not desired way and the ability to react in a dynamic way to regain a path within the funnel.

For technical applications various models of risk management emerged since the 50ies of the last century; initial point were the requirements of insurance companies to get a more reliable and valid model of the products and the consequences for the companies and customers. Beneath the accepted role of an entrepreneur in private sector and risk as a part of business life, developed concepts try to anticipate future developments, combined well known and repeated events with forecast and simulations to describe the future. These models are on the one hand tools for the strategic management, but also for operations from the internal view; they fulfill likewise a similar function, like balance sheets in the external framework. Applying a vivid risk management is in addition legally demanded and has signal effects for stake- and shareholders. Investors analyses the enterprise risk management and the results, the risk reports, for better and sustainable decisions; for the banking sector is an applied risk management fundamentally important to calculate their reserves for any credit given. Risk management is therefore one important tool for prevention of losses and estimation of potentials of an organization. All risk management systems in common are the steps of identification, estimation, decision, management and monitoring. For a single decision to make, such a model can pay off, for several decisions to make with various identified and partly dependent risk factors, which could influence the desired or not desired results, collecting and processing of data becomes over-proportional more difficult. Without a learning system with numerous manual or automatic receptors risk management will not pay off.

This chapter also gives and overview of the different kinds of risk management concepts, origins and realization: In Germany parts of several laws add up to the so called KonTraG, established in 1998 to force private enterprises to publish all relevant data for share- and stakeholders, followed by the Sarbanes-Oxley Act of 2002; the

SOX demands a enterprise-wide risk management for all stock-enlisted companies and committed the board to confirm the statements in the annual status report personally. Main emphasis is to reduce the threat of reporting invalid facts and increased responsibility for the board of directors.

Most new is the concept of the Norm DIN ISO 31000, published 2009, and adapted by public sector in several nations, including Australia and UK.

Summarizing all aspects inherent all risk management systems and methods is the notion that an effective use has to be based on an enterprise-wide application. Fragmented risk management for divisions or product lines remains incomplete and the expected support takes only this fragment into consideration. In addition without external standards and references risk management will not work. As worked out considering the measurement of performance in public sector, hard facts as reference and orientation are not very common in this sector. As researches confirmed a ratio of input, output and outcome is hard to define for public sector. For private sector several indicators can be used for consequences in the case of decisions under no certainty, including decrease of revenues of a product or a branch, decrease of market shares, and own equity, based on concrete calculations. These indicators are irrelevant for public sector. Outside a competition environment and based on a legal existence-guarantee values have to be based on other indicators beneath monetary values. I put it something differently: Public administration has to act as trustee of the public, of public funds and equipped with the authority to offer as monopolist public goods and services. With the guarantee in the background regularly not to be held personal responsible for the results of acting, the public administration has to be very careful on the market and in projects. This careful acting leads to the dilemma of more risk-averse behavior and reduces the use of opportunities, although public sector faces numerous risk factors as later seen.

Chapter 4 enlightens the effects of application in private and public sector and the necessity to adopt tools to cope with future tasks and to comply with mandatory tasks. The current financial situation left only two ways to cope with mandatory tasks: to increase the debt level or to reduce quantity and quality of public services.

By analysing the current stage of application of NPM combined with results of conservative power in public administration enshrines the effects. Especially for risk management several traditional and organizational hindrances are identified by researches: Missing personal involvement, limited accountability, limited processes to select an opportunity and pursuit gain and losses in the meaning of economic use of resources. Vague or missing measurable objectives and goals and the complex influential structure as executive of political programs restrict efficiency of tools. Important durability, based on effort to stabilize and increase liquidity, profitability, and growth have minor relevance. Likewise private sector tools will have limited effects. For an analogue application remedy can be to respect and integrate the peculiarities of public sector in tools like organization-wide risk management. Changes in behavior and culture need additional time to accept and use the tools.

In the context of effects of risk management the current situation of public finances confirms the urge; deviations in an undesired way of planned revenues and expenses will lead to additional debts. Analyses from Europe draw a sobering view. The ratio between debts and GDP was increasing for the Euro-Zone in the last 5 years, expected tendency by different analyses is up, though few states are able to present a balanced budget or expect a profit. On the local level the situation is analogue. The OECD has suggested adapting the concept of ISO 31000 as reference also for public organizations. Subsequently successful introduction and maintenance is dependent on awareness, willingness and appropriate and effective instruments to cope with a changing environment. Among the organizational structure internal and external reports and audits are necessary to show progress and adjustments. Critics show that the concentration of introducing and maintaining standards leads to more reports and focus to compliance, another slow down for a more dynamic government.

Several states started very early with concept, aims and objectives to develop and establish risk management, most sophisticated were the concepts of Australia and New Zealand and Canada; but all systems recognized the public sector peculiarities. Conversion of risk management worked out that general features, considering attitude to risk and ramification, are missing in public sector: Existence guarantees by constituency, almost unlimited financial resources, and live-long careers are only a few to name. Evolution of risk awareness has to be based on these differences.

In part II the results of two independent researches are presented and analysed, a model to measure effects of decisions to support decision makers developed as substitute for monetary values in private sector.

Focus of the first research conducted from 2009 – 2012 was to get a first impression of performances in local public administrations in Germany, flanked by several examples from Austria and Switzerland. The research was based on a questionnaire, followed by interviews with mayors or CFOs. Results confirmed the publicly discussed impression that projects are not managed properly; transfers from state and federal level are insufficient, but also self-inflicted imbalances, for example given guarantees or a mainly ignored climate change, which has to be dealt with. Annual reports about chances and threats are fulfilled but without statistical or survey-based data, the descriptions are often made by the CFO. Pure risks, for liabilities or buildings, are properly insured. Risk management and risk awareness was neither widespread nor properly installed. Customer or citizen social responsibility, similar to private sector, but also core element of public administration, was pursuit by following rules and executing political programs, accepting imbalanced budgets and the loss of financial freedom to initiate local projects among mandatory tasks. Intergeneration justice and sustainability were out of focus in weighing up with short-term political aims and objectives.

Chapter 6 presents the results of an empirical research considering the execution of legal demand presentation of chances and threats in the German municipalities. As result a range of 37 different influence factors are presented in the annual report; they can be categorized in endogenous factors what implies that roots of chances and threats are located by the local administration; exogenous risk factors are based on activities from the external environment, with limited capability to steer. Positive and negative factors are qualitatively described, whereby more negative factors are named. Remarkably a correlation between size or current debt level as key factors shows no trend: Neither greater cities nor cities with a higher level of debt in correlation to annual budget are aware of more or detailed risks. That could confirm that public sector works in a peculiar environment with own rules. Summarizing the shares of all given risk factors show the remaining input orientation, almost 50% expect an imbalance between revenues and expenses, followed by delegation of additional and complex duties without a proper financial compensation. Advances are expected by new commercial areas and their effects to businesses and population. Significant for all reports is the missing of probability or potential losses in terms of quality or quantity.

Summarizing the results leads to the estimation that risk awareness and risk management are on an initial stage in German local public administration. The risk factors, based on events (decisions or developments), identified, are focussed to the execution of mandatory and voluntarily tasks; ramifications to the customer, the citizen, are seldom explained, counter-measurements not developed. Without a proper system to process the indicators for welfare or public value and the potential threats or expected deviations, public administration are not able to cope with the constitutional task, to increase welfare. Customer social responsibility, sustainability and durability are the main fields of action, public sector has to address, by generic law and by more dynamic governance. For a systematic risk approach a binding standard has to be set by law; the spectrum of minimum requirements defined and critical thresholds determined. The identified risk factors can be used as reference, completed by expected effects and probability, based on historic or reference data.

Chapter 7 offers a model for analysing the current public value status and to process perceived data for better forecast to support decision-makers. For a holistic view I put together the expected utility of a decision and the opportunity costs, based on missed utility by not realized projects or measures. Both have to be estimated by selected subjects representing the whole spectrum of the society. They have to be selected by various determined criteria, including geographic home, age, marital status, and working place. Processing all data will lead to an expected deviation from the current public value status; this value contributes to a better understanding of ramification of decision for the society and should support decision-maker to act responsible, considering decisions and their outcome to society.

The thesis provided following key findings and main messages:

- Best practices of tools from private sector can be applied but the emulation of private business behavior is limited effective in public sector
- Spectrum of risk can be distilled and categorized for further use in reference class models
- Risk awareness is not interrelated with debts level or size of a local public administration
- County administration faces less numbers of risks and their potential threat is regarded as lower because of the financing by the cities within the county boundaries
- Potential deviation and related consequences are neither qualitative nor quantitative defined in German annual public administration reports
- By emulating private sector risk management systems, using probability and potential damages, the notion of value-at-risk will contribute to sustainable decisions
- Caused by different aims and objectives the term public value can be applied as substitute for private sector monetary values

Various steps remain to develop a fitting risk management including useful parameters as one basement for decision-makers in public sector. Especially further systematic development and a binding standard for all European states will lead to more transparency, more realistic estimation of own situation and competition, in comparison to other public administration but also as political program But the national standards lead to severe resistance, similar to the introduction of the international public sector accounting standards. Creating a topology of risks, defined by probability, potential gains and losses, and time frame, can present an actual risk situation in general or in particular for better decisions in accordance with potential freedom to act. The model of public value has to be based on valid and fast collected data from selected persons or institutions, the advance of internet ease this technical challenge.

Criteria to choose the subjects and to compute the data are necessary for application of the model. The presented model of reference class should be applied as first step of data-based forecasts and can provide a historic data base for transfer to the risk management parameters. An improved and comprehensible grade of social responsibility, durability and sustainability can be reached.

This work was written while the members of the European Union are urged to cope with refugees coming from the Arabian Peninsula and North Africa as results of the civil war and the rival political, ethnical and religious groups in Syria, Iraq and other states. The increasing number of refugees coming to Germany means on the one hand financial burdens for medical treatment, accommodation, education and administration. But on the other side these people will grow rich the society by cultural kinds and the chance to recruit qualified persons to close the gap between given and needed qualified workers. The current personal, organizational and financial challenges coming with the refugees are not content of this work.

Bibliography

Acar, M./ Guo, C./ Yang, K., Accountability When Hierarchical Authority is Absent, in "The American Review of Public Administration", Vol. 38, No. 1, March, pp. 3-23 2008

Afonso, A./ Schuknecht, L./ Tanzi, V., Public Sector Efficiency – Evidence for new EU Member States and emerging markets, European Central Bank Working Paper Series, No. 581, January 2006,

Alghalith, M., New economics of risk and uncertainty, Nova Science Publishers, New York, 2007

Akerlof, G., The Markets for "Lemons": Quality Uncertainty and the Market Mechanism, in "The Quarterly Journal of Economics", Vol. 84, No. 3, August, pp. 488-500, 1970

Alford, J.& Hughes, O., Public value pragmatism as the next phase of public management, in "The American Review of Public Administration", 38 (2), pp. 130-148, 2008

Alghalith, M., New economics of risk and uncertainty, Nova Science Publishers, New York, 2007

Allison, G., Public and private management: Are they fundamentally alike in all unimportant respects, in Sergiovanni, T. & Corbally, J. (eds.), "Leadership and organizational culture", University of Illinois Press, Urbana, pp. 214-239, 1986

Andrews, R./ Van der Walle, S., New public management and citizens' perception of local service efficiency, responsiveness, equity and effectiveness, Public Management Review, 15 (5) pp. 762 – 783, 2013

AIRMIC, Alarm, IRM, A structured approach to Enterprise Risk Management (ERM) and the requirements of ISO 31000, London, 2010

Arrow, K. & Lind, R., Uncertainty and the Evaluation of Public Investment Decisions, in "American Economic Review", Issue 60, 1970, pp. 364-378, 1970

Arthur Andersen & Co., Managing business – An integrated Approach, in "The Economist Intelligence Unit", New York, 1995, cited in Barton, T./ Shenkir, W./ Walker, P., Making Enterprise Risk Management Pay Off, Prentice Hall, Upper Saddle River, p. 139, 2002

Arvenson, Paul: Translating performance metrics from the private to the public sector, www.balancescorecard.org, retrieved 07.02.2016

Audi, R. (ed.), The Cambridge dictionary of philosophy, Cambridge University Press, Cambridge, 2009

M. Bodemann, *Management in Public Administration*,
Sustainable Management, Wertschöpfung und Effizienz,
https://doi.org/10.1007/978-3-658-22687-9

Audit Commission, Briefing: Worth the risk: Improving Risk Management in Local Government, "The Audit Commission for Local Authorities and the National Health Service in England and Wales", London, 2001

Auditor General, Victoria, Australia, Managing risk across the public sector, Melbourne, 2004

Australia National Audit Office, Future challenges for risk management in the Australian public sector, Canberra, 2005

Australian Government, Department of the Environment and Heritage, Australian Green Office, Climate Change Impacts & Risk Management, Canberra, Commonwealth of Australia, 2006

Bank-Verlag, Mindestanforderungen an das Risikomanagement, Bank-Verlag, Cologne, 2006

Banner, G., Logik des Scheitern oder Scheitern an der Logik, dms-der moderne staat, No.2, pp. 447 – 455, 2008

Banner, G., Von der Behörde zum Dienstleistungsunternehmen: Die Kommunen brauchen ein neues Steuerungsmodell, in "Verwaltungsführung, Organisation, Personalführung", 1, pp. 6-11, 1991

Barton, T./ Shenkir, W./ Walker, P., Making Enterprise Risk Management Pay Off, Prentice Hall, Upper Saddle River, 2002

Beck, S./ Benecke, M./ Felten, M/ Lipske, I, Schuster, F., Risikomanagement in Kommunen, Public Governance, Soomer, pp. 12- 15, 2013

Behn, R., Rethinking Democratic Accountability, Washington, Brookings Institution, 2001, p. 3 cited by Bovens, M., Public accountability, in Ferlie, E./ Lynn, L./ Pollitt, C.(eds.), "The Oxford Handbook of Public Management", Oxford University Press, New York, pp. 182-208, 2005

Benington, J. & Moore, M. (eds.), Public Value - Theory and practice, Palgrave Macmillan, Basingstoke, 2011

Bernstein, P., Against of The Gods: The remarkable story of risk, New York, Wiley, 1996

Bianchi, C., Improving performance and fostering accountability in the public sector through system dynamics modelling: from an 'external' to an 'internal' perspective, Systems Research and Behavioral Science, No. 27, pp. 361 – 384, 2010

Birkholz, K. et al, Public Management – Eine neue Generation in Wissenschaft und Praxis, Universitätsverlag Potsdam, Potsdam, 2006

Black, J./ Hashimzade, N./ Myles, G. (eds.), Oxford dictionary of economics, 3rd edition, Oxford University Press, Oxford, 2009

Blackburn, S. (ed.), Oxford dictionary of philosophy, Oxford University Press, Oxford, 2008

Blankart, C., Öffentliche Finanzen in der Demokratie, Vahlen, Munich, 2011

Bodemann, M., Can corporate management tools be successfully applied in public administration – A German based case study, in "Management & Marketing", Vol. 9, No. 2 (34), pp. 227-238, 2014

Bodemann. M., NKF-Klassenziel erreicht? , in "NKF-Zeitung – Journal für Doppik in Ländern und Kommunen", No. 2, Behördenspiegel, Bonn/ Berlin, p. 10, 2009

Bodemann, M., Risk Awareness als Schlüssel zum erfolgreichen Risikomanagement in: Niedostadek, A., Riedl., R./ Stember, J., "Risiken im öffentlichen Bereich", LIT, Berlin, pp. 87- 110, 2011

Bodemann, M., Technologie und Vernetzung – Integration von Verfahren in kommunale good-practice IT-Strukturen in: Hilger, D./ Schauer, R. / Thom, N., "Public Management im Paradigmenwechsel", Trauner, Linz, pp. 785-802, 2012

Bodemann, M. / Maier, D. / Sandru, M./ Weber, G., Risk awareness after the adoption of New Steering Model in German public administrations – a case study, Procedia Economics and Finance, No. 23, pp. 1046 – 153, 2015

Bodemann, M. & Olaru, M., Public value as indicator for public administration to make sustainable decisions, Proceedings of 9th European Conference on Innovation and entrepreneurship, Belfast, Northern Ireland, 09/18-09/19/2014, pp. 500-506, University of Ulster Business School and School of Social Enterprises, ISSN 2049-1050

Bodemann, M. & Olaru, M., Responsibility to customers in the context of public value management – a German case study, in "Amfiteatru economic", Vol XVI (35), pp. 171-186, 2014

Bodemann, M./ Olaru, M./ Pirnea: I., Risk awareness as key success factor for more efficient management for local public administration in Nicolescu, O.& Lloyd-Reason, L. (eds.), Challenges, Performances and Tendencies in Organisation Management, World Scientific Publishing, Singapore, 2016

Bodemann, M. / Olaru, M./ Ionela, C., Risk awareness as key success factor for more efficient management for local public administration, in "Proceedings of the 1.International management conference: Challenges, performances and tendencies in the organization management", Murigiol, 22. - 24.06.2014

Bodemann, M./ Olaru, M/ Pirnea, C., Risk awareness as competitive factor for public administration - a German case study, in "Proceedings of the IE 2015 International Conference", pp. 497-503, 2015

Bogumil, J., Administrative modernization and the logic of politics, German Journal of Urban Studies, No. 45, 2006

Bogumil, J./ Grohs, S./ Kuhlmann, S./ Ohm, Anna, Zehn Jahre Neues Steuerungsmodell, edition sigma, Berlin, 2007

Bogumil, J. & Jann, W., Verwaltung und Verwaltungswissenschaft in Deutschland, 2nd edition, Verlag für Sozialwissenschaften, Wiesbaden, 2009

Boivard, T./ Löffler, E. (eds.), Public management and governance, Routledge, London and New York, 2009

Bouckaert. Geert, Managing performance: International and national trends, Forum AP, May 17th, Rome, 2012

Bovens, M., Public Accountability, in Ferlie, E./ Lynn, L./ Pollitt, C. (eds.), The Oxford Handbook of Public Management, Oxford University Press, Oxford, pp. 182-208, 2005

Bozeman, B., Public value and public interest, Georgetown University Press, Washington, 2007

Broadbent, J. & Guthrie, J., Changes in the public sector: A review of recent "alternative" accounting research, Accounting, Auditing & Accountability Journal, Vol. 5 Iss. 2, p. 3, 1992

Brühweiler, B., Risikomanagement als Führungsaufgabe, Haupt, Berne, 2007

Buehler, K. / Freeman, A./ Hulme, R., The New Arsenal of Risk Management in "Harvard Business Review on Managing External Risk", Harvard Business Publishing Corporation, Boston, pp. 1-22, 2009

Bundesamt für Sicherheit in der Informationstechnik, Die Lage der IT-Sicherheit in Deutschland 2015, Bonn, 2015

Bundesministerium des Innern, Jedes Alter zählt, Bonn, 2016

Bundesministerium des Innern. Schutz Kritischer Infrastrukturen – Risiko- und Krisenmanagement, Berlin, 2011

Burth, A. Die Kommunalverschuldung wirksam begrenzen – Entwicklung des Modells einer doppischen Kommunalschuldenbremse in: Hilgers, D./ Schauer, R./ Thom, N., (eds.), Public Management im Paradigmenwechsel, Trauner Verlag, Linz, , pp. 209 – 224, 2012

Buurman, M./ Delfgaauw, J./ Dur, R./ Van den Bossche, S., Public sector employees: Risk averse and altruistic ?, CESIFO Working Paper No. 3851, June, 2012

Bruzelis, N./ Flyvberg, B./ Rothengatter, W., Big decisions, big risks: Improving accountability in mega projects in "International Review of Administration Science" Vol. 64 No. 3, pp. 423–440, 1998

Bryson J./ Crosby, B./ Bloomberg, L., Public value governance: Moving beyond traditional public administration and the New Public Management, Public Administration Review, Vol. 74, Iss. 4, pp. 445- 456, 2014

Bünting, H., Deutsches Wörterbuch , Isis-Verlag, Chur, 1996

Burgi, M., Kommunalrecht, C.H. Beck, Munich, 2012

Chan, J. /Xiao, X., Financial management in public sector organizations, in Boivard, T./ Löffler, E. (eds.), "Public management and governance", Routledge, London and New York, pp. 109-120, 2009

Christensen, T. et al., Organization theory and the public sector, Routledge, New York, 2007

Coleman, T., A practical guide to risk management, CFA Institute, Amazon distribution, Leipzig, 2011

Commonwealth Secretariat. A profile of the public service of Canada, Commonwealth Secretariat, London, 2003

Cottin, C. & Döhler, S., Risikoanalyse, Springer Spektrum, Wiesbaden, 2013

Crouhy, M./ Galai, D. / Mark, R., The essentials of risk management, McGraw-Hill, New York, 2006

Courtney H. et al., Harvard Business Review on Managing Uncertainty, Harvard Business School Press, Boston, 1999

Curristine, T./ Lonti, Z./ Journard, I., Improving public sector efficiency- challenges and opportunities, OECD Journal of Budgeting, Vol. 7, No. 1, pp. 1-41, 2007

Damodaran, A., Strategic risk taking, Wharton School Publishing, Upper Saddle River, 2008

De Finetti, B., Theory of probability, John-Wiley & Sons, London, 1974

deGroot, H., Performance management and cost-effectiveness of public services: empirical evidence from Dutch municipalities, Annual Conference of the European Group of Public Administration, Bucharest, September 7-10, 2011

Denhardt, R. & Denhardt, J., Public administration: An action orientation, Thomson Wadworth, Belmont, 2009

DeSantis, V./ Durst, S., Comparing Job Satisfaction Among Public and Private Sector Employees, in "The American Review of Public Administration", Issue 26 (3), pp. 327–343, 1996

De Waal, A., Achieving high performance in the public sector – What needs to be done ?, Public Performance & Management Review, Vol. 34, No. 1, pp. 81 – 103, 2010

Diefenbach, T., New public management in public sector organizations – the dark side of managerialistic 'enlightment', Public Administration, Vol. 87, No. 4, pp. 892-909, 2009

Dietlein, J., Öffentliches Recht in Nordrhein-Westfalen, C.H. Beck, Munich, 2006

Dingwall, R. & Stranglemann, T., Organizational Cultures in the Public Services, in Ferlie, E./ Lynn, L./ Pollitt, C.(eds.), "The Oxford Handbook of Public Management", Oxford University Press, New York, pp. 468-490, 2005

Dinu, V., The Need for Consumers' Protection, in "Amfiteatru Economic", XIII (28), 2009

Dixit, A., Incentives and Organizations in the Public Sector: An Interpretative Review, in "Journal of Human Resources", Vol. 37, No.4, pp. 696-727, 2002

Drennan, L. & McConnell, A., Risk and crisis management in the public sector, New York, Routledge, New York, 2007

Drexler, W., The rise and demise of the New Public Management: Lessons and opportunities for South East Europe, Uprava, letnik, VII, pp. 7-24, 2009

Drucker, P., Management, rev. edit., Collins, New York, 2008

Drucker, P., Management Challenges for the 21th Century, Butterworth-Heinemann, Oxford, reprinted edition, 2007

Duggett, M., What can we say about the Westminster Model today?, PSA Conference Manchester 2009, published also in PMPA Review, January, 2009

Dunlop, J., Public Management, draft of an unpublished paper and proposal, Summer 1979, cited by: Allison, G., Public and Private Management: Are They Fundamentally Alike In All Unimportant Respects in Sergiovanni, T. & Corbally, J. (eds.), "Leadership and organizational culture", University of Illinois Press, Urbana, pp. 214-239, 1986

Eggink, M., Innovation system performance: How to address the measurement of a system's performance, Journal of Innovation & Business Best Practices, Vol. 2012, pp. 1 -9, 2012

Ehrmann, H., Risikomanagement, Kiehl, Ludwigshafen, 2005

Erben, F. & Romeike, F., Allein auf stürmischer See, Wiley, Weinheim, 2006

Ertl, P. (ed.), Risikomanagement und Jahresabschluss, Linde, Vienna, 2006

Eurostat, Quality of life: Facts and views, European Union, Luxembourg, http://bookshop.europa.eu, 2015

Ewoh, A., Performance measurement in an era of New Public Management, Journal of Emerging Knowledge on Emerging Markets, Vol. 3, November, pp. 105 – 117, 2011

FAZ Wirtschaftsressort, Die Schulden der EU-Staaten drohen auszuufern, Frankfurter Allgemeine Zeitung (FAZ), 10.09.2009

Farneti, F. & Guthrie, J., Sustainability reporting by Australian public sector organizations: Why they report, Accounting Forum, September, 2008

Federal Bureau of Finance, Eckdaten zur Entwicklung und Struktur der Kommunalfinanzen 1999 – 2008, Berlin, July 2009.

Ferlie, E./ Lynn, L./ Pollitt, C. (eds.), The Oxford Handbook of Public Management, Oxford University Press, New York, 2007

Fernandez, S. & Rainey, H., Managing successful organizational change in the public sector, in "Public Administration Review", Vol. 66, Issue 2, March April 2006, pp. 168 – 176, 2006

Fester, T. & Thum, M., Die Pensionslasten – Eine Bedrohung zuder zukünftigen Handlungsfähigkeit der Länder, ifo Schnelldienst, Nr. 23, pp. 3 – 9, 2003

Fiorino, D., Sustainability as a conceptual focus for public administration, Public Administration Review, Special Issue, December, pp. 578 – 588, 2010

Fischhoff, B. & Kadvany, J., Risk – a very short introduction, Oxford University Press, New York, 2011

Flynn, N., Public sector management, Sage, London, 2007

Flyvberg, B., From Nobel prize to project management: Getting risks right, in "Project Management Journal", Vol. 37 No. 3 August, pp. 5 -15, 2006

Flyvbjerg, B./ Holm, M./ Buhl, S., Underestimating costs in public works projects, in "Journal of the American Planning Association", Journal, Summer, Vol. 68, No. 3, pp. 279 - 295, 2002

Flyvberg, B./ Holm, M./ Buhl, S., How (in)accurate Are Demand Forecasts in Public Works Projects, in "Journal of the American Planning Association", Vol. 71, No. 2, Spring, p. 131-146, 2005

FocusMoney, Trauma Teuerung, Nr. 26/2011, p. 45, 2011

Fone, M. & Young, P., Public sector risk management, Butterworth-Heinemann, Oxford, 2000

Forrer, J. et al., Public – private partnerships and the public accountability question, Public Administration Review, May-June, pp. 475-484, 2010

Frigelj, K., Wenn Städte in Schulden versinken, Welt am Sonntag, 29.11.2009

Fry, B. & Raadschelders, J., Mastering Public Administration, CQ Press, Washington, 2008

Gebhardt, G. Enzyklopädie der Betriebswirtschaftslehre, Schaeffer-Poeschel, Stuttgart, 2002

Fryer, K. & Antony, J., Performance management in the public sector, International Journal of Public Sector Management, No. 22 (6), pp. 478 – 498, 2009

Geys, B./ Heinemann, F./ Kalb, A., Voter involvement, fiscal autonomy and public sector efficiency: Evidence form German municipalities, Discussion Paper SP II, 2009,

Giauque, D./ Ritz, A./ Varone, F./ Anderfuhren-Biget, S., Resigned but satisfied: The negative impact of public service motivation and red tape on work satisfaction, Public Administration, Vol. 90, No. 1, pp. 175 – 193, 2012

Gilboa, I., Theory of Decision under Uncertainty, Cambridge University Press, New York, 2009

Giordano, R. / Tommasino, P., Public Sector efficiency and political culture, Banca D'Italia Working Paper, No. 786, January 2011

Girotra, K./ Netessine, S., How to build risk into your business model, in "Harvard Business Review", May, 2011

Götze, U./ Henselmann, K./ Mikus, B., Risikomanagement, Physica, Heidelberg, 2001

Gomez, P. & Meynhardt, T. Public Value: Gesellschaftliche Wertschöpfung im Fokus der Führung in Seiler, S. (ed.), "Führung neu denken – Im Spannungsfeld zwischen Erfolg, Moral und Komplexität", Orell Fuessli, Zurich, pp. 125-170, 2009

Goodnow, F., Politics and administration: A study in government, Macmillan, New York, 1900

Gough, J., Measuring perceived and acceptable risk: an application of survey approaches, Centre for Resource Management, University of Canterbury and Lincoln University, Information Paper No. 24, 1991

Gough, J., Risk and uncertainty, in "Information Paper No. 10", Centre for Resource Management, University of Canterbury and Lincoln College, 1988

Governance Institute of Australia, Good governance guide, www. governanceinstitute.com.au, 2013, retrieved 28.02.2016

Greiling, D., Performance measurement - a driver for increasing the efficiency of public services?, Protestant University of applied sciences, Darmstadt, 2005

Grimmer, K., Öffentliche Verwaltung in Deutschland, Verlag für Sozialwissenschaften, Wiesbaden, 2004

Grüb, B., Performance Measurement in Gesundheitsnetzwerken in: Hilgers, D./ Schauer, R./ Thom, N., (eds.), Public Management im Paradigmenwechsel, Trauner Verlag, Linz, , pp. 395 – 409, 2012

Gruening, G., Origin and theoretical basis of New Public Management, International Public Management Journal, No.4, pp. 1-25, 2001

Haesler, H. & Gampe I., Corporate Governance, 2002, cited in Ertl, P. & Steindl, M., Risikomanagement und Corporate Governance - Entwicklung und Inhalt, Stellenwert und faktische Durchsetzbarkeit, in: Ertl, Peter (ed.): "Risikomanagement und Jahresabschluss", Linde, Vienna, pp. 9-38, 2006

Hall, D. et al. (eds.), Business studies, Causeway Press Ltd. Harlow, 2007

Hall, J. & Jennings, E., Taking chances: evaluating risk as a guide to better use of best practices, in "Public Administration Review", Vol. 68 Issue 4 July/August, pp. 695-708, 2008

Hammerschmid, G./ Van der Walle, S.,/ Stimac, V., Internal and external use of performance information in public organizations: results from an international survey, Public Money Management, July, pp. 1 - 8, 2013

Hammond, J./ Keeney, R./ Riaffa, H. (eds.), Harvard Business Review: Making smart decisions, Harvard Business Review Press, Boston, 2011

Hampton, J., Enterprise risk management, Amacom, New York, 2009

Hansson, S., Philosophical perspectives on risk, Delft University, 2002

Hansson, S., Seven myths of risk, Royal Institute of Technology, Stockholm, 2000

Hawkins, S., The universe in a nutshell, Bantam Press, New York, 2001

Heald, D., Why is transparency about public expenditure so elusive?, International Review of Administrative Sciences, 78 (I), pp. 30 – 49, 2012

Hilgers, D./ Schauer, R./ Thom, N., (eds.), Public Management im Paradigmenwechsel, Trauner Verlag, Linz, 2012

Hill, H., Finanz- und Haushaltsrisiken, proceedings of the symposium „Aufgabenkritik, Privatisierung und Neue Verwaltungssteuerung", German University of Administrative Sciences, Speyer, 02.-04.04.2003

HM Treasury, Public sector annual reports: sustainability reporting guidance 2014-2015, Crown, London, 2015

Hohan, A./ Olaru, M./ Pirnea, C., Case study regarding the implementation of an integrated risk management system in local public administration, in "Supplement of Quality-access to success Journal", II (125), pp. 246-251, 2011

Holtkamp, L., Das Scheitern des Neuen Steuerungsmodells, dms-der moderne Staat, No. 2, pp. 423- 446, 2008

Hood, C., A public management for all seasons, in "Public Administration", Vol. 69, Spring, pp. 3-19, 1991

Hooper, D., The difference between "responsibility" and "accountability", Savannah Business Journal, December 16, 2013

Hoppe, W. & Uechtritz, M. (eds.), Handbuch kommunale Unternehmen, 2.edition, Dr. Otto Schmidt, Cologne, 2007

Holton, G., Defining risk, in "Financial Analyst Journal", Vol. 60, No. 6, pp. 19-25, 2004

Hume, D., Essay IX: Of public loan, in Green, T. & Grose, T. (eds), "David Hume – The Philosophical Works", Aalen, 1992

Hyndman, N. & Connolly, C., Accruals accounting in the public sector: A road not always taken, Management Accounting Research, 22, pp. 36-45, 2011

Innovative Verwaltung, p.21, No.1-2, 2010

Kahneman, D. & Knetsch, J., Valueing public goods: the purchase of moral satisfaction, in "Journal of Environmental Economics and Management", No. 22, pp. 57-70, 1992

Kahnemann, D. & Tversky, A., Prospect theory: An analysis of decision under risk, in "Econometrica", Vol. 47, No. 2, pp. 263-291, March 1979

Kalb, A., Public Sector Efficiency, Gabler Research, Wiesbaden, 2010

Kaplan, M., Decision theory as philosophy, Cambridge University Press, Cambridge, 2006

Kaplan, S. & Gerrick, J., On the quantitative definition of risk, in "Risk Analysis", Vol. 1, No. 1, pp. 11-27, 1981

Kegelmann, J., New Public Management, Verlag für Sozialwissenschaften, Wiesbaden, 2007

Kelly, G./ Mulgan, G./ Muers, S., Creating public value, Strategy Unit, Cabinet Office, London, 2002

Kers de Vries, M. & Balasz, K., Transforming the mind-set of organization, in "Administration & Society", Vol. 30 No. 6, pp. 640 – 675, 1999, cited by Fernandez, S. & Rainey, H., Managing successful organizational change in the public sector, in "Public Administration Review", March April, p. 169, 2006

Keynes, J., A Treatise on probability, Rough Draft Printing, Breinigsville, 2008

KGSt., Kommunales Risikomanagement, Bericht Nr. 5/2011, Köln, 2011

Kickert, W., State responses to he fiscal crisis in Britain, Germany and the Netherlands, Public Management Review, 14 (3), pp. 299 – 309, 2012

Kirbach, R., Die Rathauszocker, http://www.zeit.de/2009/30/DOS-Swap,retrieved 17.07.2009;

Knight, F., Risk, Uncertainty and profit, reprinted by Dover, New York, 2006, original published by Houghton Mifflin, Boston and New York, 1921

Köbler, G., Juristisches Wörterbuch, Vahlen, München, p. 486, 2003

Kuhlmann, S., Hat das "Neue Steuerungsmodell" versagt? Lehren aus der "Ökonomisierung" von Politik und Verwaltung, in „Verwaltung und Management", No. 3, p. 149-153, 2006

Kuhlmann, S./ Bogumil, J./ Grohs, S., Evaluation administrating modernization in German local governments: success or failure of the "New Steering Model"?, in "Public Administration Review", Sept.-Oct., pp. 851-863, 2008

Lagassé, P. (ed.), The Columbia encyclopedia, Columbia University Press, 2000

Law, J. (ed.), Oxford dictionary of business and management, Oxford University Press, Oxford, p. 577, 2009

Leadbeater, C. Personalization through Participation: A New Script for Public Services, Demos, London, 2004, cited by Dingwall, R. & Stranglemann, T., Organizational culture in the public services, in Ferlie, E./ Lynn, L./ Pollitt, C. (eds), "The Oxford Handbook of Public Management", Oxford University Press, New York, p. 468-490, 2005

Levitt, T., Marketing-Kurzsichtigkeit, in: "Harvard Business manager", Edition 02/2012, pp. 67–81, orig.1960

Lindblom, C., The science of "muddling through", in "Public Administration Review", Vol. 19, No. 2, Spring , p. 79- 88, 1958

Linna, P./ Pekkola, S./ Ukko, J., Melkas, H., Defining and measuring productivity in the public sector: managerial perceptions, International Journal of Public Sector Management, Vol. 23, No. 3, pp. 300-320, 2010

Loevenich, B., Der Umgang mit operationellen Risiken in Kreditinstituten – Vorbild für öffentliche Verwaltungen? in Niedostadek, A., Riedl, R., Stember, J., „Risiken im öffentlichen Bereich", Lit Verlag, Berlin, 2011

Mandl, U./ Dierx, A./ Ilzkovitz, F., The effectiveness and efficiency of public spending, European Commission, Economic Papers 301, 2008

Manski, C., Public policy in an uncertain world: analysis and decisions, Harvard University Press, Harvard, 2013

Manzoor, A., A look at efficiency in public administration: Past and future, in „Sage Open", October-December, pp. 1-5, 2014

Marcharzina, K., Unternehmensführung, Gabler, Wiesbaden, 2003

McPhee, I, Risk and risk Management in the public sector, Australia National Audit Office, Canberra, 2005

Menger, C., Principles of economics, Ludwig-von-Mises-Institute, Auburn, p. 18, 1976

Meurer, S., Rechnungswesen und Controlling in der öffentlichen Verwaltung, Haufe, Freiburg i. Breisgau, 2005

Meynhardt, T., Public Value Scorecard, OrganisationsEntwicklung, No. 4, pp. 79-83, 2013

Micheli, P. & Neely, A., Performance management in the public sector in England: Searching for the golden thread, Public Administration Review, July/ August, pp. 591 – 600, 2010

Mihaiu, D./ Opreana, A./ Cristescu, M., Efficiency, effectiveness and performance of the public sector, in „Romanian Journal of Economic Forecasting", No.4, , pp. 132 – 147, 2010

Monahan, G., Enterprise risk management, John Wiley & Sons, Inc., Hoboken, 2008

Mongkol, K., The critical review of New Public Management model and its criticisms, Research Journal of Business Management, 5(1), pp. 35-43, 2011

Monsen, N., Development of administrative cameralistics: An example, International Journal of Governmental Financial Management, XII (1), pp. 22-38, 2012

Monsen, N., Public Management von Einnahmen und Ausgaben, in Hilgers, D./ Schauer, R./ Thom, N., (eds.), Public Management im Paradigmenwechsel, Trauner Verlag, Linz, , pp. 225 – 236, 2012

Moore, M., Creating public value: strategic management in government, Harvard University Press, Cambridge, 1995

Moore, M., Recognizing public value, Harvard University Press, Cambridge, 2013

Moore, M. & Khagram, S., On creating public value, Working Paper No. 3, March, 2004

Moss, D., When all else fails – Government as the ultimate risk manager, Harvard University Press, Cambridge, 2002

Moynihan, D. & Pandey, S., The big question for performance management: Why do managers use performance information? Journal of Public Administration No.20, pp. 849 – 866, 2010

Mussari, R., Autonomy, responsibility and new public management, Conference on New Public Management in International Perspective, St. Gallen, 1996

National Audit Office, Supporting innovation: managing risk in government departments, National Audit Office, London, 2000

Nayer, M., Umsetzung der neuen EU-Richtlinien in Hinblick auf Risikomanagement und IKS, in Ertl, Peter (ed.), "Risikomanagement und Jahresabschluss", Linde, Vienna, pp. 39 – 64, 2006

Neustadt, R., Public management and corporate executives, in "proceedings of the National Academy of Public Administration's Panel on Presidential Management", October 7-8, 1979

Niedostadek, A./ Riedl, R./ Stember, J., Risiken im öffentlichen Bereich, Lit Verlag, Berlin, 2011

Nijkamp, P. & Ubbels, B., How reliable are estimates of infrastructure costs? A comparative analysis, in "International Journal of Transport Economics", Vol. 26, No.1, pp. 23 – 53, 1999

Novell, G., Public vs. Private Managers: A new perspective, in "Journal of Business & Economics Research", Vol. 7, No. 3, pp. 1-6, 2009

Oakley, K./ Naylor, R./ Lee, D., Giving them what they want: the construction of the public in „public value", CREST Media Change & Social Change Conference, Sept 2006, Oxford University, 2006

OECD, Overview of advances in risk management of government debt, 2005

OECD, Economic Survey of Germany, www.oecd.org, retrieved on 26.03.2010

OECD, Public sector efficiency, in Government at a Glance 2013, OECD Publishing, http://dx.doi.org/10.1787/gov_glance-2013-12-en, retrieved 16.02.2016

OECD, Risk management and corporate governance, OECD Publishing, 2014, http://dx.doi.org/10.1787/9789264208636-en, retrieved 17.04.2016

Oehler, A./ Schalkowski, H./ Wendt, S., Risikomanagement in öffentlichen Unternehmen im Spannungsfeld ziwschen Daseinsvorsorge und Steuerlast, Discussion Paper, University Bamberg, pp. 1-21, 2013

O'Flynn, J., From new public management to public value: paradigmatic change and managerial implications, in "The Australian Journal of Public Administration", 66 (3), pp. 353-366, 2007

Olaru, M./ Sandru, M.,/ Pirnea,, C., Monte Carlo method application for environmental risks impact assessment in the investment projects, in "Procedia – Social Behavioral Sciences", Vol. 109, January, pp. 940 – 943, 2014

Osborne, S./ Radnor, Z. / Nasi, G., A new theory for public service management? Toward a public service-dominant approach, The American Review of Public Administration, No. 43 (2), pp. 135-158, 2013

Ostrom, V. & Ostrom, E., Public choice: a different approach to the study of public administration, in "Public Administration Review", Vol. 31, No. 2, pp. 203 -216, 1971

Øvretveit, J., Public service quality improvement, in Ferlie, E., Lynn, L.E. jr., Pollitt, C., (eds.), „The Oxford handbook of public management", Oxford University Press, Oxford, pp. 537-562, 2005

Pečarič, M., Personal establishment and accomplishment of public service values, Transylvanian Review of Administrative Sciences, 38 E, pp. 125-143, 2013

Perry, B., Moving from outputs to outcomes – Practical advice from governments around the world, The World Bank, 2006

Peters, G., The handbook of public administration, SAGE, Los Angeles, 2007

Peterson, M., An introduction to decision theory, Cambridge University Press, New York, 2009

Pickrell, D.H., Urban rail transit projects: Forecasts versus actual ridership and cost, U.S. Department of Transportation, Washington, DC 1990

Pollitt, C., 40 years of public management reform – what we have learned, what have we forgotten, 40thAnniversary Conference "40 years of policy and politics", 19.09.2012, University of Bristol, UK

Pollitt, C., Governance and performance. A comparative perspective on contemporary Europe, Presentation to a conference organized by Norwegian Ministry of Finance and the Ministry of Local Government and Modernization, Oslo, September 24th , 2014

Pollitt, C. & Bouckaert, G., Public management reform, 2nd edition, Oxford University Press, Oxford, 2004

Pollitt, C. & Bouckaert, G., Public management reform, 3rd edition; Oxford University Press, New York, 2011

Popescu, A./ Popescu, G./ Popescu, C., Innovation's role in nowadays society and the ways to generate competitive intelligence and accountability: Case of Romania, Journal of Innovation & Business Best Practices, Vol. 2012, pp. 1-11

Porter, M., On competition, Harvard Business School Publishing Corporation, Cambridge, 2008

Power, M., The risk management of everything – Rethinking the politics of uncertainty, Demos, London, 2004

President of the Treasury Board, Canada, Integrated risk management, Ottawa, 2001

Profiroiu, M.C./ Tapardel, A./ Mihăescu, C., Performance analysis of the Romanian public administration, in "Transylvanian Review of Administrative Sciences", 40 E, pp. 183 – 200, 2013

Propper, C. & Wilson, D., Use and Usefulness of Performance Measures in the Public Sector, in "Oxford Review of Economic Policy, No. 19 (2), pp. 250-267, 2003

Province of British Columbia, Risk Management guideline for the BC public sector, Province of British Columbia, March 2012

Purdy, G., ISO 31000:2009 – Setting a new standard for risk management, Risk Analysis Vol. 30, No. 6, pp. 881 – 886, 2010

Rainey, H., Understanding and managing public organization, John Wiley & Sons, San Francisco, 2009

Rainey, H. & Bozeman, B., Comparing public and private organisations: empirical research and the power of the a priori, in "Journal of Public Administration Research and Theory", Vol. 10 (2), pp. 447 – 469, 2000

Rau, T., Betriebswirtschaftslehre für Städte und Gemeinden, Vahlen, Munich, 2007

Rehfeld, D., Rating von Kommunen, in Stephan, G. & Meurer, E.(eds.), „Rechnungswesen und Controlling", Haufe, Stuttgart, 2005

Reichard, C., The New Steering Model and the Citizen, Deutsches Institut für Urbanistik, 2004

Romeike, F. & Hager, P., Erfolgsfaktor Risiko-Management 2.0, Gabler, Wiesbaden, 2009

Rothschild, M. & Stieglitz, J., Increasing Risk: I, A Definition, Journal of Economic Theory, Vol. 2, No. 3, pp. 225-243, 1970

Rudzio, W., Das politische System der Bundesrepublik Deutschland, Leske+Budrich, Opladen, 1996

Saliterer, I.& Korac, S., Adoption und Implementierung von Performance Management auf kommunaler Ebene – zwei Seiten einer Medaille ?, in: Hilger, D./ Schauer, R. / Thom, N., "Public Management im Paradigmenwechsel", Trauner, Linz, pp. 785-802, 2012

Sartoris, J., Doppik zeigt nur die halbe Wahrheit, in „Der Neue Kämmerer", Issue 5, Dec 2008

Schedler, K. & Proeller, I., New Public Management, Haupt, Berne, 2006

Schierenbeck, H., Grundzüge der Betriebswirtschaftslehre, Oldenbourg, Munich, 1993

Schirmbrand, M., Information-Risk-Management als integrativer Bestandteil des Corporate-Risk-Management in Ertl, P. (ed.), "Risikomanagement und Jahresabschluss", Linde, Vienna, pp.109 - 136, 2006

Schmitz, T.& Wehrheim, M., Risikomanagement, Kohlhammer, Stuttgart, 2006

Schubert, T., New Public Management: Theorie, Instrumente, Wirkungen, Fraunhofer ISI, Universität Karlsruhe, 07. July 2011

Schütz, M., Risikomanagement im öffentlichen Sektor, Schweizerische Gesellschaft für Verwaltungswissenschaften SGVW, Rufenacht, Switzerland, 2006, http://www.sgvw.ch/2006/04/25/risikomanagement-im-oeffentlichen-sektor-2, retrieved 26.12.2015

Sekaly, G., Interaction of risk & control, Institute of Public Administration of Canada, Toronto, 2007

Shad, H. & Malik, A., NPM is dead, long live NPM: The strategic shift in public sector discourse, University of Hertfordshire Business School Working Paper, 2012, https://uhra.herts.ac.uk/dspace/handle/2299/5549

Shinde, S., AIG-Deals kommen Kommunen teuer zu stehen, in http://www.handelsblatt.com/unternehmen/_b=2195969,_p=,t=ftprint,doc_page=0;
retrieved 17.09.2009

Simon, H., Organizations and Markets, Journal of Public Administration, Issue 5, No. 3, pp. 273-294, 1995

Simon, H., The proverbs of administration, Public Administration Review, Vol. 6, No. 1, pp. 53-67, 1946

Simon, H., Why public administration, Journal of Public Administration-Research and Theory, Vol. 8, No. 1, pp. 1-11, 1998

Steane, P., Public Management Reforms in Australia and New Zealand, in "Public Management Review", Vol. 10. Issue 3, pp. 453 – 465, 2008

Slywotzky, A. & Drzik, J., Countering the Biggest Risk of All, "Harvard Business Review on Managing External Risk", Harvard Business Press, Boston, 2009

Smith, Adam, Wealth of nations, Bantam Dell, New York, orig. 1776, reprint 2003

Sowell, T., Basic Economics, Basic Books, New York. p. 295, 2011

Stanbury, W., Accountability to citizens in the Westminster Model of Government: More Myth Than Reality, Fraser Institute Digital Publication, Vancouver, 2003

Statistische Bundesamt, Public finance and taxes, Wiesbaden, 2014

Steel, B. & Warner, R., Job Satisfaction Among early Labor Force Participants: Unexpected Outcomes in Public and Private Sector Comparison, Review of Public Personnel Administration, Issue 10, pp. 4-22, 1990

Stiglitz, J., Economics of the public sector, 3rd edition, Norton & Company, New York, 1999

Storchevoy, M., A General Theory of the Firm: From Knight to Relationship Marketing, Saint Petersburg State University, Working Paper No. 5, p. 5, 2010

Tarantino, A., Manager's guide to compliance, Wiley, Hoboken, 2006

Taylor, F., The principles of scientific management, Cosimo, New York, reprinted 2006; Original by Harper & Brothers, London, 1911

Toma, S./ Chitijo, M./ Sarpe, D., Risk and uncertainty, Procedia Economics and Finance, No. 3 , p. 975- 980, 2012

The American Planning Association, APA Article Calls on Planning to Help End Inaccuracies in Public Project Revenue Forecasting, April 7, 2005

The Audit Commission for Local Authorities and the National Health Service in England and Wales, Briefing: Worth the risk: Improving Risk Management in Local Government, London, p. 1, 2001

Thieme, W., Kaufmännische Buchführung in der öffentlichen Verwaltung, Die öffentliche Verwaltung, No. 11, June, p. 433, 2008

Treasury Board of Canada, Integrated risk management, Her Majesty the Queen in Right of Canada, 2004

Treasury Board of Canada, Review of Canadian Best Practices in Risk Management, Her Majesty the Queen in Right of Canada, 1999

Treasury Board of Canada, Risk Management Policy, Her Majesty the Queen in Right of Canada, 2001

Trockel, S. & Heinrichs, H., Nachhaltigkeit im öffentlichen Sektor – ein integrativer Ansatz in: Hilgers, D./ Schauer, R./ Thom, N., (eds.), Public Management im Paradigmenwechsel, Trauner Verlag, Linz, , pp. 209 – 224, 2012

Tudor,T./ Mutui, A., Cash versus accrual accounting in public sector, University Babes Bolyai, Romania, retrieved from http://ssm.com/abstract=906813, 20.02.2009

Tversky, A. & Fox, C., Weighing risk and uncertainty, Psychological Review, Vol. 102, No. 2, pp. 269 – 283, 1995

UK Audit Commission, Worth the risk, CW Print Group, London, 2001.

UK Resilience/ Cabinet Office, Communicating Risk, London, 2003

US Department of Homeland Security, Risk Management practices in the public and private sector: executive summary, September 2010

Van de Walle, S. & Hammerschmid, G., The impact of New Public Management: Challenges for coordination and cohesion in European Public Sectors, Halduskultuur – Administrative Culture, Vol. 12 (2), pp. 190- 209, 2011

Van der Wal, Z./ de Graaf, G./ Lasthuizen, K., What's valued most? Similarities and differences between the organizational values of the public and private sector, Public Administration, Vol. 86, No. 2, 2008

Van Dooren, W./ de Caluwe, C./ Lomti, Z., How to measure public administration performance, Public Performance & Management Review, Vol. 35, No. 3, pp. 489 – 508, 2012

Van Dooren, W./ Bouckaert, G./ Halligan, J., Performance management in the public sector, Routledge, Oxon, 2010

Vanston, J. & Vanston, L., Testing the tea leaves: Evaluating the validity of forecasts, Research-Technology Management, Vol. 47, No. 5, pp. 33-39, 2004

Van Thiel, S.& Leeuw, F., The performance paradox in the public sector, Public Performance and Management Review, Vol. 25, No. 3, March, p. 267 – 281, 2002

Villanueva, L., The new public governance? Emerging perspectives on the theory and practice of public governance, Journal of Public Governance and Policy: Latin American Review, Vol. 1 No.1, June, pp. 126-134, 2015

Von Hayek, F., The Use of Knowledge in Society, American Economic Review, No. 4, September, p. 522, 1945

Watson, T., The evolution of public relations measurement and evaluation, Public Relations Review, 2012

Weber, M., Wirtschaft und Gesellschaft, Zweitausendeins, Frankfurt, 2008, orig. 1922

Weber, M., The Theory of Social and Economic Organization, reprint 1997, Simon& Schuster, orig. 1922

Weibel, A./ Rost, K./ Osterloh, M., Pay for Performance in the public sector – benefits and (hidden) cost, Journal of Public Administration Research and Theory, May 27, 2009

Williams, I. & Shearer, H., Appraising public value: past, present and futures, Public Administration, 2011

Williamson, O., Why Law, Economics, and Organizations, Annual Review of Law and Social Sciences, No. 1, p. 369 - 396, 2005

Wilson, W., The study of administration, Political Science Quarterly, Vol. 2, No. 2, pp. 197- 222, 1887

Wöhe, G., Einführung in die Allgemeine Betriebswirtschaftslehre, Franz Vahlen, Munich, 2002

Wolke, T., Risikomanagement, Oldenbourg, Munich, p. 9, 2007

Wollmann, H., German local government under the impact of NPM modernization and new direct democratic citizen rights, Proceedings of „International conference on reforming local government", Stuttgart, Sept. 26th, p. 4, 2002

Wollmann, H.& Marcou, G. (eds.), Production and delivery of social and public services in cross-country comparison, Palgrave: MacMillan, New York, 2006

Zalta, E.(ed.), Stanford Encyclopaedia of Philosophy, Stanford University, Stanford, available online: http://plato.stanford.edu/, 2011

Zhonghua, C. & Ye.,W., Research frontier in public sector performance management, Physisc Procedia, No. 25, pp. 793 – 799, 2012

www.coso.org/publications.htm, accessed 10.01.2016

www.destatis.de/DE/ZahlenFakten/GesellschaftStaat/OeffentlicheFinanzenSteuern/ OeffentlicheFinan-
zen/Schulden/Tabellen/SchuldenGemeinden_311213.html;jsessionid=
2B5E259E5DA0197116734DA17171D428.ca)e1, retrieved 25.03.2016

www.destatis.de/DE/ZahlenFakten/GesellschaftStaat/OeffentlicheFinanzenSteuern/ OeffentlicheFinanzen/Schulden/Tabellen/SchuldenGemeinden_

311213.html;jsessionid=2B5E259E5DA0197116734DA17171D428.cae1, retrieved 20.03.2016

www.destatis.de/DE/ZahlenFakten/GesellschaftStaat/OeffentlicheFinanzenSteuern.htm; retrieved 15.02.2016

www.de.statista.com/statistik/daten/studie/154533/umfrage/prognose-zur-entwicklung-der-finanzierungssalen-der-oeffentlichen-haushalte-imeuroruam/., retrieved 27.02.2014

www.sgvw.ch/2006/04/25/risikomanagement-im-oeffentlichen-sektor-2, retrieved 26.12.2015

www.sgvw.ch/d/dossiers/Seiten/dossier_22_sgvw_jahrestagung_fachartikel.aspx?print=1, retrieved 03.01.2010

www.time.com/time/business/article/0,8599,1890418,00.html#ixzz0vFhui2jV; retrieved 31.07.2010

*** www.diezeit.de

*** dx.doi.org/10.1787/gov_glance2013-en

*** www.ftd.de

*** www.gov.uk.

*** www.handelsblatt.de

*** www.inform-index.org

*** www.iso.org

*** www.primo-europe.eu

*** www.statista.de

The manufacturer's authorised representative in the EU is Springer Nature Customer Service Centre GmbH, Europaplatz 3, 69115 Heidelberg, Germany. If you have any concerns regarding our products, please contact ProductSafety@springernature.com

Printed and bound by CPI Group (UK) Ltd, Croydon, CR0 4YY

01/10/2026

02225834-0002